The Re-Enchantment of Political Science

The Re-Enchantment of Political Science

Christian Scholars Engage Their Discipline

Edited by Thomas W. Heilke
and Ashley Woodiwiss

LEXINGTON BOOKS
Lanham • Boulder • New York • Oxford

LEXINGTON BOOKS

Published in the United States of America
by Lexington Books
4720 Boston Way, Lanham, Maryland 20706

12 Hid's Copse Road
Cumnor Hill, Oxford OX2 9JJ, England

British Library Cataloguing in Publication Information Available

Library of Congress Cataloging-in-Publication Data

The re-enchantment of political science : Christian scholars engage their discipline /
Thomas Heilke and Ashley Woodiwiss, eds.
    p. cm.
Includes bibliographical references and index
    ISBN 0-7391-0150-1 (cloth : alk. paper)—ISBN 0-7391-0151-X (pbk. : alk. paper)
    1. Christianity and politics. I. Heilke, Thomas W., 1960– II. Woodiwiss, Ashley,
    1956–

BR115.P7 R4323 2000
261.7—dc21

00-039100

Printed in the United States of America

⊖™ The paper used in this publication meets the minimum requirements of American
National Standard for Information Sciences—Permanence of Paper for Printed Library
Materials, ANSI/NISO Z39.48–1992.

To all of our teachers, Christian or not, who have taught us the "slow boring of hard boards," we dedicate this book.

Contents

PART III: NEW THINKING IN POLICY

Acknowledgments

We owe many people a debt of thanks for helping to bring this collection to the light of day. Jan Miller, secretary of the political science department at Wheaton College helped with the correspondence and provided technical assistance. Margie Aston and Connie Leonard at the University of Kansas did likewise. We are grateful to them for getting us through many details.

Sarah Weaver at Wheaton College did outstanding work on the index. Stephanie Wetzel at the University of Kansas diligently helped with typing.

We would also like to thank the editors at the Crossroads Monograph Series for allowing us to reprint the following two monographs with minor alterations: Stacy Hunter Hecht, "The State of the States: A Perspective on Federalism and Biblically Just Social Policy," Crossroads Monograph Series on Faith and Public Policy, No. 30 (1996); and Daniel Philpott, "The Christian Case for Humanitarian Intervention," Crossroads Monograph Series on Faith and Public Policy, No. 3 (1995).

Finally, we are grateful to our spouses and children for their patience while enduring our absences and attention deficits from time to time as this collection was brought to completion.

Introduction

In a book that caused considerable excitement several years ago, Mark Noll criticized the lack of demonstrably Christian scholarship in the evangelical world, claiming that the real "scandal of the evangelical mind is that there is not much of an evangelical mind."[1] Noll challenged evangelical Christians to recover a distinct and viable life of intellectual inquiry among themselves. Not long after Noll's call, however, George Marsden resurrected a contention well known to at least some Christians. For most inhabitants of the modern academy, Marsden suggests, the notion of "faith-informed" scholarship is an "outrageous idea."[2] The purported "neutrality" of the secular liberal academy functions as a form of hostility toward the assumptions that would underlie any "faith-informed" scholarship.[3] If Noll and Marsden have their stories straight, then it appears that Christian scholars find themselves in a double-bind. On the one hand, they must face the absence among evangelicals of a tradition of academic inquiry in the social sciences and humanities (Roman Catholics may, for a variety of historical reasons, fare slightly better here). On the other hand, they must face a hostility against any such scholarship in the "mainstream" secular liberal academic institutions where much of the best and/or most recognized scholarship takes place.

But times are changing. In a recent article in *Commonweal*, for example, James Turner suggested that a recovery of intellectual inquiry is well under way at several evangelical Protestant colleges and in the evangelical Protestant world in general.[4] This development has several converging origins. First, the genealogy of excluding Christian inquiry from the academy over the past hundred years or so has been extensively traced and recorded in recent decades in works like Marsden's and many others. A number of the essays in this present collection trace various threads of this exclusion. While the explication of this genealogy is not in and of itself a refutation of its outcome, it does show that the current

1

academic culture is a much more contingent development—based on human judgments, decisions, and choices—than its triumphalist heralds of "inevitable human progress" have made it out to be. Exposure of this contingency also reveals the frequently unself-conscious premises of these judgments and decisions, an unself-consciousness that is a peculiarly prevalent feature of Enlightenment thought and that continues through to the modern behaviorist and positivist schools.[5]

Second, the separation of social scientific "fact" from religious, philosophical, or cultural "value" may now be rejected on several grounds. As Alasdair MacIntyre has convincingly shown, it is a grammatical problem, not an empirical one, if one assumes that words like "man," "woman," or "human being" are functional descriptors. Where social role is an integral part of any description of a human being, for example, "fact" and "values" are not strictly separable.[6] In the same way, if the idea of a human being, apart from a specific social role, includes an idea of function or purpose, then such descriptions include as part of their factual content an account of what moderns might call "values." Just as a piano player can be judged on the adequacy or inadequacy of her performance, so, too, a human being can be judged on how well she displays the proper functions of a human being.[7]

The positivist self-image of value-neutrality has similarly suffered from the race, class, and gender critiques of the past several decades and from contemporary Continental postmodern perspectives. The net effect of these critiques has been the recovery of *situated theorizing*. Thus, while methodological critiques of positivism and the renewed role of political theory in the recovery of a science of man do not deliver to us a Christian social science,[8] they do open the door again to the possibility of practicing a social science that includes such adjectives.

A third reason for the recovery of (evangelical) Christian intellectual inquiry has to do with positive developments within Christian theoretical work itself. Alongside MacIntyre's critiques of social science claims to predictability and of the incoherence of modern ethical theories, the most extensive and sustained critique of positivism and modern social science has undoubtedly been the work of John Milbank, who, by beginning with a Christian theological critique of secular social theory from Machiavelli onward, has shown that doing Christian social science is a reasonable and coherent proposition.[9] So swiftly and cogently have these theological/philosophical critiques coalesced that *Telos*, a journal associated with leftist politics and European varieties of Critical Theory, published a special issue in 1998 entitled "Toward a Liturgical Critique of Modernity."[10]

Milbank offers a two-pronged critique. First, he shows that social and political theory since Machiavelli and through all of its great figures and schools of thought is supported by a sometimes tacit and sometimes explicit theological narrative that stands in self-conscious contrast to the traditional (pre-Renaissance, pre-Protestant, pre-Enlightenment) Christian narrative. Second, the various currents of Western political and social thought flow within one wide but bounded streambed. All contain at or below their surface an ontology of violence that extends from the political thought of antiquity through all the modern currents and that none of their indigenous critics overcome. The ontological premises of opposition, force, and violence in human affairs remain present in every case, as do at least the shadows of a theological metanarrative, reminiscent of the shadow in Nietzsche's cave.[11] Milbank's alternative, and one that opens up at least one kind of possibility for Christian political science, is to recount a different narrative, one of peace, whose explication will set forth a different mode by which to orient our theory and praxis.[12]

Some allied developments have occurred within the ambit of Reformed and Catholic intellectual communities. In the former, there has emerged a vigorous school of Reformed epistemology that takes as its central project the rejection of the classical foundationalism that serves as the epistemological underpinning of modern thought (and hence, by extension, the social sciences). Such thinkers as Plantinga, Wolterstorff, Alston, and others in this school have argued for belief in God as a properly basic belief that overcomes the modern evidentialist arguments as set out by Descartes and Locke and which have been held as a kind of philosophical orthodoxy throughout the twentieth century.[13] Among these thinkers, Wolterstorff has made the link to political thought by arguing for the Christian acceptance of some kind of liberal arrangement along non-foundationalist lines.[14] At the same time, a small group of Catholic thinkers have undertaken from within Catholic theological perspectives a reconsideration of how Catholic thinkers ought to think about modernity and the American project, particularly as they pertain to the Catholic narrative and the tasks of Catholic scholarship.[15]

Taken together, these two developments (along with those already mentioned above) indicate an awakening of fresh and creative ways whereby Christian academics are reassessing how their theological commitments inform and shape their responses to the reigning orthodoxies that constitute their disciplines. *The Re-Enchantment of Political Science* is both an acknowledgment of this prior work and an original effort to bring some of these developments to bear in the discipline of political science.

Alongside these historical and philosophical considerations concerning the possibility of a Christian political science, it is also simply the case that Christians have begun once again to participate more openly as Christians in academic debate. As the review we have given above would indicate, Christian scholars across a spectrum of disciplines in the social sciences and humanities and with diverse theological and denominational allegiances are challenging the premise that faith-informed scholarship is either an oxymoron or simply irrelevant to serious scholarly considerations. Foundations like the Lilly Foundation and the Pew Charitable Trusts fund conferences that explore the various issues and aspects of faith-informed scholarship. Increasing theoretical scrutiny is being given to the "neutrality" premises of the secular academy, as illustrated, for example, by the Wolterstorff-Audi exchange regarding the place of religious language and justification in public policy debates.[16] The intellectual life of Catholics and evangelical Protestants alike is receiving significant public nurture through high-quality publications like *First Things* and *Books and Culture*. In the academy, where even an interest in the historical effects of Christianity was somewhat subdued in recent decades, there is a renewed interest in the past, present, and potentially future effects of religion broadly and Christianity specifically on social, political, and economic structures, institutions, and phenomena. This work has been descriptive, analytical, and normative. It has engaged historians, philosophers, political theorists, and even behavioral social scientists.[17]

But, someone might ask, is such a hyphenated form of social inquiry necessary or beneficial? Our short answer to such paternalism is: necessary for what? Beneficial for whom? A much better question, we suggest, is this: what has happened in our social and political situation that would make an explicitly Christian social science interesting?[18] Several essays in this collection attempt to answer this question in a variety of ways. Whether or not such studies would be "useful" and to whom can only be demonstrated in the doing. We remain confident, however, that the dissolution of positivism through the gradual exposure of its normative and conceptual incoherencies has, at the least, made new forms of Christian inquiry interesting. The essays collected in this volume demonstrate sober-minded empirical and normative evaluations of social and political phenomena. They speak within disciplinary frameworks, but in a Christian voice. Such speaking need not be doctrinaire shouting, but rather a dialogical engagement that takes place with full awareness that Christians may often have more to learn from their non-Christian social science colleagues than they have to teach.[19] We trust the current collection demonstrates such engagement.

This book belongs to the field of political science. And in this field, too, questions concerning the relationship between religion and politics—at theoretical, historical, and behavioral levels—are receiving renewed and increasing attention. As in so many developments, however, political science is a latecomer in the revival of faith-informed scholarship; we intend here to help forward this scholarly agenda. While the essays in this volume argue for such "new Christian thinking," they also demonstrate that it has already commenced, being located in various subfields of the discipline.

Much of the work that has established new paths out of the morass inflicted by positivism has been done by theologians and philosophers. For most political scientists, this kind of work is naturally associated in their own discipline with the work of political theorists or historians of political thought. The present volume, however, is not exclusively a work of political theory; it represents a variety of subfields in political science. In every case where questions of political philosophy are not the immediate concern, one may imagine an underlying claim about the insufficiency of Weberian or positivist neutrality, but this is a working premise of investigation, not an argued refrain. Working from such a premise, when it is acknowledged, is not a methodological shortcoming. Much of "value-free" social science also makes reference to a wider order of being that may not be explicit in the work itself. A continuing tacit reference to such an order tends to make social scientists intellectual philistines; to avoid such philistinism is therefore one moral task to which our vocation calls us.[20] Christian social scientists offer one such possibility that now has renewed viability in our late modern climate.

Such an effort raises another question that is not identical to the one concerning necessities and benefits. Despite our rejection of Weberian neutrality or positivist "objectivity," would this kind of resurgence make any difference to the topics, methods, and results of social-scientific or humanistic inquiry in political science? We argue that such a perspective can, indeed, make a distinct and not merely quirky contribution. The form of inquiry we advocate here asks for "the opening of the academic mainstream to scholarship that relates one's belief in God to what else one thinks about."[21] While the answers to specific questions will likely vary wildly, "with God in the picture, contemporary issues may be viewed in fresh and promising ways."[22] It is our intent to show how this claim may be true for political science. Accordingly, this collection undertakes a broad disciplinary conversation concerning the identity and ends of Christian political science. It shows along both normative and empirical dimensions that the community of Christian scholarship has a distinctive and substantive voice from within its own narrated tradition to offer the discipline of political science and the practice of politics that such an academic discipline might inform.

At least three important Christian traditions are given voice here—Reformed, Anabaptist, and Roman Catholic. Luther's political theology comes in for critical scrutiny along the way. Eastern Orthodox Christianity and its variants do not appear, nor do the many voices of American Christianity that do not fit neatly into one of these major categories. While this may be a fault, it is inevitable for at least two reasons. First, and most obviously, this is an introductory volume, not an exhaustive encyclopedia, if such a thing were even possible. Exclusions are inevitable. Second, thinking systematically about politics has not developed as an integral part of every tradition of Christian thought and practice. Some (Wesleyanism and Lutheran pietism, come to mind here as examples) are not noted for systematic engagement with political questions in the same way that, say, Roman Catholicism and several branches of Calvinism are.

The two chapters of the first section examine broad issues of Christian theological orientation and their potential effects on disciplinary considerations. The second part, containing four essays, presents specific examples of new Christian thinking in political theory. These essays are good examples of how intellectual, evangelical ferment taking place in other disciplines (particularly theology, history, and philosophy) is beginning to have its proper effects in political science. Part Three contains three examples of "faith-informed" public policy and foreign policy studies.

In the opening chapter, Michael LeRoy argues that there has been no "one way" for Christians to think about and engage political questions. Some of the paths taken have been more helpful than others. For evangelical Protestants, LeRoy proposes an approach that follows those of Augustine/Calvin and rejects Luther. He argues for a "method of Christian understanding of politics that is in dialogue with the scriptures, reason, and empirical reality." He then goes on to show how such an approach would position itself in the current profession of political science and how it compares with other approaches evangelical Protestants, liberal Protestants, and Catholics are currently taking in questions of politics.

In the second chapter, Thomas Heilke argues for the possibility of attaching Christian adjectives to political science in such a way that a specific Christian perspective on the question of politics emerges while at the same time legitimately claiming to be an activity of "objective" social-scientific inquiry. To make such a claim involves a critique of the currently hegemonic forms of political science inquiry, which is the task of the second part of the chapter. The third section outlines a program of inquiry that takes a specifically Christian perspective as its beginning point.

Together, these two chapters pose a variety of questions that open up the possibility of Christians practicing a political science that denies the need to bifurcate one's scholarly life from one's "private" life of faith commitments. To do so, one must show how various forms of the Christian tradition provide resources for making reasoned political judgments and for engaging in theoretical *and* empirical political inquiry that is of scholarly interest and relevance to non-Christians.

The second section of the book moves to the area in which the preponderance of identifiably "Christian" scholarship on political themes has historically focused—political theory. In each case, however, these essays show forms of new thinking that are emerging in the evangelical world.

In its focused critique of the liberal exclusion of "religious" discourse from the public square, Ashley Woodiwiss's chapter serves as a complement and extension to the two chapters in part 1. Woodiwiss contends that, in all its forms, a consistently argued liberalism is ultimately hostile to all viewpoints that, in the words of Stanley Fish, "owe their allegiances not to its procedures—to the unfettered operation of the marketplace of ideas—but to the truths they work to establish." Woodiwiss takes up John Rawls as the specific interlocutor in his critique, but extends the claim more widely. In a manner consistent with the arguments of the first two chapters, Woodiwiss asks what the story of liberalism would look like if it were told by religious believers rather than the liberal victors. He thereby establishes a strong basis for rejecting the liberal version of its own story.

Brink, in turn, focuses on aspects of the liberal-communitarian debate that concern not only faith-informed claimants, but all political scientists and practitioners. Brink argues that this debate is unresolvable, because both sides begin with an essentialist account of human identity, disagreeing chiefly over what the essence of such identity might be. He proposes to engage the debate from a different perspective by turning to the resources for grappling with questions of human identity that are found in one stream of the "Imago Dei" tradition of Christian theology. The relational understanding of the Imago Dei doctrine, as opposed to the predominantly essentialist interpretation found in liberal and communitarian doctrines, offers an account of human identity that allows us to escape the libertarian-communitarian impasse and to critique the very premises of the debate. Like Woodiwiss, Brink questions the characterization of the self that is given by contemporary liberals, opposing it with a philosophically more satisfying account to be found in one stream of the Christian tradition.

Beginning with Theodore Lowi's analysis of the regulatory expansion of the American state (coupled with its decreasing legitimacy and increasing ineffectiveness in securing laudable community enhancing policy outcomes), Timothy Sherratt introduces the neo-Calvinist political theory of Abraham Kuyper as a means of analyzing these developments and prescribing solutions for them. As in other chapters in this volume, Sherratt shows that a political science that avails itself of analytical and prescriptive resources that are found in a specifically *Christian* tradition has a good deal to offer the non- and even anti-Christian mainstream discipline.

In the fourth chapter of part 2, Professor Woodiwiss extends the critique of his first chapter, turning now to the question of Christian citizenship, not in the kind of democratic regime that Rawls seems to advocate but in a more "agonistic" democratic regime. Woodiwiss contends that Christian citizens (and all members of particularistic communities) are better served in a democratic regime that more openly acknowledges the ineliminable conflicts of an open society in which there is a multiplicity of seemingly incompatible ends than in a deliberative democracy that unself-consciously excludes contending voices. Beginning with a critique of such regimes, Woodiwiss moves to a characterization of an agonistic democracy and ends with the question of how Christians would function as peaceable citizens in such a regime. The task of Christian political theory, he argues, "is the cultivation of Christian citizenship for the contemporary agonistic democracy."

Part 3 of the book is perhaps the most uncommon from a disciplinary perspective. Whereas Christian readings of politics are a core part of the tradition of political philosophy and political theory from the fourth century to the twentieth, it is more unusual to hear a definitively Christian voice in the contemporary areas of policy studies, unless it is in specifically political advocacy work. Clarke Cochran, writing out of a Roman Catholic perspective, and Stacey Hunter Hecht, writing out of a Reformed background, show how such policy studies are possible within a Christian framework using standard scholarly tools of analysis. Daniel Philpott addresses a specific concern within the sphere of international relations and foreign policy in a similar way, writing out of a natural law tradition.

Examining the provision of health care by Catholic agencies of various kinds, Professor Cochran argues that "Catholic social theory and Catholic practice possess distinctive resources as they bear upon health care delivery and health care politics . . . [and that] ecclesiology may represent a potentially significant concept for thinking about the institutional and policy challenges of the next century and for understanding the behavior of religious groups in policy and politics." Ecclesiology drives, modifies, or informs institutional behavior in important ways, because the way in which "churches and other religious organizations" think of themselves as churches may "partly explain variations in their approaches to policy arenas." The specific ecclesiology of a particular tradition will, if such things matter at all, affect the way the church organizes itself for action, and this organization will affect what kinds of institutions are created. Thus, while Catholics build hospitals (which may over time become entangled with local, state, federal, and private-sector bureaucracies), Protestants build community clinics (which may remain somewhat more independent of bureaucratic interference). These differences can be traced to differing ecclesiologies, and such doctrinal differences may also affect the abilities or inabilities of these service institutions to adopt to changing legislative, regulatory, and social climates. The delivery of these services by religious organizations, moreover, is not a trivial portion of such services in American society. This chapter is not, therefore, merely an example of a Christian doing the sort of political science everyone else does, too. Rather, the particular faith commitments of this particular political scientist help him to recognize what others might, because of their Weberian methodological and theoretical commitments, miss. Professor Cochran's essay is a work in "Christian" political science in the sense that existence within a tradition of faith directs a scholar to particular political questions that may not appear to a researcher working outside of that tradition.

Next, Stacey Hunter Hecht's chapter is an example of evaluating specific public policy agendas and developments through a Christian scholarly lens. While such evaluations have become a routine and published part of the activities of an array of Christian advocacy and lobby groups, they are only gradually becoming visible to mainstream political science as serious scholarly work. It is worth noting the somewhat different political principle of equality Professor Hecht reads out of Abraham Kuyper's political thought in contrast to Professor Sherratt. Christian political science will not be univocal in its evaluations and interpretations.

Finally, Daniel Philpott offers a Christian defense of interstate humanitarian intervention on the basis of natural law and just war traditions. Without explicitly saying so, Philpott demonstrates the intellectual strength of these traditions by showing their nondogmatic call for making judgments in specific, difficult situations. Philpott shows how Christians can pay attention to international balances of power, international legalities, and the strategic interests of states at the same time as they do not eschew the moral problems of international action. There is a long history of Christian reasoning in these traditions, and Philpott shows how their resources remain applicable and directly helpful in evaluating and conducting contemporary affairs. This relevance of Christian reasoning is especially pertinent in light of post-Cold War developments, in which we find a renewed interest in humanitarian pleas, clearly separated, as they now can be, from bipolar strategies of global positioning. The moral problems of humanitarian intervention are not uniquely Christian, being "fully accessible to, and fully demanding upon, all reasoning humans, unaided by special revelation." Philpott argues, however, that "a particular Christian case for humanitarian intervention complements the more widely accepted one." This "complement" brings resources to bear on the problem that other approaches lack. Philpott does not intend thereby either to merely "supplement" the efforts of the nation-state or its agents, or to underwrite them. He seeks, rather, to inform, speak to, and criticize them by thinking critically about them from within a Christian tradition that is in dialogue with political actors who may or may not be working within that tradition.

In sum, the chapters in this collection demonstrate the growing theoretical sophistication of faith-informed political science. As the ranks of explicitly Christian Ph.D.s and avowedly Christian scholars continue to swell within the social sciences, we hope that alongside the usual learning, thinking, and criticism that takes place in the reading of any argument, scholars may gain encouragement from the efforts made by these contributors to show that faith and intellect need not become divorced in the practice of modern social science.

Notes

1. Mark Noll, *The Scandal of the Evangelical Mind* (Grand Rapids, Mich.: W. B. Eerdmans, 1994), 3.
2. George Marsden, *The Outrageous Idea of Christian Scholarship* (New York: Oxford University Press, 1997), 10 and 67.
3. Marsden, *Christian Scholarship*, 34-37; 172-82.
4. James C. Turner, "Something to be Reckoned With: The Evangelical Mind Awakens," in *Commonweal* 126, 1 (Jan. 15, 1999): 11-13.
5. Alasdair MacIntyre, *After Virtue,* 2d ed. (Notre Dame: University of Notre Dame Press, 1984), 55-56.
6. MacIntyre, *After Virtue*, 121ff.
7. Such a rethinking of the content of our descriptive categories, however, extends beyond the human phenomena and, by this, extension support the more restricted claims regarding only the human. Leon Kass, a physician and biochemist by training, parallels

MacIntyre's argument in important ways, but he gives greater attention to the claims of the modern natural sciences to have uncovered an "ethically sterile nature" over against the "morally freighted life lived by human beings" (Leon Kass, *The Hungry Soul: Eating and the Perfection of Our Nature* [New York: The Free Press, 1994], 5). This form of knowing rejects teleology and regards knowledge of natural phenomena as useless for ethical inquiry (Kass, *Hungry Soul*, 4). Its development and its claims, as the history of sociology and modern political thought shows, have not been tangential to social science concerns. In the first place, modern philosophy "following the lead of modern science, insisted on the absolute distinction between facts and values, a distinction rooted in the view that nature itself is "objective" and indifferent to all human concerns with better and worse or with the good, the just, and the beautiful" (Kass, *Hungry Soul*, 4; Cf. Kass, *Toward a More Natural Science: Biology and Human Affairs* [New York: The Free Press, 1985], 318-45). Second, political inquiry has generally been a subset of philosophical inquiry. Third, the link between the two can be no better illustrated than in the persistent efforts of modern political inquiry to model itself epistemologically and methodologically on the natural sciences and the regular failures that have resulted from such moves. (For one history of this effort and its failures, see Thomas Spragens, Jr., *The Irony of Liberal Reason* [Chicago: The University of Chicago Press, 1981]). Kass shows, however, that by proceeding as it has, natural science itself has neglected much that properly belongs to the class of natural material and biological phenomena. Kass's arguments add force to MacIntyre's work, because they attack positivistic claims where those claims have always been believed to be strongest—in the realm of the natural sciences themselves.

8. Kass, for example, is a committed Jew, and he argues for a natural teleology that seems not to require theistic premises (*Toward a More Natural Science*, 249-75).

9. John Milbank, *Theology and Social Theory: Beyond Secular Reason* (Oxford: Blackwell Publishers, 1990).

10. *Telos* 113 (Fall, 1998): 3-134. Russell Berman's introduction to the volume provides an interesting historical/theoretical effort at situating this new critique within the tradition of Critical Theory and its concerns for human emancipation—an argument for overcoming the too facile association of leftist thought with secularism. See, "Creation and Culture: Introduction to 'Toward a Liturgical Critique of Modernity,'" 3-10.

11. See Friedrich Nietzsche, *The Gay Science*, aphorism 108.

12. For a more thorough summary of Milbank's critique and an example of how it can lead to both a retheorizing and as a point of response to other postmodern alternatives to the Western tradition, see Thomas Heilke, "On Being Ethical without Moral Sadism: Two Readings of Augustine and the Beginnings of the Anabaptist Revolution," *Political Theory* 24 (August, 1996): 493-517.

13. For a brief description of this view, see Alvin Plantinga, "Reformed Epistemology," in Philip Quinn and Charles Taliaferro, eds., *A Companion to Philosophy of Religion* (Cambridge, Mass.: Blackwell Publishers, 1997), 383-89. For an interesting history of this perspective and its quite impressive success within the American philosophic academy, see Kenneth Konyndyk, "Christianity Reenters Philosophic Circles," *Perspectives* (November 1992): 17-20.

14. See Robert Audi and Nicholas Wolterstorff, *Religion in the Public Square: The Place of Religious Convictions in Political Debate* (Lanham, Md.: Rowman & Littlefield Publishers, Inc., 1997).

15. For examples, see Kenneth R. Craycraft, Jr., *The American Myth of Religious Freedom* (Dallas: Spence, 1999); David Schindler, *Heart of the World, Center of the Church: Communio Ecclesiology, Liberalism, and Liberation* (Grand Rapids, Mich.: Wm. B. Eerdmans, 1996); and Michael Baxter, C.S.C., who coauthored with Stanley

Hauerwas, "The Kingship of Christ: Why Freedom of 'Belief' Is Not Enough" (originally delivered at a symposium sponsored by the DePaul University Law School on the separation of church and state in the United States) in Stanley Hauerwas, *In Good Company: The Church as Polis* (Notre Dame, Ind.: Notre Dame University Press, 1995): 199-216.

16. Audi and Wolterstorff, *Religion in the Public Square*, passim. An examination of this topic from a more restricted, legal, and constitutional perspective may be found in Michael J. Perry, *Religion in Politics: Constitutional and Moral Perspectives* (New York: Oxford University Press, 1997).

17. For examples of each kind of work, consider the following: Nicholas Wolterstorff, *Until Justice and Peace Embrace* (Grand Rapids, Mich.: Wm. B. Eerdmans, 1983); Stephen V. Monsma, *When Sacred and Secular Mix: Religious Nonprofit Organizations and Public Money* (Lanham, Md.: Rowman & Littlefield, 1996); James McClendon, *Systematic Theology: Ethics* (Nashville: Abingdon Press, 1986); Joshua Mitchell, *Not by Reason Alone: Religion, History, and Identity in Early Modern Political Thought* (Chicago: University of Chicago Press, 1993); Oliver O'Donovan, *The Desire of the Nations: Rediscovering the Roots of Political Theology* (Cambridge: Cambridge University Press, 1996); J. C. D. Clark, *English Society, 1688-1832: Ideology, Social Structure, and Political Practice during the Ancien Regime* (New York: Cambridge University Press, 1985); the various single-authored and coauthored works of Lyman Kellstedt, John Green James Guth, and Corwin Schmidt on political behavior among religiously affiliated American voters. The second and third editions of Kenneth Wald's textbook, *Religion and Politics in the United States* (Washington, D.C.: Congressional Quarterly Press, 1992 and 1997) contain excellent bibliographies covering a variety of subfields of study along various social-science and historical lines.

18. Stanley Hauerwas, *Wilderness Wanderings: Probing Twentieth-Century Theology and Philosophy* (Boulder, Colo.: Westview Press, 1997), 82-83.

19. Richard J. Mouw and Sander Griffioen, *Pluralisms and Horizons: An Essay in Christian Public Philosophy* (Wm. B. Eerdmans, 1993), 107-9.

20. For an even-handed summary and review of this same Weberian problem in the dispute between one particular school of political philosophy and the behavioralists in the 1950s and 1960s, see William T. Bluhm, *Theories of the Political System: Classics of Political Thought and Modern Political Analysis* (Englewood Cliffs, N.J.: Prentice-Hall, Inc., 1978), 63-70.

21. Marsden, *Christian Scholarship*, 4.

22. Marsden, *Christian Scholarship*, 4.

Part One

Disciplinary Reconsiderations

Chapter 1

From Worldviews to Research Programs: Toward a Christian Political Science

Michael K. Le Roy

My concern . . . is that we Christian political scientists, through our profes-
sional socialization, may have too uncritically accepted the social sciences' self
rhetoric . . . as Christian scholars we are called to be open to the possibility
that our long-held and cherished views of our profession may well be in need
of spiritual discernment and conceptual revision.[1]

Ashley Woodiwiss

The Christian practice of the discipline of political science runs parallel to Gabriel Almond's characterization of political science itself: a
room full of "separate tables," in which members of each school of
thought engage in a discussion with themselves, or when pressed, a
shrill monologue with the "other tables" present in the room. Almond's colorful illustration uses the metaphor of separate tables to
describe the divisions that characterize the professional practice of
political science. In his view, conflict within the discipline is characterized by methodological and ideological divisions. This divides the
discipline into four camps, which Almond refers to as "Soft Left,
Hard Right, Soft Right, and Hard Left." Each of these tables share
particular methodological and ideological commitments that impair
their respective views of disciplinary history and political reality.
Political science practiced by Christians is no doubt a long way from
even approximating the kind of typological coherence of the wider

profession, but it does risk making many of the parallel errors of its secular counterpart. This chapter examines the current research practices of Christian political scientists, which I contend have been defined by the discipline itself rather than by rigorous theological reflection, and suggests an alternative model for guiding research in the discipline. The goal is to avoid the pitfalls of secular practice within the discipline *and* encourage a more coherent research program in political science from a Christian perspective.

The First Great Divide: Inductive v. Deductive

At times it would seem that the only great divide in Christian political science has already been established along methodological lines. The differences in the Christian practice of the discipline parallel that of Aristotle's inductive method and Plato's deductive approach to understanding and apprehending knowledge of the natural order. Socrates articulates so-called "first principles" and then deduces from them what the nature of the state, citizenship, and labor should look like when it is based upon these principles. The most interesting aspect of the *Republic* is the rather humorous and disturbing result that flows from this process. Children are taken from parents and the aged are banished.[2] Readers are left wondering whether Socrates plays this game with his reader in order to teach his disciples about the cost of wisdom, or to make a mockery of this particular approach. In any case this tends to be the model employed by Christian and other political thinkers since the Socratic age. Principles are teased out of moral texts, and then used to chasten institutions and practices of subsequent ages. Whether because it is the legacy of St. Augustine or because of Christian attachments to holy scripture, the deductive approach has taken firm hold in Christendom and Christian approaches to political science. The failure of the Christian church to recognize Galileo's discoveries is the direct result of a logically deduced Christian "worldview" that could not tolerate the discovery of realities that did not conform to this worldview.

Christian disdain for "scientific," methodical thinking about reality is actually at the root of the division we now find within the Christian practice of political science. While it is true that science itself can become an idolatrous religion, this particular preconception about the utility of scientific methodologies has circumscribed natural scientific thinking about Christian models of inquiry, and fully stunted the Christian practice of social science. Mark Noll's analysis of Christian thinking about science is instructive on this point. Noll argues that nineteenth- and twentieth-century battles concerning the interpretation of scripture as statements of empirical fact have led evangelicals and fundamentalists to reject all or most scientific methods, arguments, and findings.[3] One of the many interesting observations of Noll's analysis is that the Christian response to inductive scientific methods was to invent a deductive natural science. In the late nineteenth and early twentieth centuries, a few natural scientists were encouraged to conduct their scientific inquiry with the assumption that *literal* interpretation of particular biblical texts (primarily the Genesis accounts) provides the *Christian* framework for understanding the physical world. And yet, the particular reading of scripture upon which these scientists' inquiries rested was an interpretation that was out of step with traditional Christian interpretation. Noll appropriately invokes leading thinkers in the Christian tradition (i.e., St. Augustine, Galileo, and Bacon), who all conclude that to interpret scripture as making final statements about nature and the physical world "retard[s] a God-honoring understanding of nature" that can complement the truth of scripture by means of reason and experience.[4] While evangelical errors on this count have been most severe in the natural sciences, this same pattern of thinking is in evidence in Christian thinking about the social sciences.

The failure to believe that God can work as effectively through reason and experience as He does through scripture are as much rooted in theological tradition as they are in contemporary thinking. But the problem is not merely with the deductive approach to social science. It also rests in a Christological approach to social and political ethics, which is overly individualist and pietistic. In his essay on "Christ and Power," John Howard Yoder identifies two currents of theological and philosophical reflection that have been uncritically merged to create a Christian social ethic which holds that Christ's teachings are not relevant to social and political life.

> In line with the personal appeal which has been so central in Protestant faith since Luther, even more since Pietism, and especially since the merging of Protestant existentialism with modern secular personalism—and even more especially since Freud and Jung imposed upon everyone in our culture the vision of man as a self-centered reacting organism—it has seemed quite evident that the primary message of Jesus was a call most properly perceived by an individual, asking the hearer for something that can be done most genuinely by an individual standing alone.[5]

The implication of such an argument is that Jesus' social reality and social ethics are somehow distinct from the Christ event. The reason given in support of this is that Jesus came for "spiritual reasons" and not to deal with issues relevant to politics or social organization. However, Yoder responds to this argument by reminding us that Jesus actually is intimately aware of the political and the social realms of human existence and that the message of the Gospel is relevant to these realms. In fact, human beings receive far more instruction from Jesus on how to handle complex social and political problems than they do matters of doctrine. "We have the record of Jesus' dealing explicitly with whether he should be king or whether we should love our enemies, with what we should do with wealth; only very indirectly can we get from his teachings any help on the metaphysics of incarnation."[6] To these concrete social circumstances we also receive statements about Christian duties to pay taxes and teachings on violence. This does not even include the Pauline admonitions to pray for government and to obey those in authority. In fact, it could be credibly argued that the New Testament gives far more guidance to Christians in the area of Christian civic and social ethics than it does to pastors in the area of church leadership.

Students of the Pauline letters are acutely aware of the fact that an understanding of Paul's letter to the Phillippians necessitates an understanding of the social and political order at Phillippi. This is also true of Corinth, Rome, and Ephesus. Just as we should seek to understand nature from biblical and physical analysis, so too we should seek to understand the political and social order using the resources of scripture alongside reason and experience. Analysis of the texts of Augustine and Calvin on the principle of obedience to political authority reveals that their instructions are rooted in scripture, but also in a firm understanding of social and political knowledge generated by secular scholars. In addition, Augustine and Calvin engage the prevailing inductive analyses of politics of their age. For Augustine, this means an engagement with Plato, while Calvin engages Aristotle's forms of government. Their analysis of scripture leads them to posit principles that leave little doubt about their interpretation, namely, that obedience to political authority is essential on the condition that political authority leaves space for the Christian life.

Almost all of the great figures in Christian thought have engaged in this activity, but most of them generally emphasized biblical teaching to Christian people rather than proclamations to the wider culture, or to the powers and principalities that have reigned in a given context. In fact, most of the moral teachings in the Bible are aimed at the instruction of the people of Israel about their need to obey God's law, or admonitions in the New Testament to obey secular authority, unless it inhibits Christian freedom. With the exception of Augustine, most Christian thinking about government occurs in a European Christian cultural context and so obedience is emphasized again and again, even among the reformers. Augustine is one of the first to help Christians make sense of the Church's relationship to secular government when he teaches that the minimum purpose of government is to provide order, and as a result, peace:

> It is important for us also that this people should possess peace in this life, since so long as the two cities are intermingled we also make use of the peace of Babylon—although the People of god is by faith set free from Babylon, so that in the meantime they are only pilgrims in the midst of her. That is why the Apostle instructs the Church to pray for kings of that city and those in high positions, adding these words: 'that we may lead a quiet and peaceful life with all devotion and love' [1 Tim 2:2]. And when the prophet Jeremiah predicted to the ancient people of God the coming captivity, and bade them, by God's inspiration, to go obediently to Babylon, serving God even by their patient endurance, he added his own advice that prayers should be offered for Babylon, 'because in her peace is your peace' [Jer 29:7] – meaning of course, the temporal peace of the meantime, which is shared by good and bad alike.[7]

The strong suggestion of this passage is that even Babylon can be used to serve God's ultimate purposes. Rather than emphasizing what divides Christians and non-Christians, Augustine is at pains to teach Christians that they can find limited common cause with non-Christians. The political order can be relevant to both the good and the bad. Rather than offering a wish that the leaders of Babylon remain un-Christian, Augustine admonishes his followers to pray for those in authority.

Augustine is capable of this view because he is engaged with the leading political theories of the day found in the *Republic* of Plato and Scipio's *On the Republic*. He considers the dominant body of thinking about civil authority and public life, and he engages it. He is a scathing critic who vilifies Plato's prideful utopianism and Scipio's sophistry that describes the Roman Republic as just, but he is also cautiously capable of seeing that God might actually work through the arguments of these philosophers. Instead of simply rejecting the philosophers' arguments that a commonweal is possible where all citizens have a common sense of right, Augustine appropriates this argument and then subverts it by replacing an un-Godly definition of justice with God's own definition. What Augustine seeks to promote is the goal of a commonweal itself, but one that is guided by the love of God and the love of neighbor. Augustine's biblical reading of the political order is informed by reason and empirical observation, which comes through critical engagement with secular knowledge.

John Calvin describes government in a way reminiscent of Augustine, but this is a government in which Christians are actually called to participate in what Calvin describes as a Christian's highest calling. Calvin, like Augustine, invokes Paul's teaching to make the case for the Christian view of government:

> For it is just as if it had been said, that it is not owing to human perverseness that supreme power on earth is lodged in kings and other governors, but by Divine Providence, and the holy decree of Him to whom it has seemed good so to govern the affairs of men, since he is present and also presides in enacting laws and exercising judicial equity. This Paul also teaches when he enumerates offices of rule among the gifts of God, which, distributed variously, according to the measure of grace, ought to be employed by the servants of Christ for the edification of the Church (Rom, xii. 8).[8]

Calvin goes so far as to characterize government as a gift from God that is evidence of His grace. Because of the possession of power, Calvin refers to those who serve in government as having the "highest of Christian callings." While Geneva under Calvin is sometimes repressive, Calvin's sophistication and understanding of politics is enhanced by his willingness to concede that some questions, such as the specific form of government that God would endorse, are unanswerable merely by means of the examination of scripture. However, what is most notable is the fact that he too invokes the classical typology of Monarchy, Aristocracy, and Polity to characterize the options, and then uses scripture, reason, and experience to derive his conclusion.

> And if you compare the different states with each other, without regard to circumstances, it is not easy to determine which of these has the advantage in point of utility, so equal are the terms on which they meet. Monarchy is prone to tyranny. In an aristocracy, again the tendency is not less to the faction of a few, while in popular ascendancy there is the strongest tendency to sedition. . . . Owing, therefore, to the vices or defects of men, it is safer and more tolerable when several bear rule, that they may thus mutually assist, instruct, and admonish each other and should anyone be disposed to go too far, the others are censors and masters to curb his excess. This has already been proved by experience, and confirmed also by the authority of the Lord Himself, when he established an aristocracy bordering on popular government among the Israelites,

> keeping them under that as the best form, until He exhibited
> an image of the Messiah in David. . . . All this, however, is
> said unnecessarily to those to whom the will of God is a suffi-
> cient reason. For if it has pleased Him to appoint kings over
> kingdoms, and senates or burgomasters over free states, what-
> ever be the form which he has appointed in the places in
> which we live, our duty is to obey and submit.[9]

This lengthy quotation is instructive, because it helps to exposit a method of Christian understanding of politics that is in dialogue with the scriptures, reason, and empirical reality. Calvin can find no bibli-cal support for endorsing any particular type of government, and so he uses his faculties of reason and his own experience to come to a conclusion. Those who know Calvin know that he is personally dis-posed to aristocracy, but he is not so beholden to his own opinion that he is incapable of reasoning.

The Second Great Divide in Political Science: First Things or Baptized Behaviorism?

Christian research of political subjects takes so many forms in the twentieth century that it is difficult to know exactly where the line should be drawn between writing that qualifies as "Christian scholar-ship" in the discipline of political science and other forms of dis-course that are related. I recognize that such a strategy risks mar-ginalizing certain forms of discourse, but in the interest of understanding what might constitute Christian scholarship, it seems as though this strategy is inescapable. The problem is that much of what is written in the professional journals by Christians is most definitely "scholarship," but generally only Christian inasmuch as the author professes a Christian commitment. Conversely, other writings on politics found in *First Things, Christian Century,* or *Christianity To-day* are most definitely Christian, and often exhibit a very high de-gree of theological literacy and sophistication, but are not usually in any way informed by political science scholarship. Christendom is also flooded with an extensive literature that is characterized by a low level of theological literacy and a very ill-informed foundation in po-litical science. Christian political science, as it has developed in the twentieth century, risks succumbing to the same sectarianism to which the secular profession has fallen prey, unless it recognizes and seeks to capitalize on its key distinctives.

The first key division within contemporary Christian scholarship in political science turns on the inductive/deductive division, and is partly informed by a deeply rooted historical antipathy toward science that easily spills over into the social sciences. This is likely reinforced by the fact that the progenitors of the modern practice of the discipline have done little to incorporate "deductive" Christian principles into their research. Modern social scientific theorists like Marx, Weber, Durkheim, Dewey, and others have even defined their "social science" as intentionally antagonistic to the Christian church, religious belief, and practice. An interesting example is the international study of religious belief and faith practice. Until very recently, social scientists have almost universally maintained that advanced industrial societies are experiencing a gradual drift away from traditional religious values. While the United States has stood out as a significant counter-example to this perceived trend, the "secularization hypothesis" has become an axiom in the study of advanced industrial democracy. What forms the substance of a highly contentious debate in sociology has been uncritically accepted by political scientists of all stripes.

Talcott Parsons's theory of secularization in *The Social System* appears to be the departure point for most political scientists who view religion as an historical artifact. Parsons's book argues that sacred systems of belief once pervaded all human ideas, endeavors, and creations. The grip of the sacred is characterized as totalizing and virtually unassailable. Unassailable that is, until the "forces of modernization," which owe a debt of gratitude to the Protestant Reformation and the Renaissance, succeeded in driving a wedge between the claims of the sacred and human faculties of reason. This inevitable historical process will eventually result in the demise of the sacred at best, or the privatization of all things sacred at the very worst.[10]

The most significant incorporation of Parsons's ideas by the political science community is found in Seymour Lipset and Stein Rokkan's analysis of cleavage structures in society as they mobilize citizens to create and participate in political parties.[11] Lipset and Rokkan's analysis of the French Revolution is the high water mark of church-state conflict where these institutions contested crucial questions of public morality and education. According to their analysis, this conflict was fiercest in Catholic countries, but it was virtually nonexistent in Protestant countries due to the way in which Protestant churches became actual "agents of the state."[12] Since the development and mobilization of parties along the lines of a church-state cleavage, as well as other cleavages (which include a center-periphery cleavage, rural-urban cleavage, and class cleavage) western democratic systems have become "frozen" in place largely due to the lack of new voters entering electoral systems with universal suffrage.[13] The implication of this argument is that "Christian political movements" are relevant only as historical phenomena, not evidence of the continued political relevance of religious belief and practice.

What is interesting and problematic about this particular conception of religion in the context of politics is its rather exclusive emphasis on religious institutions to the detriment of individual religious believers and unbelievers. The role that the Catholic Church has played in many European countries has no doubt been a significant factor explaining the presence and permanence of religiously based parties over time. Research by Richard Rose and Derek Urwin in 1969 provided an empirical confirmation of the "freezing hypothesis" that occurred ironically during a time situated on the threshold of explosive social change.[14] Through an analysis of western party systems, they concluded that the constellation of party systems was indeed the same as that which emerged in the 1920s.

The problem with viewing religion as an historical artifact has very little to do with the empirical analysis done to explain the emergence of systems; rather, it tends toward a static view of religious mobilization and a wooden interpretation of religious faith and practice. According to the view laid out by Lipset and Rokkan, church-state conflict peaked in the late eighteenth century, suggesting that the role of the church as a player in politics has been declining since that time. Cleavages that are more salient replace religious cleavages and relegate the church to the social position of a private spiritual advisor with a limited public role. This static understanding of religion's role in politics presumes that the political concerns of religious people are also historical issues with no present urgency. And yet, education, family policy, abortion, euthanasia, and third world debt relief are all domains in which churches enter the public square to mobilize citizens in western societies.

Lipset and Rokkan's focus on the institutional church as "the agent" of religious mobilization has led scholars interested in religious or "values-based" explanations to focus on overly narrow measures of religious commitment in western countries without sufficient attention to the religious context of a given country. In his important study of cultural values in advanced industrial democracies, Ronald Inglehart claims that "the available evidence strongly suggests that we are witnessing an intergenerational decline in the subjective importance of God in the lives of these publics. This decline seems gradual in some countries, but in Western Europe and Japan, it seems pronounced."[15] In his analysis of voting behavior and political participation, Russell Dalton suggests that there is a strong correlation between religious orientation and political behavior, but he relies very heavily on declining church attendance to support his assertion that "there are indications that the religious cleavage may be following the same pattern of decline [as] the class cleavage."[16]

The study of religion in comparative politics is not unlike that of the study of religion in most of the twentieth century manifestations of social sciences. Comparative politics in particular, like the social sciences in general, was conceived to transcend the ideological and value-laden analyses of earlier students of political science. It is a hybrid of sociology and more classical approaches to the study of power, politics, and institutions.[17] Interestingly enough, the incorporation of sociological method into the comparative analysis of political systems brings with it a bias that appears to support early sociological presuppositions about religion. Jeffrey Hadden recognizes that:

> Few forecasts have been uttered with more unshakable confidence than sociology's belief that religion is in the midst of its final death throes. Writes Gerhard Lenski in the introduction to *The Religious Factor* in 1961, "from its inception [sociology] was committed to the positivist view that religion in the modern world is merely a survival from man's primitive past, and doomed to disappear in an era of science and general enlightenment. From the positivist standpoint, religion is, basically, institutionalized ignorance and superstition."[18]

Sociologists now recognize the extent to which their methods were intertwined with an uncritical acceptance of secularization as an inevitable social process.[19] An examination of the literature on political behavior seems to suggest that students of comparative politics accept this assumption without much evaluation, in which they seem to deal with religion as an "historical artifact." According to those who would understand religion as an historical artifact, religion was an important factor in the organization of twentieth-century politics, but its relevance is waning in contemporary politics.

Such a picture is no doubt a very unfriendly one for faithful Christians who would consider rigorous study of politics. Twentieth-century political science does seek to marginalize the church and religious belief as the object of human devotion, but this secular discussion is really no different from the one encountered by Augustine. Plato's *Republic* and Scipio's commentary on this text both envision a polity where devotion to justice could supplant devotion to God. But rather than writing it off as "irrelevant" for Christian consumption and not worth engaging, Augustine engages this literature because it is the narrative that competes with social and political truth proffered by the scriptures. By engaging the Platonists, recognizing "the good" in some of their arguments, and rejecting that which is anathema, Augustine embodies Paul's admonition about Christ and culture that is potentially the most salient for Christian social scientists: "But examine everything carefully, hold fast to that which is good."[20] Twentieth-century evangelical Christians have essentially written off social scientists rather than trying to engage them in any serious manner. Instead of examining and interpreting their data, which can be done, they have dismissed them out of hand. In so doing, they have failed to understand the methods, discoveries, and innovations current in the professions. This makes Christians less able to interpret and critique the discourse of the age and more likely to engage in the kind of groundless editorializing that characterizes much of American Christendom's political discourse.

Even the most contemporary examples of this approach are numerous. Many conservative Christians have come to equate the broad practices, methodologies, and theories of social science with ethical relativism without seeming to understand what they criticize.[21] The problem seems to involve confusion over the difference between moral relativism and cultural relativism of social science.[22] The ideas, methods, and discourse of twentieth-century social science have led Christians to consider that the most valuable Christian discourse flows from a return to "First Principles." These scholars rightly acknowledge that Christian examination of politics has been underway since the moment Christ admonished the Herodians to "Render to Caesar the things that are Caesar's and to God the things that are God's" (Matt 22:22). Christ's answer gives us only a glimpse as to what our relationship to political authority should be, but it is clear that the political order is somewhat distinct from, but still under, the dominion of God.

Most Christians have interpreted this to mean that the political order, in its ideal form, should serve God's purposes. This is a point upon which Christian thinkers since Augustine have agreed with near unanimity. However, the point made by Christ raises a host of questions that will remain unresolved until the moment of his return. What form should government take? What is political justice? Who should rule? What is the proper relationship between the Christian church and civil authority? What is the proper relationship between Christians and civil authority? When (if ever) should citizens and/or Christians disobey political authority? What are the limits of political power? What are the ends of political power? What are the appropriate uses of power? These are just of few of the normative political questions that have been debated and contested by Christians from Augustine and Aquinas to Calvin and Luther. Almost all of the questions are still the subject of considerable debate as they are fashioned and refashioned by the challenges of the ages.

The answers to these questions form the basis of the first division within the Christian practice of political science. We inherit our theological divisions from Europe where Catholics, Lutherans, Calvinists, and Mennonites all defined their relationship to Caesar's coin in distinct ways. Political theory and practice for these groups was dependent upon at least two factors: theological first principles, and the context in which these principles were applied. While Christian thinking about politics has strongly emphasized the former it has done little to consider the importance of the latter. The great strength of *deductive Christian political reflection* is that it has helped to clarify the most important normative questions about the Church's relationship to the political order. The great weakness of this approach lies in its apparent inability to contend with the empirical realities of politics. By empirical realities, I mean that this approach is rarely sensitive to political science theory, institutional design, function, social and cultural context, and sometimes realities of human behavior.

One recent example comes to mind. A symposium published by the journal *First Things* in 1996 entitled "The End of Democracy? The Judicial Usurpation of Politics" dealt with the proposition:

> The government of the United States of America no longer governs by the consent of the governed. With respect to the American people, the judiciary has said in effect said that the most important questions about how we ought to order our life together are outside the purview of "things of their knowledge."[23]

The contributors to the symposium engaged in analysis of Supreme Court decisions that for Christians have been difficult to reconcile with an orthodox faith. These included a decision about homosexual rights (*Romer v. Evans*, 1996), equal access to the Virginia Military Institute (*United States v. Virginia*, 1996), and abortion (*Planned Parenthood v. Casey*, 1992). The analysis by most of the contributors of the symposium focused on whether or not the courts had the authority to decide the cases in the way that they did. The fact that they decided them in a way antagonistic to Christian principles led them to the conclusion that the Supreme Court did not have the authority to usurp democracy. What followed from this was a suggestion that Christians should engage in civil disobedience, and should perhaps even consider preparation for "tyrannicide."[24] I do not object to the authors' moral outrage with many of these decisions, but I do object to the haste, and minimal political analysis, with which the authors seemed to come to their conclusions.

As a political scientist I found it disturbing that Christians would make the claims that they made in this rather lopsided symposium without an awareness of a rather extensive body of literature that documents the abandonment of moral discourse in the public square as well as in the Congress. Analysts of all stripes have concluded that reforms of Congress over the past 100 years have resulted in decentralized power, legislative individualism, crumbling traditions, proliferation of subcommittees, and the weakening of party discipline. All of these factors have contributed to unwillingness by members of Congress to implement policies that reflect the public will on controversial questions of social morality.[25] This means that most of these questions of the public will are left up to the courts. Rather than legal clarification, which can be made through the legislative process, the Congress has preferred to make vague and ambiguous legislation that insures reelection because of the inability to pin members of Congress down on specific issues. This leaves interpretation and clarification up to the other two branches of government. Our democratic system may indeed be in need of overhaul, but Congress has given up its hegemonic power in equal measure to the other branches' usurpation of it. However, it appears as though the Christian legal scholars and political theologians are not interested in engaging the findings of political science.

This is not to say that theological reflection on the nature of science, ideas, culture, art, and politics is not important. On the contrary, such reflection is at the center of the academic enterprise. Whether one is a Christian, Hindu, atheist, or unreflective "Sheila," our assumptions about the nature of reality, human identity, and social relations are foundational to our thinking on all other matters. For orthodox Christians this means that we *must* try to know God's creative design in all aspects of his Creation. We *must* seek to understand the corrupting effects of sin in the whole of the created order. The most difficult task is that we *must* also humbly, and with God's help, seek the transformation of a corrupted humanity and social order until Christ comes again. But we must do so in a spirit of humility, seeking truth where truth is best found.

Toward a Christian Program of Political Science Research

It appears as though there are at least four different categories for political scholarship, and that these can be arrayed on at least two continua. The first continuum is the level of theological sophistication that is brought to bear in the attempt to understand a particular research question. The second concerns the level of disciplinary awareness and methodological sophistication that informs our attempts to understand the nature of truth in the social and political spheres of interaction. Unfortunately, because of the "great divide" articulated earlier, Christian scholarship is becoming divided between two camps. One behaves as though the profession of political science does not exist, and the other behaves as though theological principles cannot be integrated with the social scientific problems of mainstream research. The typology is presented in figure 1.

Figure 1: Christian Scholarship Typology

Theological Sophistication		
Disciplinary Engagement	High	Low
High	Christian Scholars	Baptized Behaviorists
Low	First Things	Culturalists

The goal of this typology is not to rate, or berate, the quality of the general contributions, but to clarify what is Christian political science, and what is not. The ideal that is suggested here is that Christian political science should be rooted in theological principles that are informed by theologically chastened political science research.

The "Culturalists" in this model refer to those "Christian" contributors who are characterized by a relatively low level of theological and biblical sophistication, and a minimal awareness of and engagement in the discipline of political science. Examples of this type of contribution are numerous. They tend to be highly ideological, coming from the left or the right, with claims that are particular to a specific political context. As such they are not relevant to Christian thinking about a problem outside of a specific cultural context. Examples of their writings include Doug Bandow's libertarian text *Beyond Good Intentions*, Robert McAfee Brown's *Saying Yes and Saying No,* and Jerry Falwell's *Listen America!* These contributions are a valuable part of any political discourse in a democracy because they provide alternatives that are attractive to participants in the culture, but they do not advance Christian knowledge of politics.

The second group consists of those with mainstream political science training and minimal theological grounding. My moniker for them is meant to be fun, rather than to ridicule, because these scholars contributions have been pathbreaking. These researchers, such as Corwin Smidt, Lyman Kellstedt, and Paul Weber are most definitely engaged in scholarship recognized by the discipline at large. Their writing and research contributes to the discipline's understanding of political phenomena, and their approach has relevance for a wide variety of political contexts. Eminent political scientists such as Berkeley's Aaron Wildavsky and Daniel Elazar have taken an interest in their work and sought to build on their nascent theories. Many Christians are even becoming interested in their findings. However, these scholars are operating in a discipline without careful Christian scrutiny of the assumptions and theories of the discipline. Christian practice within the discipline has not yet had the benefit of a Christian scholar who can evaluate the basic assumptions of the discipline. This is necessary because it would assist Christian political scientists with the most important task that they face: How do we participate in the theoretical debates that dominate the discipline? If Christians are to do more in the discipline than remind the profession that they must include "a religion variable" in their analysis, then we must start to engage the theories that now dominate the discipline. For example, it is incumbent upon Christians to critically evaluate, and where possible, modify and appropriate theories like the culturalist theory proposed by Ronald Inglehart, or theories of rational choice suggested by a number of economically oriented scholars. To fail in this task will perpetuate the habit of assuming that private theological commitments and public scholarship have no relationship.

The First Things approach to political science scholarship has already been criticized for its empirical and theoretical insularity. For historical reasons Christians have often been far more comfortable engaging in purely normative political science. Scholars like H. R. Niebuhr, Carl Henry, Mark Amstutz, Jim Skillen, and others have continued in the "inductive" tradition whereby normative propositions are postulated from theological principles. These scholars have helped thousands think more carefully about the nature of politics from a theological perspective. Their contributions have been essential for the practice of politics. Christian induction continues to fall short for many reasons, and in a way, post-modernism makes this all the more difficult. Teasing out "biblical principles" by those who use inductive methods is always vulnerable to the argument that they are engaging in "morally selective" preaching, or only telling part of the story to promote a particular ideological agenda. Moreover, few Christians from this tradition have taken up the onerous task of presenting empirical evidence that their "ideal" is better than any other ideal. One illusion is that this critique is asking them to quantify and make scientific their research agenda. Not so. There are a wide variety of systematic methods (comparison and case study) used, as we have seen, by figures like Augustine and Calvin. Finally, their induction has led them to the conclusion that it is not worth trying to have a conversation with the empiricists, because their respective agendas are too far apart.

The two sides of the argument (the First Things group and the Baptized Behaviorists) now find contemporary expression as Christians attempt to do "Christian Political Science." Both sides have unthinkingly positioned themselves in terms of the secular categories of the profession, namely, induction vs. deduction, or normative vs. empirical, or Christian vs. secular. But where are we left with this approach? Christians who have been students at Christian colleges, and thus trained to reflect theologically on most things, are now trained by secular institutions. They generally feel frustrated by the lack of sophistication we see coming from Christian quarters in political science and the normative vacuum we find in mainstream political science. Ironically, there are movements afoot in the secular practice of the profession that may provide a way out of this impasse.

Innovative scholars in the secular profession who are dissatisfied with the normative vs. empirical dichotomy are seeking to make moral claims that they can support with rigorous, systematic scholarship. For example, Robert Putnam believes that democracy is an important normative good that is worth defending. He roots his discussion in De Tocqueville's analysis of democracy in the nineteenth century, where civil society is the moral foundation upon which the democratic polity is built. However, Putnam does not stop at moralizing. His thirty-year analysis of Italian democracy reveals that social capital, his concept that includes civic trust and social interdependence, is the key to a vital and responsive democracy. His book and subsequent analyses of social capital in the United States are both committed to the enterprise of discovering what might improve the moral climate of society and democracy.[26] This includes analyses of voluntarism, television watching among citizens, economic inequality, and a host of other morally rooted projects. He is not explicitly Christian in his analyses, but his research could be one example of work that is compatible with a Christian moral framework.

Scholarship that flows out of reasoned Christian conviction and is supported by rigorous, theologically chastened, social scientific research is most likely to produce the type of Christian scholarship that will speak a different kind of truth. If Christians believe that limited government is good, then they should be able to demonstrate this theologically *and* empirically. If Christians believe that interest group participation in politics is morally problematic, they should be willing to make the theological case and present evidence for such a position. If one believes that Christians are better represented in a political party, one should be willing to test one's assertions. Professor Kenneth D. Wald summarizes the goal of the project that is before us:

> The fundamental challenge to the field, in my view, is to integrate our work with the discipline at large—be it work on American politics, comparative politics, or political theory.
> . . . This perception rests on my assumption that we ought not to become a self-contained ghetto with our own journals but should try whenever possible to bring our views to the attention of the profession.[27]

However, if recognition in the discipline were our only goal, our project would be for the sake of pride rather than for the City of God. With this in mind, it is fitting that Augustine should also characterize the goal of our truth-seeking.

> If they find a Christian mistaken in a field which they themselves know well and hear him maintaining his foolish opinions about our books, how are they going to believe those books in matters concerning the resurrection of the dead, the hope of eternal life, and the kingdom of heaven, when they think their pages are full of falsehoods on facts which they themselves have learnt from experience and the light of reason? Reckless and incompetent expounders of Holy scripture bring untold trouble and sorrow on their wiser brethren when they are caught in one of their mischievous false opinions and are taken to task by those who are not bound by the authority of our sacred books. For then, to defend their utterly foolish and obviously untrue statements, they will try to call upon Holy Scripture for proof and even recite from memory many passages which they think support their position, although they understand neither what they say nor the things about which they make assertion [quoting 1 Tim. 1:7].[28]

What is the agenda for this truth seeking work? First of all, I should qualify my comments by stating that the setting of such an agenda needs to be an enterprise that is shared by the Christian community of scholars in political science. But at least let me begin by making the following motion for our joint consideration.

First, I would propose that Christian scholars in political science begin by developing a list of research questions that need our most urgent attention. This list may be drawn from a combination of sources, both from the wider profession of political science *and* our various theological traditions. The development of this list should also include a thoroughgoing defense of the meaning and purpose of our questions on theological grounds, and this "defense" of each question should be debated within the community of Christian scholars.

Second, I would suggest that the methods used by political scientists be scrutinized in light of theological and normative criticisms often leveled against the empirical social sciences. Do these criticisms have merits? What do Christian scholars think of the claim that *social science methods* exalt empirical reality at the expense of God's special revelation found in the scriptures and exhibited in the life and teachings of Jesus Christ? Such a debate may conclude that social science methods are inconsistent with the Christian practice of the discipline, or on the other extreme we might conclude that they are wholly compatible with Christian learning in political science. More likely than not I am guessing that we will acknowledge what we now practice: the methods are not inherently good or evil, but may be used for either purpose depending upon the meaning of our work.

Finally, I propose that Christian political scientists actively but humbly engage Christians who might speak, write, and lobby in error without any knowledge of the contributions of the discipline of political science. Christian political action that is ignorant of deeper knowledge of politics and process sorely damaged the standing of Christians in the public square. This is not a call for the chastisement of theology by political science, but an effort to enhance and improve theological pronouncements that may be issued by the Christian church and its servants.

This essay is intended as a conversation starter among Christians in political science who are now beginning to develop a collective consciousness within the discipline of political science. I am increasingly convinced that this conversation is necessary to begin to lay the foundation for the kind of serious Christian scholarship that can only be produced by a community of scholars. This communal effort must replace our individual and often quixotic approaches to the practice of the discipline of political science. Without it I fear that the Christian practice of political science will merely be like Miguel de Cervantes' description of Don Quixote as "a muddled fool, full of lucid intervals."

Notes

1. Ashley Woodiwiss, "Counter-Cultural Christianity and Political Science: Some Thoughts," *CPS Newletter* (Spring 1996), vol. 5, no. 2.

2. Allan Bloom, ed., *The Republic of Plato* (New York: Basic Books, 1968), 221-50.

3. Mark Noll, *The Scandal of the Evangelical Mind* (Grand Rapids, Mich.: Wm. B. Eerdmans, 1994), 177-208.

4. Ibid., 204.

5. John Howard Yoder, *The Politics of Jesus* (Grand Rapids, Mich.: Wm. B. Eerdmans, 1972), 135. Here Yoder is criticizing the individualistic ethical responses offered by Rudolf Bultmann, *Theology of the New Testament* (New York: Scribner's, 1951); and Roger Mehl, "The Basis of Christian Social Ethics," in Bennett, ed. *Christian Social Ethics in a Changing World.*

6. Ibid., p. 136.

7. For a theological justification of this principle see Augustine's seminal work, *The City of God* (New York: Penguin, 1972), 892.

8. John Calvin, *Institutes of the Christian Religion* (Grand Rapids, Mich.: Wm. B. Eerdmans, 1989), 653-54.

9. Ibid., 656-57.

10. Talcott Parsons, *The Social System* (Glencoe, Ill.: The Free Press, 1951) and a summary from C. Wright Mills, *The Sociological Imagination* (Oxford: Oxford University Press, 1959) 32-33.

11. S. M. Lipset and Stein Rokkan, "Cleavage Structures, Party Systems, and Voter Alignments: An Introduction," *Party Systems and Voter Alignments* (New York: The Free Press, 1967) 1-67.

12. Ibid., 15.

13. Stein Rokkan, *Citizens, Elections, and Parties*. (Oslo: Universitetsforlaget, 1970).

14. Richard Rose and Derek Urwin, "Social Cohesion, Political Parties, and Strains in Regimes," *Comparative Political Studies* 2, no. 1 (1969): 7-67; and "Persistence and Change in Western Party Systems since 1945," *Political Studies* 18, no. 3 (1970): 287-319.

15. Ronald Inglehart, *Culture Shift* (Princeton, N.J.: Princeton University Press, 1990), 187.

16. Russell Dalton, *Citizen Politics in Western Democracies* (Chatham, N.J.: Chatham House, 1988), 161.

17. Harry Eckstein, "A Perspective on Comparative Politics," *Regarding Politics* (Berkeley: University of California Press, 1992), 103-4.

18. Gerhard Lenski, *The Religious Factor* (New York: Doubleday, 1961), 3 op. cit., J. Hadden, "Toward Desacralizing Secularization Theory," *Social Forces* 65, no. 3 (1987): 587.

19. This recognition begins with the pioneering work of David Martin, "Towards Eliminating the Concept of Secularization," in *Penguin Survey of the Social Sciences*, ed. Julius Gould (New York: Penguin, 1965); Charles Y. Glock and Rodney Stark, *Religion and Society in Tension* (New York: Rand McNally, 1965), among others.

20. I Thessolonians 5:21.

21. Francis A. Schaeffer, *A Christian Manifesto*, revised edition (Westchester, Ill.: Crossway, 1982), 18. Tim LaHaye and Jerry Falwell have also made this equation in a number of their characterizations of the notion of pluralism.

22. For a careful examination of the difference between ethical relativism and cultural relativism in social science by a Christian author, please see Charles E. Garrison, *Two Different Worlds* (Newark: University of Delaware Press, 1988).

23. "The End of Democracy?" *First Things*, November 1996, 19.

24. The strong suggestion of civil disobedience is suggested by Robert Bork, "On Judicial Oligarchy," and Charles Colson, "Kingdoms in Conflict." Tyrannicide is alluded to in Robert P. George, "The Tyrant State," *First Things*, November 1996.

25. These include Richard Fenno, *Home Style* (Boston: Little Brown, 1978); Bruce Cain, John Freejohn, and Morris Fiorina, *The Personal Vote* (Cambridge, Mass.: Harvard University Press, 1987); and Walter J. Oleszek, *Congressional Procedures and the Policy Process* (Washington, D.C: CQ Press, 1989).

26. Robert Putnam, *Making Democracy Work* (Cambridge, Mass.: Harvard University Press, 1991).

27. Interview in Gregory M. Scott, *Political Science: Foundations for a Fifth Millenium* (New York: Prentice-Hall, 1997) 366-67.

28. Augustine, *The Literal Meaning of Genesis*, trans. John Hammond Taylor (New York: Newman, 1982), 1:42-43, quoted in Noll, *Scandal of the Evangelical Mind*, p. 203.

Chapter 2

At the Table? Toward an Anabaptist Political Science

Thomas W. Heilke

What would it mean for there to be an "Anabaptist political science"? The question seems, on its face, to be either absurd or so belligerently partisan that the word "science," a least, should be exchanged for another. To unpack this question in a less reactive mode, however, I propose the following considerations. First, let us ask, what is "Anabaptist"? Second, what is "political science" as an activity of enquiry both with respect to its objects and its ends? Finally, what would the adjective (Anabaptist) supply to the subject (political science) that would make it a distinctive activity while remaining a "social science"? Would there be room at the social science table for such a manner of investigating social, political, and historical phenomena?

Anabaptism and Social-Scientific Historiography

The date of January 21, 1525, serves as a convenient birthday for Anabaptism. On that day, Conrad Grebel, the son of a Zurich patrician, "rebaptized" George Blaurock, a Roman Catholic priest, at the home of Felix Manz, in Zurich.[1] That act of rebaptism had, as its logic began to unfold, profound ecclesiological and political-theoretical consequences. It was, moreover, not a singular originating act of Anabaptism. "Anabaptist" refers historically to a somewhat amorphous grouping of religious movements originating in Switzerland, Germany, and the Low Countries that had in common an anticlericalism and anti-pedobaptism, and usually a belief in the necessity of living according to a rigorous ethical standard as part of a specifically "Christian" life. Most of those groups that survived the early years of heavy persecution and who avoided the millenarian excesses of the Münsterites accepted the doctrines of nonviolence and nonresistance to evil, which they found displayed in the life of Jesus, as a component of their ethical standard. Other aspects of their ethics included a conception of the church as a brotherhood and as separated from political power; the practice of peace and agape as central to Christian ethics; and, a prophetic stance toward the powers that be. "Anabaptist" will refer in this chapter to the modern inheritors of this ethic who still practice it in a communal context.

An interesting debate has been fermenting largely within the confines of Anabaptist historiography for the last few years over the question of Anabaptist identity. The characterization of Anabaptism that I have given here, and its actual historical development, has come into dispute, and what is distinctly "Anabaptist" or even distinctly of Anabaptist heritage (among groups like the Mennonites, Amish, Swiss Brethren, and so forth) is a matter of contention. This dispute about Anabaptist identity itself focuses attention in a helpful way on the question of social science "objectivity," which will receive some scrutiny in this chapter. The dispute is more or less divided between so-called "evangelical" interpreters of Anabaptism and social science or "real-historical" interpreters. Some social science accounts of Anabaptist identity seem to reduce historical manifestations of Anabaptism to expressions of resentment, powerlessness, or illegitimacy.[2] In this view, Anabaptist doctrines developed historically in response to specific historical conditions, but they cannot be said to have developed *prima facie* out of principled responses to such conditions. Instead, they are "real-political" adaptations to specific circumstances.[3]

In the accounts of so-called evangelical interpreters of Anabaptism, however, Anabaptist doctrines regarding violence, separatism, and the like cannot be reduced to real-political principles of survival or to anticlericalism or the like. Anabaptists themselves, these authors suggest, had something else in mind, a more positive agenda by which they identified themselves. It might be described as "recovery" or "restoration."[4] What they sought to "recover" or "restore" was a community context in which they could practice what they called a "God-pleasing life." In Platonic or Aristotelian terms, we might call it a "good life."[5] Anabaptists found the image of such a life in the stories of the Old and New

Testaments. It was given both in the form of specific commands, but especially in the form of narratives that illustrated what a life that embodied such commands might look like. In contrast to the real-historians, the evangelical interpreters insist on the essential pertinence of this embodiment for identifying a common normative thread in Anabaptism and for identifying a common heritage that informs contemporary concerns and practices of Anabaptist churches.

This dispute seems peripheral to our concerns here, but it plays into the argument of the present chapter in at least two distinct ways. First, if the tradition of Anabaptism is a sound, living tradition, some disagreement at the level of the identity and meaning of the tradition is to be expected.[6] It does mean, however, that we attenuate any strong claim of precise identity, which will impinge on any conclusions we might draw about a determinative social science done from an Anabaptist perspective: it cannot be ideological. Second, to ask what is Anabaptist is to ask not a question with an obvious sort of answer, but to engage immediately the central issue of this chapter, namely, that in any form of enquiry, the ethical perspective or the inquirer matters to the choice of the objects of enquiry and to its substantive outcome.

Let us consider as one example of substantive Anabaptist inquiry and its problems a series of essays on pacifist historiography of American history that were the outcome of a conference at Bethel College in Newton, Kansas, in 1992.[7] In this collection, we find essays on various aspects and episodes of American history written by historians who are members of "peace churches" (usually Anabaptist churches in which nonviolence and nonresistance are the ethical norms for members) and who write history from the perspective such churches supply. What kind of history do they write, and what difference does a peace perspective make to its substance?

An Example: Pacifist Historiography in American History

In "Was the 'Good War' a Just War?" Ken Brown examines the motives and public justifications for the entry of the United States into the Second World War. At the outset, such an examination clearly has its methodological difficulties:

> The problematic nature of counterfactual reasoning looms in assessing any historical event. No one ever knows with cer-

tainty what might have happened had other choices been made. To say that Hitler could have been stopped by less costly means is counterfactual; to say that he could not have been stopped except by war is equally unprovable. Such statements are based on prior assumptions about human nature and society and as such are outside the realm of proof. In any attempt to make sense of history, counterfactual judgments cannot be avoided. We attempt to verify faith presuppositions that we cannot verify, and whether we are political "realists" or theological "pacifists," we move quickly into realms of faith. The war is historical fact. Alternative scenarios are speculative.[8]

Keeping in mind the problems of such an approach, which all too easily tempt the writer to self-authenticate whatever principles he or she may hold, Brown begins his argument not from a pacifist perspective but from just war reasoning. This beginning point is justified by the observation, which Brown leaves unstated, that "just war thinking necessarily draws on pacifist presuppositions for its rationale—that those who resort to violence bear the burden of proof." Both traditional just war theorists and strict pacifists begin with the common premise that violence and especially the harming of innocents are evils to be avoided.[9] Addressing both *jus ad bellum* and *jus in bello* criteria of just war theory, Brown asks how "good" (just) the seemingly most justifiable war in American history actually was.[10] He locates at least three points of contestation.

First, the American rational for fighting the war was neither "to save the Jews or to stop the [atomic] bomb." It was to avenge Pearl Harbor, and American entry into the European theater was based on Germany's alliance with Japan. Second, Allied behavior in the war violated *jus in bello* principles in several arenas. Brown cites various incidents of individual Allied soldiers committing wartime offences,[11] but he is especially interested in the wartime violation of *jus in bello* principles by the Allied governments as a matter of policy. In particular, he targets the British policy (in which Americans and other Allies participated) of terror bombing German cities throughout much of the war. Alongside just war concerns regarding this policy, Brown cites the apparent ineffectiveness and military wastefulness of an enterprise that seems to have been based as much on revenge as sound strategy.[12] Brown argues (contra Michael Walzer) that the massive obliteration of German civilian targets could not be defended morally as an act reasonably taken in response to a "supreme emergency." Alongside evidence of its ineffectiveness, saturation bombing seemed to "violate the most funda-

mental human values—which is what happens in war—in order to preserve those values."[13]

In similar fashion, William E. Juhnke scrutinizes the Truman administration's decision to drop the atomic bomb on Japan. A close examination of the five options the Americans had for ending the war with Japan[14] leads Juhnke to a now common conclusion that the nuclear
carnage at Hiroshima and Nagasaki was anything but inevitable.

As with the end of the war, so with its beginning, pacifist historical
revisionism asks whether the historical events leading up to and including Pearl Harbor, for example, were inevitable. Ken Brown is especially
interested in the lost opportunities of Allied leadership: he cites evidence
from Robert Fearey's recollections of Japanese-American diplomacy before the outbreak of the war in the Pacific that the Roosevelt administration might have negotiated a Japanese withdrawal from China and Indo-
china and a partial lifting of the embargoes against Japan, but that it
made almost no effort to do so.[15]

But, to echo Juhnke's pedagogical question, so what? That history is
not uniperspectival is no longer news, if it ever was. The question that
confronts us is, rather, what kind of history shall we tell? What legiti-
mates a particular telling, and why should anyone listen? The history
that nonresistant pacifists have to tell is clearly, though not always, "revisionist." Like other forms of revisionism, it takes a new perspective on
the standard story that has been told up to this point. In particular, it
questions the logic of "historical necessity," arguing that history involves opportunities and choices, not merely necessary acts and outcomes.[16] It is therefore a revisionism that is based in part on counterfac-
tuals, and the competent pacifist historian takes the fragility of such a
method into account. It is, however, a "revisionism with a vision."[17]
Three characteristics of this vision particularly stand out.

First, pacifist revisionism accepts a moral, pedagogical role for the
writing of history:

> The living of human history matters because moral choices
> are not only real but important; they make a difference for
> how the world is to go and what is to happen to our neigh-
> bors. Therefore the writing of history, when rightly done,
> ought to somehow render the decisiveness of the choices peo-
> ple make. Yet often the historian puts a premium on being
> able to lay over events the grid of an explanatory cause/effect
> connectedness such that things really had to go the way they
> finally did. The more convincingly the historian can demon-
> strate that necessity, the better sh/he believes the job has been
> done.[18]

The evangelical historian, on the other hand, rejects precisely such determinism, pointing out, rather, the turning-points and situations of decision where things could well have gone another way. It is at these intersections that the prevalent political realist conception of how history goes may be called into question as we open our vision to other possibilities.

Second, with every due regard for the multiple perspectives that might be brought to bear on any particular historical event or series of events, pacifist revisionism seeks truth:

> In calling for a pacifist re-envisioning of American history, then, we are not merely asking the world to pay attention to our peculiar fiction. We rather propose to offer a telling of American history that is convincingly truthful, that explains more phenomena more completely and satisfactorily than alternative narratives, and that has power to persuade those willing to listen. This is more than a call to redress a prevailing overemphasis on militarism, or to allow a small place for peacemakers to stand on the historiographical stage. This is a struggle for the identity of America, waged by people sufficiently aware of their own presuppositions that they can avoid becoming hostage to any ideology that would narrow their vision. Themes as great and as humanizing as peace, justice, community and conflict resolution are large enough for all our energies.[19]

The truth that is spoken is spoken out of community practice. The alternative interpretations emerge from alternative practices—of repentance and forgiveness—that inform the Anabaptist church. But if the church is the context of practice and the origin of practical claims about social practice and social truth for the Anabaptist historian and/or social scientist, then how does he or she avoid speaking only to the converted? Does it make sense to evaluate historical deeds and political claims according to standards the doers and claimers reject?

> [T]he fundamental duality with which the Christian speaking to the environing society must reckon is not the difference between church and state as social institutions, nor between interpersonal relations on the face-to-face level and large group relations or between legalism and "playing by ear,"—although these differences will ultimately also be involved—but the difference between faith and unbelief as the presuppositions of his ethical message. To his Christian breth-

ren the Christian addresses a testimony whose sole norm is Jesus Christ and whose adequate basis is the faith commitment of the brother spoken to. Outside the circle of faith, the presupposition cannot be the commitment of the individual spoken to and challenged, but only Christ's objective claim on him.[20]

If "Christian ethics is for Christians,"[21] of what does Christian history or Christian political science (written for non-Christians, or for Christians who do not accept the Anabaptist interpretation of the "norm of Jesus Christ") consist?

The question leads to a third principle of Anabaptist historiography and social science, which John H. Yoder once formulated as the use of the "middle axiom." He used it in the context of analyzing a Christian *witness* to the state, which may, perhaps, be distinguished from the Christian *study* of history and politics. As I will argue presently, however, the two are not as distant from one another as notions of "objectivity" would lead us to believe. So-called middle axioms are principles of conduct posited to rulers by peace-church (Anabaptist) members. They are "middle," because they appeal to categories of conduct that the ruler can understand, but that also have reference to Anabaptist language. They might include the following: "the sword is not the source of creativity"; "manhood is not brutality"; "if you wish peace, prepare for it"; "war is not a way to save a culture"; "social creativity is a minority function"; "the nation is not the morally primary community"; "practicality must have a longer time frame."[22] Beginning with these sorts of principles, the Anabaptist social scientist conducts his or her investigation into social, political, or historical phenomena just as some other social scientist might begin with Weberian, Machiavellian, or Marxist principles as a basis for asking questions and seeking answers.

But why "Anabaptist" rather than simply Christian? The difference between the Anabaptist church on the one hand, and magisterial or "Constantinian" churches on the other, revolves largely around their disparate conceptions of the role of the church in the world. For the Anabaptist, as for all non-Constantinian free churches, the Christian church is the establishment of a separate kingdom whose principles take precedence over the claims of clan, nation, or state. Violence, moreover, is unjustifiable in this kingdom and for its members. Here history is written not by men (or women) in power, but by the weak, the oppressed, and the outsider, whose perspectives, interests, and claims of importance may stand in radical contrast to those of the world's powerful and successful who believe that by force and violence they can make history go

in the direction they determine.[23] Anabaptists are critical of the links
magisterial churches tend to make between the fate of any particular im-
perium and the fate of the church. They are equally dubious of claims
Christians may make concerning the justification for violence to uphold
"civilization" or some such transcendent good as it is represented in the
continuation of a particular political regime.

The middle axioms of the Anabaptist are based on the basic principles of nonviolence and Christian separation, and they are used as a
principle of evaluation at the intersection between Christian principles
and state behavior. Thus, the "Christian social critique will always speak
in terms of available, or at least conceivable, alternatives. It will not request from the state the establishment of a perfect society, but will call
rather for the elimination of specific abuses."[24] The standards for such a
critique are found in the "kingdom of God," but the utterance of critique
is neither utopian nor "extremist," because "[t]he fact that the world to
which we speak is in rebellion guarantees that the Christian social critique can never lead too far." Instead, "[t]he world can be challenged, at
the most, on one point at a time, to take one step in the right direction, to
approximate in a slightly greater degree the righteousness of love."[25] It
may be that "the judgment of Christians who are well informed will often differ little in substance from the intelligent judgment of other social
critics,"[26] but that does not vitiate the substance of the critique nor does a
Christian speaking from the standpoint of a kingdom that makes a particular claim to sovereignty lose his voice when he is in agreement with
those who make claims from another standpoint.

Progress: The Meaning of Political Science

What, then, may these Anabaptist historians with their anti-
Constantinian and pacifist perspective teach us about doing political science? Let us begin with the meaning of modern social enquiry. Like that
of Anabaptism, the meaning of modern social enquiry can be captured in
a narrative. Like the story of Anabaptism, any particular story about social inquiry may be contested, but I propose here to trace one thread of
meaning that begins approximately with two lectures at the Sorbonne in
1750 and that has one ending in contemporary theories of secularization
or modernization.

In 1750, a young prior, Anne Robert Jacques Turgot delivered two
lectures at the Sorbonne in Paris that together, in the words of Frank and
Fritzie Manuel, "framed a new conception of world history from remot-

est antiquity to the present and constituted the first important version in modern times of the ideology of progress."[27] The methodological question animating the lectures was the following: How is it that mathematics is more advanced than physics, which in turn is more advanced (in the sense of providing more certain knowledge) than other ways of interpreting the external world?[28] Accepting, as he did, Locke's sensationalist psychology,[29] Turgot argued that the reception, new combination, and reflection on the material impressions in the mind is the "ultimate assurance of the inevitable and indefinite advancement of the human mind."[30] He believed there was a "basic drive in human nature to innovate, to create novelty, to bring into being new combinations of sensations."[31] When we look from this basic human tendency to the variety of ways of knowing, we notice that mathematics treats ideas only, but that physics, although it expresses its findings or "reflections on the material impressions in the mind" in a mathematical way, must operate with these impressions from the external world in such a way that the abstract purity of the ideas are lost. The process of purification, based on a new mathematizing combination and reflection on our material impressions proceeds slowly as it moves through each of the individual sciences, because human beings tend to anthropomorphize nature, giving it human/divine attributes that are mere projections of their own nature.[32] It was Turgot's claim that historically, humankind had moved from an anthropomorphic view of nature to a more metaphysical and finally a mechanical view. We had, in other words, moved from a "godded" world to a world described by abstract (metaphysical) concepts (which, for Turgot, refer to nothing real) and finally to a world in which we make "proper" observations of the mechanical interactions of bodies, which itself leads to mathematical expression and empirical experimentation. This gradual process of purification in each of the mechanical or natural sciences (astronomy, navigation, geography, physics, chemistry, biology, and so on) would expand to the arts, politics, and ethics.[33] It was a movement forward—progress—whose constant core of meaning was the gradual attainment of certainty, expressed in mechanical/mathematical terms, about the natural and human worlds. This progress was "based on an interpretation of history" in which humankind is "slowly advancing" toward "a condition of general happiness" and the laborious process of civilizational advancement would be justified by this conclusion. It would, moreover, be "the necessary outcome of the psychical and social nature of man." Otherwise, it would not be independent and autonomous, but "at the mercy of any external will," which would make it not the product of human progress, but the outcome of Providential will.[34]

Accordingly, neither the Greeks nor the medieval Europeans with their cyclical conceptions of cosmological order had a notion of progress in the modern sense, nor did the limited beginnings of the notion of advancement in the Renaissance arrive at the full-blown notion of continual human material and intellectual advance in history.[35] It is only in the Enlightenment that Bacon's and Descartes's hope of unlocking the secrets of nature for the amelioration of the human condition are combined with aspirations for the same in man's social and political life into a philosophy of history in which material and intellectual advance, unhampered and unaided by Providence, is the *telos* and the certain expectation of human endeavor.[36] Such progress is based on the principle of "universal reason implanted in man," which, having supplanted the superstitions, prejudices, and passions embodied in religion, will lead to an endless betterment in the human condition.[37] The Christian might well interject here with the observation that the role of the Holy Spirit in history has now been supplanted by human activity and/or by natural processes.

This historical sentiment of progress is manifested in contemporary political science in a variety of ways. One influential tradition, which finds some of its roots in the French positivism of Comte and St. Simon, combines a progressivist material teleology of history with a technocratic agenda of political mastery. For Comte, as for Turgot, human progress is equivalent to the acquisition of certainty concerning the operations of nature by way of a mathematizing discourse concerning all natural phenomena. As did Turgot, so Comte also foresaw the application of positivist (scientistic) principles he supposed he had found in natural scientific reasoning to the governing of society. Human affairs would be properly ordered in accordance with positive principles:

> Nothing more remains to be done, as I have already explained, than to complete the positive philosophy by including in it the study of social phenomena, and then to sum them up in a single body of homogenous doctrine. When these two tasks have made sufficient progress, the final triumph of the positive philosophy will take place spontaneously, and will reestablish order in society.[38]

The Comtean dream of a positivist society is not as distant from the classical liberal political aspirations that animate the American polity and American social science as one might imagine. In Thomas Spragen's analysis, "the technocratic view of politics" that finds its home in a wide variety of ideological schools of thought "is an offspring of the liberal tradition." The "central continuities" they have in common consist in their "similar conceptions of human knowledge and its political utility."[39] First, argues Spragens, technocrats, including the Comtean variety, "embraced and expanded on the fundamentally positivistic conception of knowledge they found embedded in liberal rationalism." Among other things, this "embrace" "anticipated the establishment of a secure and incontrovertible base for human knowledge in clear and distinct perceptions"; like Turgot, the technocrats believed that "the achievements of the mathematizing sciences were paradigmatic for the progress of knowledge"; and, finally, being firmly rooted in the progressivist paradigm of history, they looked forward to a time "when knowledge would escape all residual mystifications, [and] become expressed in a language freed from metaphysical confusion" or any other obscurantist forms of knowing.[40]

Second, technocrats also followed early adherents of liberal rationalism in their belief that "the realm of positive knowledge" included knowledge of moral precepts. Positive knowledge of human morality was ultimately of the same order as positive knowledge of material phenomena: the former would bring about order and moral progress in human affairs just as the latter had brought about an expansion of (progress in) technological power.

Eventually, however, technocrats like Comte and his followers amended the liberal model of knowledge and its social implementation. In particular, they departed from the liberal conception of what reason could accomplish and how it would do so. Accordingly, their model of a "rational" society was quite different from the original liberal image:

> For the liberals, reason and common sense—freed from their enslavement and corruption by superstition, myth, and dogmatism—were expected to fasten directly and unproblematically on the goals and standards they themselves considered to be "natural" and "self-evident." Central among these self-evident truths were the goals of liberty, equality, justice, and natural rights. For [the technocrats], "liberty," "justice," and "rights" were consigned to the realm of metaphysical nonsense—empty and "negative" abstractions without grounding in the world depicted by modern science. Their own goals were rather vaguely conceived ones of social harmony, organization, peace, and happiness, all of which were conceived to be more consonant with a naturalistic and mechanistic view of the world and of human nature.[41]

Similarly, we see in Comte and other technocrats a notion quite different from original liberalism of how (liberal) progress would be accomplished:

> if the technocrats agreed with the liberals in conceiving that political progress would be achieved by the spread of reason, their scientific elitism rendered this process remarkably despotic—even if it was covered over with a heavy gloss of sincere benevolence. The rationalization of the social order, in their accounts, was to come not so much through democratic persuasion and accommodation as through the expert social management of well-meaning "doctors of morality." Technocratic praxis assumed not a representational mode, but the mode of authoritarian intervention.[42]

But what does any of this have to do with political science? I have suggested that contemporary political science has its own story, or is part of a larger story of the investigation of certain kinds of (human) phenomena. To see how the story I have traced cursorily to this point ends up being part of the story of American political science, we must consider certain aspects of that academic activity.

Progress and Democracy: The Meaning of American Political Science

Let us begin with two generally accepted characteristics of American political science. First, as a separate, distinguishable academic discipline, political science is principally an American invention of the late nineteenth century. Second, and closely tied to this historical circumstance, American political science has been largely (but tacitly) understood to be an academic activity in the service of American democracy to strengthen and preserve that democratic regime.[43]

Several criticisms may be levied against political science thus conceived. First, there has been a strong tradition of value neutrality or value-noncognitivism in American political science since the Second World War. This value-noncognitivism was understood by its proponents as a necessary corollary to making social science more "scientific" in the positivist sense. To be "scientific," political science would, along with the other social sciences, have to be "purged of its metaphysical and normative components."[44] At the same time, however, many proponents of such a positivist science seek either to aid a particular regime or kind of regime, or their writings betray the desire to implement the findings of social (political) science in the technocratic manner of Helvetius, St. Simon, Comte, Bentham, and their intellectual progeny.

In the case of the former, one might ask why a "value-neutral" social scientist prefers one regime over another. On the basis of his or her proclaimed neutrality, it would appear that the choice of regimes is arbitrary. It would seem that the social scientist is not a thoughtful citizen or scholar when he or she chooses, but a vulgar partisan:

> When he says that democracy is a value which is not evidently superior to the opposite value, he does not mean that he is impressed by the alternative which he rejects, or that his heart or his mind is torn between alternatives which in themselves are equally attractive. . . . by saying that democracy and truth are values, he says in effect that one does not have to think about the reasons why these things are good, and that he may bow as well as anyone else to the values that are adopted and respected by his society. Social science positivism fosters not so much nihilism as conformism and philistinism.[45]

For technocrats, on the other hand, the claim to value neutrality is coupled with a claim to technical expertise, which is to say, manipulative power.[46] Both claims are, at the very least, debatable. The implementation of technical expertise as a political act for the sake of "social harmony" or some such ideal is itself a "value," or better, a normative standard for which one must argue;[47] it is not an obvious historical necessity. The claim to such expertise in the realm of human affairs, moreover, has been soundly repudiated by the critiques of Alasdair MacIntyre and others, who have shown that such claims can be made good only if human life is predictable in the manner of nonanimate physical phenomena along the lines of law-like generalizations, which it radically is not.[48] The claim to managerial effectiveness in business and politics is therefore a "contemporary moral fiction":

> The dominance of the manipulative mode in our culture is not and cannot be accompanied by very much actual success in manipulation. I do not of course mean that the activities of purported experts do not have effects and that we do not suffer from those effects and suffer gravely. But the notion of social control embodied in the notion of expertise is indeed a masquerade. Our social order is in a very literal sense out of our, and indeed anyone's control. No one is or could be in

charge. . . . Belief in managerial expertise *is* then, one more
illusion and a peculiarly modern one, the illusion of a power
not ourselves that claims to make for righteousness. . . . For . .
. the realm of managerial expertise is one in which what pur-
port to be objectively-grounded claims function in fact as expressions of arbitrary, but disguised, will and preference.[49]

Thus, while knowledge is not, despite their ostensible claims, a "neutral"
quality for either the liberal-democratic social scientist or the technocrat,
both lack an argument for its proper use. Both seem to suffer from a
philosophical naïveté that originates in the entirely unself-critical optimism of the Enlightenment itself, in which the form and use of the new
knowledge delivered by the sciences of nature was generally taken to be
self-evidently salutary for social and political purposes.[50] At this juncture, too, one finds an entree for (Christian) social scientists whose study
is informed by more carefully developed normative principles.

But, setting aside for the moment the philosophical incoherence of
claims to value-neutrality, we may consider more closely those "values"
that the support of American democracy seems to entail. Even if the
value-noncognitivist does not seem able to offer self-consistent reasons
why democracy is worthy of support over against, say, tyranny, a Christian social scientist is not limited by such discourse. Christian believers
and nonbelievers alike who seek coherent criteria for distinguishing
between different kinds of political regimes will look to arguments concerning the noble and the base (the just and the unjust), the good and the
bad, the political and the nonpolitical, and concerning social purposes
with respect to the good for man.[51] And the various Christian traditions,
including Anabaptism, will themselves provide resources for such judgments. The axioms I listed earlier are one example where such judgment
might develop.

Christian judgment about such matters will occur on at least three
levels. First, the Christian social scientist will, on the basis of empirical
evidence and ethical argument, make reasoned judgments about the
relative "goodness" of any particular regime over any other. In this, he
or she may not differ much from any other person, lay or professional,
for whom good citizenship poses a question requiring reasoned judgments. Second, he or she will make similarly grounded judgments about
the relative merits of any particular regime at any particular time and
place. Given the self-declared ends of a regime as well as the Christian
conception of the purposes for political rule, how is regime *x* perform-
ing?[52]

Third, and perhaps not least, the Christian can move from the critical study of actual regimes to a metacritique of the language the value-noncognitivist social scientist uses in his analysis and description of these same regimes:

> Social scientists see themselves compelled to speak of unbalanced, neurotic, maladjusted people. But these value judgments are distinguished from those used by the great historians, not by greater clarity or certainty, but merely by their poverty: a slick operator is as well adjusted as, he may be better adjusted than, a good man or a good citizen.[53]

The "purely descriptive concepts" of social science themselves betray unavoidable "value judgments," and the Christian political scientist cannot sidestep such implicit claims if he or she is to engage these "value-neutral" students of phenomena about which he or she, too, is asking questions. As Leo Strauss points out, the distinction between "democratic" and "authoritarian" in American social science generally carries approbation for the former and disapproval of the latter. Similarly, when social scientists follow Weber in speaking "of three principles of legitimacy, rational, traditional, and charismatic,"

> their very expression "routinization of charisma" betrays a Protestant or liberal preference which no conservative Jew and no Catholic would accept: in light of the notion of "routinization of charisma," the genesis of the Halakah out of Biblical prophecy on the one hand, and the genesis of the Catholic Church out of New Testament teaching, necessarily appear as cases of "routinization of charisma."[54]

For the Christian social (political) scientist (for whom "Christian" is not a contrived label formed out of arbitrary value preferences, but an adjective pertaining to a consistent and coherent view of the world as a whole and how a human life should be lived in that world), an empirical study of any given political regime, a moral evaluation of it, and the questions that direct one's empirical glance are closely integrated parts of a single activity.[55]

But to return more specifically to the American scene in political science. The general characteristics of value-noncognitivist social science, in both its academic and its technocratic manifestations, manifest themselves in specific ways in American social and academic life.

First, as writers like Spragens and Thomas Szasz show, there is "an influential tradition within American social thought that is properly characterized as technocratic," and that tends to replicate the scientific management aspirations of St.-Simon and Comte.[56] It is not merely the case that the utopian novels like Edward Bellamy's *Looking Backward* or B. F. Skinner's *Walden Two* are important features of the American literary landscape; rather, the self-proclaimed expertise of technocrats has been brought to bear on American domestic and foreign policies with frequently disastrous and deeply corruptive results. Those social sciences that foster technocratic claims have thus become at times the handmaiden(s) of corrupting forces acting on the constitutional framework of the American regime.[57]

Second, and somewhat in contradiction to the first point, political science has often become an academic discipline that supports the status quo. As Charles Lindblom has argued, most political scientists (apart, perhaps, from a few Marxists and a growing number of Foucauldian poststructuralists) are "strongly disposed to see the main outlines of putative democratic political systems as benign." Accordingly, he finds a "Pollyanism" in mainstream political science that defines "political parties by reference only to their useful functions," interprets "political socialization as education rather than impairing," and finds, "without explanation or argument on the point, common good more than conflict and exploitation in the governmental process." Consequently, for example, "political science could . . . find in citizen apathy a source of political stability without considering that it might perhaps as well have found it to be a source of opportunities for elite exploitation of the masses."[58]

In similar fashion, American Political Science Association president Theodore Lowi complained in his departing reflections on the state of the discipline in 1992 that the hegemonic subfields in political science engage largely in apologetics for the status quo. Indeed, he argued, the character of political science—the objects of its study and its methods of studying them—are a "dependent variable": political science is itself a political phenomenon, the "product of a regime" that, like any regime, "tends to produce political science consonant with itself." In the case of American political science, this consonance is manifested in "the thought-ways and methods of a modern bureaucratized government committed to scientific decision-making" that inform many of the methods and questions in political science.[59] Thus, the questions political scientists ask and the methods by which they find answers replicate the processes of the state they study. In Lowi's analysis, there are "three principal consequences of following Leviathan too closely":

> First, we have as a consequence failed to catch and evaluate
> the significance of the coming of economics as the language

of the state. Second, we have failed to appreciate how this language made *us* a dismal science like economics. Third, having been so close to Leviathan, we failed to catch, characterize, and evaluate the great ideological sea changes accompanying the changes of regime.[60]

In short, contemporary American political science is insufficiently aware of itself and insufficiently critical of the objects it studies. Here, too, we find openings for Anabaptist and other nonconformist political scientists.

Third, and closely related to Lowi's observations, the uncritical commitment of American political science to democracy has led not only to "benign interpretations" of the democratic political system that ignore with seeming naïveté the power differentials and possible power manipulations in such a system, but also to a social science that tends to serve those in power (the elite) without any reflection that such service might disadvantage the already disadvantaged. Such naïveté leads to "patterned impairments" or "learned incompetencies" that reflect "parents' desires to *control* rather than edify their children, an older generation's desire to *control* rather than edify the younger generation, clerics' desires to *control* rather than edify an errant mass, and political and economic elites' desire to *control rather than edify* the masses." Such a pattern "constantly recommends to political scientists, as well as to all of us, hierarchy, obedience, deference, faith, inequality, and stability."[61] Political scientists seem too rarely to see the coercions and injustices of such patterns for what they are, even though there is a rich tradition of critiquing precisely such patterns in the sub-field of political philosophy. Its subject matter would seem to make political science "the discipline that is and that must be most centrally concerned with structures of power that can dominate people's lives and consciousness in ways that are often neither necessary nor desirable." Insofar as its "value-neutrality" and/or the philistinism of its practitioners allow its agenda to be shaped and distorted by political power, however, it misses its most enobling opportunity.[62]

Fourth, and more optimistically, it appears that the self-proclaimed value-neutrality of political science, especially in a democratic setting, leaves open, if unintentionally, a door for choosing the topic of research. As Lindblom has it, political science from the 1940s to the present has developed a fairly sophisticated account of *how* to *do* research, but in the choice of *what* to research, political scientists remain amateurs;[63] there are no decisive prescriptions of this kind in political science.

All four of these trends in political science offer openings for the Christian political scientist. I am not implying that a Christian can or should preach "salvation" to political science, nor that his or her choice of topics and perspectives will in particular cases be much different from the approaches of other thoughtful and self-aware practitioners of political science research. Rather, I am pointing out the problems and openings in this tradition that an able scholar can exploit for new directions and new perspectives to inform his or her work.

These trends in political science are not restricted to the study of American politics. "Modernization" or "secularization" theories show the pervasiveness of the progressivist paradigm even in the study of non-American, nondemocratic politics. In Claude Welch's editor's introduction to a reader in "Political Modernization," it is assumed that modernization—the increasing use of technologies to produce consumer goods and to control nature, central control of social institutions, the "systematization" of administrative control of society, economic expansion[64]—are inevitable. This inevitability, for all of the problems it raises and human costs it incurs, is nevertheless taken to be at least benign, and more likely positive. "Can we identify stages of growth through which all states and society *must past*?" asks Welch.[65] Such change engenders disruption, which produces resistance. Evaluating this resistance produces a "value-laden" language: "Does ethnocentrism *seriously jeopardize the prospects* for modernization? Are other groups as *receptive to change* as the Japanese and Baganda, or might *traditional values* (including group solidarity) of other peoples pose *insuperable obstacles* to modernization?"[66] Resistance notwithstanding, the outcome is assured, and that is a good thing: "Societies differ in their speed and ease of adaptation, but "traditional beliefs" (as contrasted with "rational" ones?) can ease the "pains of transition" if they are "astutely utilized." "Traditional beliefs," however, may also be a hindrance: "Primordial sentiments do not disappear overnight, but rather after a long and often acrimonious period of transition." The outcome is not guaranteed—"stagnation" or "political 'decay'" may set in, but the optimism of progress remains at the core of the investigation.[67]

Almond and Powell's treatment of secularization contains similarly loaded language. Secularization "is the process whereby men become increasingly rational, analytical, and empirical in their political action," and the "secularization of culture is the process whereby traditional orientations and attitudes give way to more dynamic decision-making processes" with more "scientific" (read: "rational") habits of decision-making.[68] The *development* toward secular rationality is not inevitable, but the advantages of its greater efficiency and organizational power are clear.[69] This perspective, and the more general notion that the various goals of modernization—economic growth, governmental effectiveness, military effectiveness, democratization—are mutually compatible and even mutually reinforcing, has been heavily criticized by some political scientists.[70] Criticism from within political science, however, has tended not to see alternatives, but to seek for solutions to the problems modernization causes with resources from within the modernization impulse itself.[71] Confronted with the standard categories of American political science, the Anabaptist political scientist might question the coherence of value-noncognitivism, she might question the power imperative of specific regime "values" even in a democratic polity, she might question the idolatrous (and empirically dubious) characteristics of a doctrine of progress, and she might suggest new directions for research based on the kinds of middle axioms we noted earlier that emerge from a pacifist, minority standpoint.

Let us note, too, that the story of modernization and secularization can be told differently, and political science is not and need not be monolithic in its approach, as is indicated in Manfred Halpern's analysis of social change in the Middle East and North Africa. He interprets modernization not as a positive and incontrovertible force, but as a powerful invader, perhaps irresistible at the extremes, but perhaps also susceptible to modification on the terms of those whom it threatens with sweeping change. "Tradition" is not a set of vestigial behaviors whose destruction is celebrated, but an inheritance of rich life-ways whose unwilled passing is mourned.[72] On the whole, however, dogmas of modernization and secularization remain in good part pieces of the larger liberal myth of progress that continues to inform large tracts of social science research even as it continues to serve as a foundational myth in American political culture.[73]

It is worth mentioning as well that critiques of political science, political regimes, and political practices do occur within the "Christian world." At a recent International Studies Association conference, where I served as a panel discussant, a graduate student presented her findings on American evangelical missionary attempts to evangelize in Latin America during the 1980s. She found that in Guatemala, for example, social indicators (financial savings, material standard of living, etc.) were somewhat improved after conversion, because the American evangelical version of Christianity, at least, included economic and social practices that improved one's material position (fathers, for example, are encouraged to keep steady employment where possible and to stay at home with their families in the evenings, rather than going out to drink and gamble). Republican foreign policy perspectives of the time (regarding the threat of world communism, for example) tended also to be part of the "Gospel message" that these conservative evangelical missionaries brought with them. In this part of their message, they were considerably less successful. The new Guatemalan Christians did not see the gospel politically scripted in the way the missionaries did, and so they looked for and took up other political views.

After I had expressed some amusement at the ability of the gospel to subvert the political ideology of the missionaries bearing its message, a Mennonite theologian who happened to be in the audience introduced himself and suggested that I had missed a deeper point. Insofar as the American missionaries were introducing disciplines inclining toward the cohesion of the *nuclear* family and toward specific economic practices, were they not merely replicating the basic consumption unit of late-modern American capitalism? Did this perhaps imply the preparation of Guatemalan society for a consumerist ethos along American lines? Could we not imagine another possibility for the shape of Christian community, less hostile to the message of the gospel and less amicable to the consumerist suburban model of American evangelicalism? One's blindness to the mendacious nuances of the status quo, I learned, may be deep indeed.

Why Anabaptist? The Lure of Classical Political Theory

One direction that Christians have taken in response to the problems of modernity and modern political thought is a return to classical political theory. This path has been mediated for American political scientists through the writings especially of Leo Strauss and Eric Voegelin, and their intellectual heirs. Alongside Strauss's ambiguous relationship to religion in general and Voegelin's ambiguous relationship to Christianity in particular,[74] an Anabaptist might point to a more particular problem that Christians confront in the tradition of classical political thought.

John Milbank has identified this problem as a difference between the fundamental ontology of peace that the Christian tradition embodies and the ontology of dialectic and conflict of all pagan ethics that the virtue traditions of Plato and Aristotle attenuate but do not, ultimately, overcome. Thus,

> Plato and Aristotle's account of the virtues founders on certain antinomies they lack the resources to resolve. In fact, within the terms of the antique *mythos*, their attempt to oppose virtue to difference fails, and their versions of virtue are always deconstructible to difference after all.[75]

In the Christian account, argues Milbank, "one has a variant of virtue that is *not* deconstructible to difference, but is, in a sense, reconcilable with an analogically understood difference." Consequently, the "reconciliation of virtue with difference" is possible for the Christian, because Christianity "more emphatically construes virtue as that which aims towards, and is possible within a fundamental condition of peace." More specifically,

> If the *polis* can adjudicate to all their roles, and assign a virtuous way of life, then justice must be possible. And a justice that is living together in agreement, rather than mere mutual toleration, implies a real peace that is more than just suspended warfare. However . . . Plato and Aristotle found it finally impossible, because of the gravitational pull of Greek *mythos*, to imagine a civic or an ontological peace that was more than suspended warfare.[76]

For the Christian, however, whose non-dialectial and non-heroic conception of virtue emerges out of an ontology of peace, and which cannot, therefore, be deconstructed into another dialectical of difference, "the ethical action itself . . . seeks a *telos* which is the further promotion of creative freedom—not, indeed for anything, but for precisely what charity will unpredictably require, according to its own higher prudence." "By contrast," concludes Milbank, "for the antique understanding, virtue remained essentially a heroic power to restrict a preceding violence, to organize formally a material field, and to rein in forces around a stable, non-ecstatic centre."[77] As Milbank goes on to show, however, the Christian alternative is severely attenuated by the Christian turn to Constantinian forms of Christianity in the fourth century.[78]

In consequence, the Anabaptist who presumes the "ontological priority of peace to conflict," at least in the story that God reveals about Himself,[79] a return from the values-chatter of modern emotivism (which is at the core of both modern American liberal society and American social science) to the virtue-ethics of antiquity is insufficient. He or she must "sketch out a 'counter-history' of ecclesial origination, which tells the story of all history from the point of view of this emergence," and he or she must then "describe the 'counter-ethics' or the different practice, which emerges."[80] At the more narrow level of political science, this means that a critical stance over against the implicit and explicit normative basis of political science inquiry and a critical stance over against the empirical "findings" of political science requires not a retreat into a "New Science of Politics"[81] based on principles discovered in antiquity, but a move to a new metanarrative basis of peace from which to understand and critique political phenomena. The nature of political rule and the claims of political rulers may, from this standpoint, take on an entirely different character.[82] At the least, out of "a new, nonpolitical social practice" arise the possibilities of a new awareness of the power-discourse behind claims to legitimacy and justice, but that, unlike similar awareness by deconstructionist philosophers like Foucault, does not rest on a further dialectic of difference, but on a "reconciliation of virtue with difference." This reconciliation is not available for Christians who accept a Constantinian ethic of joining themselves personally or corporately to the interests of the state.[83]

To repeat, this new perspective of peace does not mean that Anabaptist political science becomes the utopian effusion in social science language of the dreams of Hegel's "beautiful souls." Rather, critical engagement with political problems is informed by a counternarrative that holds open the possibility of new forms of community and that speaks to the powers that be from that stance, even while it acknowledges that this stance is unavailable outside the realm of faith.[84]

Conclusions

If the critical stance assumed by an Anabaptist political scientist is unavailable outside of the acceptance of specific faith claims, in what way can he or she communicate that critical perspective that is not a mere talking to oneself? I have argued the following concerning contemporary political science:

(1)   By a variety of accounts, contemporary social science finds its epistemological roots in classical liberalism;

(2)   The epistemology of liberalism, when applied to a science of *human* phenomena, makes such a science ethically incoherent;

(3)   overlooking this epistemological problem, we find American social science to be largely unreflectively working on behalf of American democracy;

(4)   this activity of marshalling knowledge for the use of the regime tends to make political science oriented toward the status quo and to work in the interests of those in power;

(5)   other orientations are possible.

The Anabaptist does not talk only to herself for at least two reasons. First, the activity of the church is visible to the world as a concrete witness to an alternative way of being. It is out of both this concrete form and its not-yet-realized aspirations that the Anabaptist speaks. Second, the Anabaptist speaks to the secular powers and social scientists in a common vocabulary, making claims to ultimate justice, goodness, and perfection that the secular powers may also make and the specific criticisms of which they will therefore be more likely to understand. These middle axioms are developed out of a principled reflection on the claims and deeds of secular powers in contrast with the claims (and deeds) of those whose membership is in the Kingdom of Heaven. The Anabaptist rejects the ethical schizophrenia of Lutheran theology and of the closely related liberal public/private split. He likewise rejects the Roman Catholic distinction between laity and clergy or "professional" practitioners of religion. He also rejects the overlap between church and state of Constantinian Catholicism and the Magisterial Reformation. Consequently, his social science must be part of an integrated witness to the powers that be. In this, it may, on specific matters, speak similarly to other, non-establishment voices. It may also suffer corruption. That is a matter for correction under God's grace. It may, moreover, be ignored, scorned, or suppressed. If obedience and not historical effectiveness is the prime directive, however, then that, too, is left to God's care. The Anabaptist is a "supportive resident alien," being neither a manipulator of social forces nor an apologist for seeming political necessity. If permitted to join the scholarly and practical discussion of political questions, the Anabaptist would offer a vibrant voice at the table.

Notes

1. Cf. George Williams, *The Radical Reformation* (Philadelphia: The Westminster Press, 1962), 119-27; and, Heinold Fast, "Conrad Grebel: The Covenant on the Cross," in *Profiles of Radical Reformers: Biographical Sketches from Thomas Müntzer to Paracelsus*, ed. Hans-Jürgen Goertz and Walter Klaassen (Kitchener and Scottdale: Herald Press, 1982), 118ff.

2. I have given an extended argument for this characterization of (some) social science interpretations of Anabaptism in "Theological and Secular Meta-Narratives of Politics: Anabaptist Origins Revisited (Again)," *Modern Theology* 13, no. 2 (April, 1997): 227-52. The most important works in this school of interpretation include: C. P. Clasen, *Anabaptism: A Social History, 1525-1618* (Ithaca and London: Cornell University Press, 1972); James M. Stayer, *Anabaptists and the Sword*, 2nd ed. (Lawrence: Coronado Press, 1976); and Hans-Jürgen Goertz, *Die Täufer: Geschichte und Deutung* (München: Verlag C.H. Beck, 1980). James M. Stayer, Werner O. Packull, and Klaus Deppermann, "From Monogenesis to Polygenesis: The Historical Discussion of Anabaptist Origins" *The Mennonite Quarterly Review* 54 (1975): 83-122, provide a good re-

view of the arguments, as does James M. Stayer, "Was Dr. Kuehler's Conception of Early Dutch Anabaptism Historically Sound? The Historical Discussion of Anabaptist Münster 450 Years Later," *Mennonite Quarterly Review* 60, no. 3 (1986): 261-62. For a review of the fragmentation in Anabaptist historiography, see especially James Stayer, "Let a Hundred Flowers Bloom and Let a Hundred Schools of Thought Contend," *The Mennonite Quarterly Review* 53, no. 3 (1979): 211-18.

3. Stayer, Anabaptists and the Sword, 6.

4. Walter Klaassen, "The Nature of the Anabaptist Protest," *The Mennonite Quarterly Review* 55, no. 4 (1971): 298-300. Cf. H. W. Meiheuizen, "The Concept of Restitution in the Anabaptism of Northwestern Europe," trans. William Keeney, *The Mennonite Quarterly Review* 54, no. 2 (1970): 141-58; Frank J. Wray, "The Anabaptist Doctrine of the Restitution of the Church," *The Mennonite Quarterly Review* 28, no. 3 (1954): 186-96. Central works from the "evangelical" perspective, crudely categorized, include: Harold Bender, "The Anabaptist Vision," *Church History* 13 (1944): 3-24; Denny Weaver, *Becoming Anabaptist: The Origin and Significance of Sixteenth-Century Anabaptism* (Scottdale: Herald Press, 1987); John H. Yoder, "'Anabaptists and the Sword' Revisited: Systematic Historiography and Undogmatic Nonresistants," *Zeitschrift für Kirchengeschichte* 85, no. 2 (1974): 127-39; Kenneth R. Davis, "Vision and Revision in Anabaptist Historiography: Perceptional Tensions in a Broadening Synthesis or Alien Idealization?" *The Mennonite Quarterly Review* 53, no. 3 (1979): 200-207; Werner Packull, "A Response to 'History and Theology: A Major Problem of Anabaptist Research Today,'" *The Mennonite Quarterly Review* 53, no. 3 (1979): 208-11.

5. Klaassen, Neither Protestant nor Catholic, p. 20.

6. Alasdair MacIntyre, *Three Rival Version of Moral Enquiry: Encyclopaedia, Genealogy, and Tradition* (Notre Dame, Ind.: University of Notre Dame Press, 1990), 58-103.

7. James C. Juhnke and Louise Hawkley, eds., *Nonviolent America: History through the Eyes of Peace* (Newton, Kans.: Mennonite Press), 1993.

8. Ken Brown, "Was the 'Good War' a Just War?" in Juhnke and Hawkley, eds., *Nonviolent America*, 88-89.

9. Stanley Hauerwas, *Against the Nations: War and Survival in a Liberal Society* (San Francisco: Harper and Row, Publishers, 1985), 137-38.

10. For a pacifist remark on that particular war, see Donald F. Durnbaugh, "War and Patriotism from Historic Peace Church Perspectives," in Juhnke and Hawkley, *Nonviolent America*, 176-77.

11. Brown, "Good War," 90.

12. Brown, "Good War," 94-95; Stephen Toulmin, "The Limits of Allegiance in a Nuclear Age," in *Just War Theory*, ed. Jean Bethke Elshtain (New York: New York University Press, 1992), 280-98, at 283; Freeman Dyson, *Weapons and Hope* (San Francisco: Harper and Row, 1984), 60-62, 115-20, 149.

13. "The moral cost of fighting Hitler was less tangible but more devastating than the physical destruction of Europe. In fighting him on his own terms we were forced to descend to a similar depravity of means. Eichmann carted people to the ovens. The Allied air forces carted the ovens to the people. . . . In adopting terror bombing and esca-

lating it to its technological culmination at Nagasaki, we embraced what A. J. Muste called 'the logic of atrocity'" (Brown, "Good War," 100-101).

14. Juhnke outlines the following five options: "1) modify surrender terms, 2) demonstrate the bomb, 3) wait for Russia to intervene, 4) invade Japan, and 5) drop the bomb without warning." All five, Juhnke claims, "were given at least some consideration by decision makers of the era" (William E. Juhnke, "Teaching the Atomic Bomb: The Greatest Thing in History," in *Nonviolent America*, ed. Juhnke and Hawkley, 109).

15. Brown, "Good War," 90-91.

16. Brown, "Good War," 91-93.

17. Charles Chatfield, "Revisionism with a Vision," in *Nonviolent America*, ed. Juhnke and Hawkley, 15-20.

18. John Howard Yoder, "The Burden and the Discipline of Evangelical Revisionism," in *Nonviolent America*, ed. Juhnke and Hawkley, 23-24.

19. James C. Juhnke, "Manifesto for Pacifist Reinterpretation of American History," in *Nonviolent America*, ed. Juhnke and Hawkley, 13-14.

20. John Howard Yoder, *The Christian Witness to the State* (Newton, Kans.: Faith and Life Press, 1964), 29.

21. Yoder, Christian Witness, 28.

22. Yoder, "Burden and Discipline," 23.

23. Yoder, "Burden and Discipline," 35-36; *Priestly Kingdom*, 138-39, 140, 82-92.

24. Yoder, Christian Witness, 38.

25. Yoder, Christian Witness, 39.

26. Yoder, *Christian Witness*, 35, also 45.

27. Frank E. Manuel and Fritzie P. Manuel, *Utopian Thought in the Western World* (Cambridge: The Belknap Press, 1979), 461.

28. Robert Jacques Turgot, "A Philosophical Review of the Successive Advances of the Human Mind," in translated and ed. Ronald L. Meek, *Turgot on Progress, Sociology, and Economics* (Cambridge: Cambridge University Press, 1973), 45.

29. Bury, *Progress*, 161, 165; Manuel and Manuel, *Utopian Thought*, 463; Robert Jacques Turgot, "On Universal History," in *Turgot on Progress*, 84-88, 93-94, 100-101.

30. Manuel and Manuel, *Utopian Thought*, 463.

31. Manuel and Manuel, *Utopian Thought*, 464.

32. Turgot, "Philosophical Review," 45-46.

33. Turgot, "Philosophical Review," 56-58; Turgot, "Universal History," 94-105, 116-18.

34. J. B. Bury, *The Idea of Progress: An Inquiry into Its Growth and Origin* (New York: Dover Publications, Inc., 1955), 5. Cf. Turgot, "Philosophical Review," 55, 59; Turgot, "Universal History," 64.

35. Bury, *Progress*, 7-36; John Passmore, *The Perfectibility of Man* (New York: Charles Scribner's Sons, 1970), 195-99.

36. Bury, *Progress*, 127-28; cf. René Descartes, *Discourse on Method*, trans. Donald Cress (Indianapolis: Hackett Publishing Company, 1980), 33; Francis Bacon, *The New Organon* (Indianapolis: Bobbs-Merrill Company, Inc., 1960), 15-16.

37. Bury, *Progress*, 150.

38. Auguste Comte, *Introduction to Positive Philosophy*, ed. Frederick Ferré (Indianapolis: Hackett Publishing Company, Inc., 1988), 30.

39. Thomas A. Spragens, Jr., *The Irony of Liberal Reason* (Chicago: University of Chicago Press, 1981), 121, 128-31.

40. Spragens, *Irony of Liberal Reason*, 122.

41. Spragens, *Irony of Liberal Reason*, 125-26.

42. Spragens, *Irony of Liberal Reason*, 126.

43. Rogers M. Smith, "Still Blowing in the Wind: The American Quest for a Democratic, Scientific Political Science," *Daedalus* 126 (Winter 1997): 253-87 at 255-59, 263, 273; Charles E. Lindblom, "Political Science in the 1940s and 1950s," *Daedalus* 126 (Winter 1997): 225-52 at 248.

44. Spragens, *Irony of Liberal Reason*, 170.

45. Leo Strauss, *What Is Political Philosophy? and Other Studies* (Chicago: The University of Chicago Press, 1959), 20. "Our social science may make us very wise or clever as regards the means for any objectives we might choose. It admits being unable to help us in discriminating between legitimate and illegitimate, between just and unjust, objectives. Such a science is instrumental and nothing but instrumental: it is born to be the handmaid of any powers or any interests that be. What Machiavelli did apparently, our social science would actually do if it did not prefer—only God knows why—generous liberalism to consistency: namely, to give advice with equal competence and alacrity to tyrants as well as to free peoples" (Leo Strauss, *Natural Right and History* [Chicago: The University of Chicago Press, 1953], 3-4; also 5-80).

46. Alasdair MacIntyre, *After Virtue: A Study in Moral Theory*, 2d ed. (Notre Dame, Ind.: University of Notre Dame Press, 1984), 86.

47. Spragens, *Irony of Liberal Reason*, 172.

48. MacIntyre, *After Virtue*, 88-108; Hannah Arendt, *The Human Condition* (Chicago: The University of Chicago Press, 1958), 43-45; Yoder, *Christian Witness*, 44.

49. MacIntyre, *After Virtue*, 107.

50. Spragens, *Irony of Liberal Reason*, 173; Strauss, *Natural Right*, 23; MacIntyre, *After Virtue*, 55, 59.

51. Strauss, *Political Philosophy*, 23, 19, 21, 22.

52. Yoder, *Christian Witness*, passim. Cf. John Howard Yoder, *The Original Revolution* (Scottdale, Pa.: Mennonite Publishing House, 1972), 76.

53. Strauss, Political Philosophy, 21.

54. Strauss, Political Philosophy, 21.

55. Although it is certainly possible to think of being Christian as a "value-preference" or "life-style choice," I will bracket that possibility for purposes of this discussion: the telling critiques that have been levied against the incoherence of "values chatter" in general (which I have briefly summarized in the preceding paragraphs) work equally well against the "religious preference" form of that discourse.

56. Spragens, *Irony of Liberal Reason*, 176.

57. Examples of such corrosive activity includes especially the involuntary incarceration of individuals not for punishment for deeds done, but for treatment of psychological conditions deemed "deviant" or open to therapeutic intervention. Such treatment

tends to fly in the face of the central liberal doctrines of human rights and individual responsibility. Abuses of this kind in American society are well documented (Spragens, *Irony of Liberal Reason*, 179-83; cf. Thomas Szasz, *Ideology and Insanity: Essays on the Psychiatric Dehumanization of Man* (Garden City, N.Y.: Doubleday, 1970), 98-112, 113-39).

58. Lindblom, "Political Science," 247.

59. Theodore Lowi, "The State in Political Science: How We Become What We Study," *American Political Science Review* 86 (March 1992), 1.

60. Lowi, "The State in Political Science," 5.

61. Lindblom, "Political Science," 247 (italics in original).

62. Smith, "Still Blowing in the Wind," 276.

63. Lindblom, "Political Science," 244.

64. Claude E. Welch Jr., "The Comparative Study of Political Modernization," *Political Modernization: A Reader in Comparative Change*, ed. Claude E. Welch Jr. (Belmont, Calif.: Wadsworth Publishing Company, Inc., 1967), 4.

65. Welch, "Political Modernization," 2 (my italics).

67. Welch, "Political Modernization," 12-13 (my italics).

68. Welch quotes Sinai: "Men came to believe for the first time that it would be possible to rearrange society on rational principles . . . All these social, economic, political and cultural revolutions helped to break the 'cake of custom' of traditional society, and to create our modern world of incessant change and innovation and of enduring achievements" (I. R. Sinai, *The Challenge of Modernisation* [London: Chatto and Windus, 1964], 18-19, in Welch, "Political Modernization," 4).

69. Gabriel A. Almond and G. Bingham Powell, Jr., *Comparative Politics: A Developmental Approach* (Boston: Little, Brown and Company, 1966), 24-25, 33.

70. Almond and Powell, *Comparative Politics*, 57-63.

71. Samuel P. Huntington, "The Goals of Development," in *Understanding Political Development*, ed. Myron Weiner and Samuel P. Huntington (San Francisco: Harper-Collins, 1987), 6-11.

72. I take this to be the gist of Huntington's review, "Goals," 11-28. One social science example to the contrary is Peter Berger's *Pyramids of Sacrifice: Political Ethics and Social Change* (Garden City, N. Y.: Doubleday, 1976).

73. Manfred Halpern, *The Politics of Social Change in the Middle East and North Africa* (Princeton, N. J.: Princeton University Press, 1963), 1-37.

74. Katherine S. Newman, *Falling from Grace: The Experience of Downward Mobility in the American Middle Class* (New York: Random House, 1988), 1-19.

75. See *Faith and Political Philosophy: The Correspondence between Leo Strauss and Eric Voegelin, 1934-1964*, trans. and ed. Barry Cooper and Peter Emberley (University Park, Pa.: The Pennsylvania State University Press, 1993); Murray Jardine, "Eric Voegelin's Interpretation(s) of Modernity: A Reconsideration of the Spiritual and Political Implications of Voegelin's Therapeutic Analysis," *The Review of Politics* 57, no. 4 (Fall 1995): 581-605.

76. John Milbank, *Theology and Social Theory: Beyond Secular Reason* (Oxford, England: Blackwell Publishers, 1990), 331.

77. Milbank, Theology and Social Theory, 331.

78. Milbank, Theology and Social Theory, 363.

79. Milbank, Theology and Social Theory, 417-23; Yoder, Priestly Kingdom, 135-47.

80. Milbank, Theology and Social Theory, 363; John H. Yoder, The Original Revolution, esp. 13-104.

81. Milbank, Theology and Social Theory, 381.

82. Voegelin, *The New Science of Politics: An Introduction* (Chicago: The University of Chicago Press, 1952), chapters 1 and 2.

83. Milbank, Theology and Social Theory, 406-11.

84. Yoder, *Priestly Kingdom*, 80-88, 135-47, 172-95; cf. John Howard Yoder, *The Royal Priesthood: Essays Ecclesiological and Ecumenical*, ed. Michael G. Cartwright (Grand Rapids, Mich.: Wm B. Eerdmans, 1994), 143-67.

85. Yoder, *Christian Witness to the State*, 29.

Part Two

New Thinking in Theory

Chapter 3

Rawls, Religion, and Liberalism

Ashley Woodiwiss

Much has been made of Rawls's "practical" or "political" turn from his *Theory of Justice* (1971) to his *Political Liberalism* (1993).[1] Both secular and religious Rawls watchers wrestle over the issue of whether and to what extent *Political Liberalism* represents a fundamental break with the theoretical underpinnings of *Theory of Justice*. Does *Political Liberalism* reflect continuity or discontinuity in Rawls's overall project? For my purposes here, I leave that intramural debate to Rawlsian scholars. Rather, I will simply go with Charles Kelbley who notes in his review of *Political Liberalism:* "Much, indeed most, of the content of this new book continues to argue in support of his original theory of justice, but the new, perhaps even startling, focus of *Political Liberalism* has the effect of requiring us to understand the theoretical underpinnings of the original theory and its applications quite differently. A number of new ideas, such as 'reasonable pluralism,' 'the burdens of judgment,' 'overlapping consensus,' and 'public reason' are the agents of this change in focus and understanding."[2]

Such a view permits both sides to thrash out just how much remains of *Theory of Justice* after all the new ideas have been sifted through. Scholarly religious assessment of *Political Liberalism* has focused chiefly upon Rawls's concept of "public reason," and here, I want to assess the problem with Rawls's public reason that has most concerned them.

In part one I identify this problem as one of "exclusionism." Whether or not "exclusionism" is particular to Rawlsian liberalism or whether it must be seen as a fixed article in what Jean Hampton describes as "the common faith of liberalism"[3] is the subject of part two. My conclusion that exclusionism is indeed an ineliminable part of liberalism pushes me, in the third and final section, toward a particular reconceiving of the nature of the liberal regime from a perspective internal to a particular, religiously traditional, and nonliberal community.

The Problem with Political Liberalism

> Political liberalism assumes that, for political purposes, a plurality of reasonable yet incompatible comprehensive doctrines is the normal result of the exercise of human reason within the framework of the free institutions of a constitutional democratic regime. Political liberalism also supposes that a reasonable comprehensive doctrine does not reject the essentials of a democratic regime. Of course, a society may also contain unreasonable and irrational, and even mad, comprehensive doctrines. In their case the problem is to contain them so that they do not undermine the unity and justice of society.[4]

Rawls makes this claim in the introduction to his *Political Liberalism*. There he discusses how this work with its new ideas should be understood vis-à-vis his previous *Theory of Justice*. He draws attention to the following problem: while in a well-ordered society there might be widespread and overlapping consensus as to the principles of justice as fairness (the topic of *TJ*), nevertheless in a modern democratic society the reasons why citizens of certain subcommunities of the liberal regime do in fact agree to justice as fairness may not agree with the reasons of other groups. For Rawls, this is the modern situation of "reasonable pluralism." There may be agreement on the principles but no agreement on the reasons for the agreement. Rawls employs the concept of "public reason" to construct a model of public deliberation for the peaceable negotiation of differences between such (potentially rival) subcommunities. As such, his concept is central to his justification of the modern pluralist liberal regime.

Roberto Alejandro suggests that we understand Rawls as engaged "in what might be termed a hermeneutic and archeological enterprise."[5] As archeology, Rawls is after the discovery of political principles that are deeply embedded in our practices and institutions and which reflect a fund of commonly held beliefs about the best way to sustain our common democratic society. As hermeneutics, Rawls seeks to articulate those principles for the end of achieving and sustaining social stability (or what I call, *regime maintenance*). But criticism has been loud and consistent over Rawls's efforts to line-draw between reasonable and unreasonable doctrines and the role that the concept of public reason plays in his theory.

For instance, Alejandro claims that Rawls's paradigm "comes up with a 'political liberalism' that is self-justified. Rawlsian justice guarantees social unity to the extent that its premises are *justified in advance*."[6] For Alejandro, the problem is not that Rawls reads politics out of his account, as some of his critics have claimed, but that he employs a particular political methodology that sets up a public political discourse "concerned with the exclusion of divisive issues that might threaten the stability of a well-ordered society."[7] In this line of argument, "public reason" and the other ideas that Rawls employs must be seen as political tools whereby he constructs a "public" after his understanding of regime needs. This is architectonic political philosophy masquerading as a pragmatic turn.[8]

In a similar line of argument, William Galston faults the kind of line-drawing that Rawls employs in his discussion of the reasonable and the unreasonable. Particularly in the most troubling issue for liberals, that of religion, Galston sees Rawls as not taking the fact of religious diversity "seriously enough." Rather, Rawls is involved in inherently contestable line-drawing when he talks of extending toleration only to reasonable doctrines, which he defines in the extended quote above. Galston replies: "This criterion packs far too much into the idea of 'reasonable.' I can easily imagine religions that thoughtfully reject the essentials of democracy while finding it possible to reach a range of practical accommodations with democratic requirements." Galston indicts him further, as when Rawls claims that a key component of public reasonableness includes "accepting the methods and conclusions of science when not controversial."[9] After listing a partial account of those groups for whom particular claims of science are fully controversial, Galston claims: "If 'not controversial' means 'not challenged by any religion,' then virtually nothing of contemporary science can be included in public reason. But if we construe 'not controversial' to exclude the claims of dissenting religious groups, then once again, as with an overly restrictive definition of the reasonable, we fail to take deep diversity seriously enough."[10]

For critics like Alejandro and Galston, the nature of Rawls's project in *PL* is too (politically) exclusive in what he reads in and out of public discourse by means of "reasonableness." Indeed, Jean Hampton makes the argument that Rawls's use of "reasonable" as an excluding device is itself "an illiberal idea."[11] If Rawls's concept can be scored on these terms, just what have religious scholars made of "public reason"?

Coming to Terms with Rawlsian Exclusionary Liberalism

To identify Rawlsian liberalism with exclusion leads to the following unsettling question: What does his theory means for traditional religious communities; that is, those communities possessed by the kind of comprehensive doctrines that Rawls can only partially allow into the public discourse of the modern liberal regime? There appear to be three major responses to Rawlsian exclusionary liberalism from among religious scholars: (1) the view that such exclusion is necessary and beneficial both for the liberal regime and the religious voice; (2) the view that exclusionary liberalism needs to be softened by making even more room for the religious voice; and, (3) the view that such exclusionism constitutes too high a price for religious communities to pay for inclusion in the Rawlsian liberal regime.

Another term for exclusion when it deals with religion is "privatization." Paul Weithman rejects the notion that Rawlsian political liberalism is guilty in this matter. While acknowledging that Rawls does constrain the religious voice in his theory, Weithman argues that "Rawls would allow religion greater scope in political discourse than is often thought." Taking on a number of such critics, Weithman maintains that, while religious reasons cannot suffice for public reason, "religion is not, however, completely prohibited from public or political discourse." In this view, religion can serve as an important intellectual resource in political argument. Meanwhile, what Weithman identifies as the goods of "mutual respect, trust and assurance of every last citizen that society corporately and others singly respect" he views as better secured in our day by the discipline of Rawlsian public reason than by arguments invoking any religious authority. Weithman's reasoning here is historical and contextual. In explaining just why the Supreme Court could use religiously grounded arguments in *Zorach v. Clauson* (1952) but no longer can or ought to, Weithman comments: "In the intervening forty years, pluralism has increased, as has the suspicion of religious authority and religious argument. It seems to me very doubtful that the Supreme Court could now rely on religious arguments to justify its verdicts without arousing suspicions that the fundamental interests of some are being sacrificed illegitimately."[12]

From this vantage point, the concept of public reason serves the political needs of the contemporary pluralist regime. In so doing it also provides beneficial discipline to religious communities who would seek an active part in the public discourse of such a regime. This kind of religionist view I call Rawlsian exclusionary liberalism *sola*, for it leaves intact the liberal modern regime, and requires the religious voice to undergo some disciplinary training before it can speak.

David Hollenbach represents a second scholarly religious response to Rawlsian exclusionary liberalism. Dissenting from Weithman, Hollenbach argues that Rawls has not gone far enough with his notion of public reason as set out in *Political Liberalism.* Hollenbach acknowledges that the Rawlsian "well-ordered" society is one in which as Rawls states, "A reasonable and effective political conception may bend comprehensive doctrines toward itself, shaping them if need be from unreasonable to reasonable."[13] That Rawlsian political liberalism has this effect does not trouble Hollenbach. But Rawls misses the historical fact how, in American practice, religiously motivated voices have been, at times, central to this public bending of comprehensive doctrines. Hollenbach cites John Courtney Murray's influence on Catholic social thought and Martin Luther King Jr.'s contribution (one which Rawls himself cites approvingly in *Political Liberalism,* 247 and 250) to the formation of public reason. Hollenbach maintains, "Rawls's theory, even as interpreted by Weithman, needs to make considerably more room for such a role for religion in public life."[14] Such a view may be considered as Rawlsian exclusionary liberalism *plus.* From this perspective Rawls has much to offer, but religion is here explicitly enlisted as a necessary supplement for liberal regime maintenance. Where the *sola* perspective requires no such external supplementation, the *plus* view demands that liberalism solicit a public theological justification.

Rejecting this latter incorporationist view, Timothy Jackson claims that Rawls does not require the Christian citizen to abandon the highest virtue/value of the Christian tradition, *agape,* so much as to subordinate it to social ends. But such subordination eventuates in the compromise of her integrity. When Rawls requires Christians to "bend" their comprehensive doctrines for the sake of an overlapping consensus in the operation of public reason, he is "demanding too large a sacrifice." Rawls poses as the central political problem: "How is it possible that there may exist over time a stable and just society of free and equal citizens profoundly divided by reasonable though incompatible religious, philosophical, and moral doctrines?"[15] Jackson responds thus: "The strong agapist doubts that a sacrifice of virtue for a desirable civic accord is practically possible, given that she sees agape as the necessary condition for the substantive realization of all other human goods. Acting out of a loving motive is the best (finally the only) way to further lasting public peace and social cooperation, but these are secondary effects."

For Jackson, the liberal quest for consensus "must not be permitted to overrule other moral commitments."[16] From this perspective, which can be understood as the perspective internal to traditional religious communities, Rawlsian exclusionary liberalism prohibits that which is the *sine qua non* of identity, integrity and authenticity. To embrace

Rawlsian public reason may work civic peace for political society in the aggregate, but the cost for certain communities may be too high. Such a rejectionist view I label, Rawlsian exclusionary liberalism *not*.

In sum, religious scholars consider Rawls's "public reason" and its exclusionary quality as problematic. The level of concern on the part of such scholars range from Weithman's downplaying of the problem, to Hollenbach's efforts to accomodate the religious voice to it, to Jackson's rejection of Rawls's account. To be fair, Rawls acknowledges openly that public reason has its limits and seeks to confront the issue of exclusion head-on. Unfortunately, he fails to solve the problem. Rawls argues that he has abandoned his originally preferred "exclusive view," which held that, "on fundamental political matters, reasons given explicitly in terms of comprehensive doctrines are never to be introduced into public reason." Rather, he now embraces an "inclusive view" which allows citizens "in certain situations, to present what they regard as the basis of political values rooted in their comprehensive doctrine, provided they do this in ways that strengthen the ideal of public reason itself." Just what kind of situations count and which do not, he makes clear by citing favorably the religious based claims of abolitionists and Martin Luther King Jr., but rejecting those of contemporary pro-lifers in the abortion debate. Rawls's meek attempt at navigating through this patently political claim rests on a watery historicism: "This brief discussion shows that the appropriate limits of public reason vary depending on historical and social conditions. The ideal may best be achieved in different ways, in good times by following what at first sight may appear to be the exclusive view, in less good times by what may appear to be the inclusive view."[17] It appears that Rawls is in fact involved in gatekeeping; now permitting this, now rejecting that religiously-based public argument. Obviously, the distinction here is not so much between exclusion and inclusion but between a strong and a weak version of exclusion.[18]

I end this first section with an observation: the existence and demand for exclusion is an ineliminable part of Rawlsian theory. As Hampton puts it as she considers how Rawls uses the notion of reasonableness to adjudicate the abortion debate: "Perhaps we should simply treat this footnote on abortion as a regrettable mistake on Rawls's part—an illiberal moment in the book that can (and should) be excised from the text without affecting the liberal theory put forward there. But I worry this was no simple mistake. In particular, I worry that there is something about Rawls's theory of liberalism that encourages anyone who embraces it to use the notion of 'reasonable' in the illiberal way it is used in this footnote."[19] Insofar as the identity and integrity of the religious voice of traditional religious communities are concerned, Rawls walks the beat. He may be made to look like the good cop or the bad, the hard cop or the soft, but policing the public square is the thrust of his posture toward the speech and actions of traditional communities of faith.

In the remainder of this chapter, I wish to argue that the best way to get at the character of Rawlsian exclusionary liberalism is from the perspective that best comprehends the effect of his theory; that is, from the perspective of membership within a particularistic community.[20] From such an internal perspective, the *sola* and the *plus* religionist accounts contribute to a kind of regime maintenance that would be acceptable if the regime's relationship with traditional communities of faith were unproblematic or easily reconcilable. But the *not* religionist viewpoint is both a more accurate historical understanding of that relationship and a better political perspective whereby such communities may begin the reassessment of how to negotiate their place in the regime of modern liberalism. As such, my argument takes me into a broader consideration of liberalism itself.

The Problem with Liberalism

In this section I want to place Rawls into two historical contexts: (1) the more immediate context of contemporary liberal political philosophy, and, (2) a longer context in terms of the history of liberalism. I conclude this section by endorsing Jean Hampton's view that in *Political Liberalism*, Rawls must be seen as a keeper of the liberal faith. The significance of this last point is spelled out in detail below and in the final section of this chapter.

The shift that has occurred within Rawls's theoretical project corresponds to a larger shift in liberal justificatory strategy. The shift might be seen in terms of contemporary liberals deriving their insight and inspiration from Aristotle rather than Kant. Developing largely as their response to the "communitarian critique of liberalism" (Sandel, MacIntyre, Taylor, etc.), defenders of the liberal regime have shifted their ground as to what constitutes the proper reading of religion in the liberal regime.[21] The pervasive *neutrality thesis* of the 1970s and early 1980s employed in liberal argumentation (and which drew heavy direct inspiration from Rawls's *Theory of Justice*) has given way to a new justificatory project employing what I call a *neo-Aristotelian thesis*.

Signs that the old orthodoxy was losing its grip surfaced early in the 1980s, when William Galston took the issue head-on in his article, "Defending Liberalism." In a book two years before he had employed a neo-Aristotelian (rather than the standard rights-based) argument to show how a liberal might account for "justice and the human good." But it was in this later article that he claimed that the then standard neutrality-based defense of liberalism was "fundamentally misguided."[22] This defense, when *applied* in public discourse, judicial proceedings, administrative guidelines, etc., fuelled the perception of "liberalism as morally empty." There, Galston maintains that the reconstruction of liberal theory is a crucial and necessary link for the revival of liberal politics. This same sense of urgency continues in Galston's recent work, *Liberal Purposes* (1991).

A new generation of liberal scholars appears now to positively delight in talking about virtue, religion, community, and flourishing. The neutralists have been superseded by an alternative perspective, one which Michael Perry describes as a form of "neo-Aristotelian liberalism."[23]

I use this apt description for the body of literature considered here, especially as it pertains to their handling of the place of religion in the liberal state. While certain differences separate such scholars as Galston, Kymlicka, Macedo, and Perry (differences in tone as well as content) what unites them is a shared rejection of defending liberalism the way it has been done for the last two decades and a commitment to respond directly to the kinds of criticisms that communitarians, conservatives, and leftist critics have made in the past decades concerning liberalism's apparent inability to provide for a substantive account of community, virtue, and religion. Where the neutrality thesis took religion off the table, the neo-Aristotelian thesis puts it back on.

In her critical assessment of the variety of approaches that liberals have taken to justify the liberal state, Margaret Moore points out what the neo-Aristotelians have concluded: "Neutrality cannot be achieved because neutrality itself requires justification."[24] Taking rights seriously occurs when we believe them to be linked in some important way to our sense of the grand scheme of things; that is, to our understanding of the Human Good. To privilege no account of the Good, thus privileging "neutrality," seems a fragile reed upon which to rest the liberal project. Liberalism must be able to promise more. As Galston concedes: "Aristotle was right: Core political principles shape the character of every aspect of the community. Like every other form of political community, liberalism is a regime."[25]

But does this rejection of neutrality entail what the neutralists previously considered anathema to the idea of a liberal state; namely, "perfectionism"?[26] Yes and no. This newer thesis exhibits "perfectionist" tendencies when it identifies specific liberal virtues that are essential for a flourishing liberal polity, the necessity of shared ends which forms the communal identity, and when it argue for religion's ineliminable place within the liberal regime. However, a sense of hesitation is also discernible in this literature. Celebrating the richness of the liberal tradition and the resources it possesses, a condition that makes it possible to speak of a liberal conception of the Good Life, the neo-Aristotelians nevertheless mount a project that Galston is willing to describe only as one of "minimal perfectionism."[27] Along with the talk of shared ends, virtues, etc., there exists within the new thesis a continuing commitment to autonomy, the plurality of ends worthy of human choice, and a profound reluctance to allow state coercion to override freedom of choice. Neo-Aristotelian perfectionist liberalism does two things at once: like Aristotle, it treats the existing and historical realities of the community (e.g., the religious character of the people) as the necessary materials with which political philosophy and statesmanship must be concerned. But as *liberals*, these thinkers are concerned, having now let the wolf in the door, that the talk of community, virtue, religion, etc., be properly domesticated so that it becomes pet, not predator, in the liberal household. This is to embrace religion even as it tries to control it. Or as Galston puts it, "What is distinctive about liberalism is not the absence of a substantive conception of the good, but rather a reluctance to move from this to full-blown public coercion of individuals."[28]

In the neo-Aristotelian thesis, the remedy for neutrality comes by way of a recovery of original liberal sources (especially Locke for the discussion of religion) and a reappreciation for the everyday sentiments of the common citizen (as the proper basis for prudential liberal policies). Galston faults Rawls for his misreading of Locke's doctrine of religious toleration as an argument justifying a more general doctrine of liberal neutrality. He states, "Locke's argument is not only less sweeping than, but actually contradicts, the contemporary conception of neutrality."[29] And Michael Perry argues that while all liberals are "committed to a tolerant, democratic politics," it is important to remember that John Locke based his arguments on his Protestant theology, not some "Liberalism as neutrality [which is] a phantom, a will o' the wisp."[30]

As for the everyday sentiments of citizens, Galston invokes a classic Tocquevellian argument in maintaining that "the level of religious commitment among Americans is demonstrably higher than is the case for all other Western countries." Consequently, the juridical nature of the neutrality thesis that forms most of the controversial twentieth-century Supreme Court cases on religious practice, while accepted by many elites, "was not firmly rooted in a popular consensus."[31]

The net effect of such a misunderstanding by the neutralists led to their disastrous conclusion that religion was dispensable in thinking about and defending liberalism. They had misconceived the relationship between religion and the liberal regime. Following his Tocqueville-like analysis of the matter, Galston contends that in some ways "religion and liberal politics need each other. Religion can undergird key liberal values and practices; liberal practices can protect—and substantially accommodate—the free exercise of religion."[32] Perry claims that neutralism "entails repression of the essentially political nature of religion," robbing it of its public place. He replaces neutrality with his model of "ecumenical politics," which recognizes that the fundamental standards of American political morality "derive from the religious traditions of American society, in particular the biblical heritage."[33]

To this point, the neo-Aristotelian thesis might elicit support from the perspective I am adopting here. For members of traditional communities of faith this is the kind of history to which they subscribe; the kind of cultural read of religion's place in the American soul (or psyche) they wish to give; the kind of relationship between religion and liberalism in which they wish to believe. So what is the problem? I believe members of traditional communities of faith will find most troubling just how the neo-Aristotelians portray the nature of the relationship which exists between the liberal regime and religion.

Moore, in her analysis of liberal political philosophy, acknowledges her preference for perfectionist accounts over those of the neutralists. But she shows that when perfectionists talk about such things as community there is a distinctive way of talking about it. She notes how in Will Kymlicka's theory, "community is valuable only if it allows for meaningful choice, only insofar as it supports a framework in which individual autonomy can be exercised. Community has no independent value of its own. What is really doing the work in Kymlicka's theory are traditional *liberal* principles."[34] Substitute the term *religion,* for that of *community,* and one easily gets the idea of what is at work here. The literature of the neo-Aristotelian thesis, for all its willingness to talk about religion, has a rather tailored account of religion in mind. It is religion (employing Rawls's term) bent in service to the liberal state.

This stands out in the neo-Aristotelian literature whenever traditionalist religious communities and the kinds of arguments they make are under investigation. Such arguments are held to be based on nonliberal principles. Neo-Aristotelians consequently consider such forms of discourse or arguments that these communities regularly employ within their shared life as not permitted in the modern liberal public square. In this literature a politically correct form of religion suitable for the liberal regime comes through. Traditionalism it is not. Galston states that neither "juridicalism nor fundamentalism can serve as an adequate basis for a liberal society." But he gives a rather broad read of fundamentalism for he later claims "ways of life that require self-restraint, hierarchy, or cultural integrity are likely to find themselves on the defensive, threatened with the loss of both cohesion and authority." Later when he celebrates the liberal regime's inculcation of a sense of critical self-reflection he acknowledges that such "is bound to have an effect on our ability to maintain those commitments, especially the ones resting on tradition, unquestioned authority, and faith."[35] We see evidence then of what Rawls describes as the work of political liberalism in bending "comprehensive doctrines toward itself." While I am not sure quite what Galston means by commitments based on "unquestioned authority," of this I am certain: if liberalism indeed necessitates such effects, then traditionalists might be forgiven if they wonder why they should continue to commit themselves to propping up this regime. But these liberals seem complacent in concluding that over time, in the liberal regime, there will be certain ways of life which may simply not win out. While traditionalist communities may survive in liberal societies, they must do so at the margins, and only with vigilance.

Thus Stephen Macedo, in celebrating the citizenship, virtue, and community he finds in liberal constitutionalism, notes how the distinguishing political fact of the liberal regime, its "aspiration to public reasonableness," requires that "appeals to inner conviction or faith" be ruled out in public justification.[36] This may lead to public positions "that religious fanatics will find deeply objectionable." But in his view, liberalism "cannot help but shape people's lives broadly and deeply and relentlessly over time" so that "nuns criticize their bishops and even the Pope; authorities of all kinds come into question. Certain types will find the liberal culture hospitable (artist, entrepreneur, arguer, and playboy) and others (devout and simple) will find the going tough."[37] More recently, and in direct employment of Rawlsian public reason, he asserts: "We will sometimes accommodate dissenting groups, but we must remind fundamentalists and others that they must pay a price for living in a free pluralistic society."[38]

Finally, Michael Perry's model of ecumenical political dialogue puts only the bar of "public accessibility" to those religious arguments that seek entrance to the public square. But religious groups, communities, and arguments can pass through only when they argue "in a manner neither sectarian nor authoritarian." Traditionalist communities in their public arguments must avoid appeals to local premises or experiences (sectarian) or to persons and institutions (authoritarian) "that have little if any authority beyond the confines of one's own moral or religious community." In avoiding these, the community demonstrates its acceptance of "fallibilism and pluralism" as the two essential assumptions necessary for ecumenical political dialogue to work.[39]

A review of the neo-Aristotelian literature as it pertains to religion thus gives grounds for concern to members of traditional faith communities. While open to the view that religion has much to offer the modern liberal state, the neo-Aristotelians read religion is such a way as to marginalize and silence traditionalist voices. As a response to this situation, members of traditionalist communities must give serious reflection to just what is the relationship between their faith commitments and the principles that underlie liberal modernity. Moore has shown how liberalism, however defined or defended, "is itself a conception of the good, on all fours with other conceptions of the good, and deeply antithetical to many moral and religious conceptions. It is committed to the value of autonomy and its principles presuppose the importance of protecting individual autonomy above all else." As she notes, real Christian communities in Canada and the United States find such an emphasis militantly opposed to their long-term survival. "Their cultural survival depends on devaluing the exercise of autonomy and emphasizing instead living according to the word of God."[40] The policing of traditionalist religious communities in America by the liberal state requires the regime to possess its own religious narrative, disciplined by cogent philosophic argument. Rawls's selective argument for an "inclusive" view of the limits to public reason gives strong credence to the view that the defenders of the liberal regime are now fully prepared to use religion in service to their "well-ordered" society. Or, as Macedo has put it in his characteristically blunt way, "Liberal civic education is bound to have the effect of favoring some ways of life or religious convictions over others. So be it."[41]

The question that the member-based perspective would lodge against both Rawlsian public reason and the neo-Aristotelian thesis is: must liberalism *as a whole* be inimical to the priority commitments of members of traditional communities of faith? Or, put differently, is Rawlsian exclusionism in fact "an illiberal idea"? Is liberalism itself illiberal insofar as its rhetoric of reason, reasonableness, and public reason masks an ineliminably exclusionary project?

Religion and Liberalism

Although Hampton considers Rawls's theory illiberal, she does not extend the argument to the tradition of liberalism itself. In this section, I wish to trace out an emerging narrative of suspicion which makes such an extension. As articulated specifically by religious scholars it gives added weight to the argument I am making here; namely, that members of traditional communities of faith who wish to preserve their integrity and identity need to rethink their location within the controlling regime of liberal reason.

In what follows I wish to develop a twofold argument: (1) the historical emergence of liberalism and the modern state as a project of domination over traditional communities of faith, and, (2) the permanent exclusionary structure of liberal thought. Taken together these two conditions spell out the politically problematic situation that confronts the members of traditional communities of faith.

How are we to understand the historical emergence of liberalism and the modern liberal regime? Standard accounts, of course, trace the emergence of the modern state as a direct *result* of the "wars of religion." As Rawls states:

> During the wars of religion people were not in doubt about the nature of the highest good, or the basis of moral obligation in divine law. The problem was rather: How is society even possible between those of different faiths? What can conceivably be the basis of religious toleration? Thus, the historical origin of political liberalism (and of liberalism more generally) is the Reformation and its aftermath, with the long controversies over religious toleration in the sixteenth and seventeenth centuries. Something like the modern understanding of liberty of conscience and freedom of thought began then.[42]

Notice how Rawls's posing of the problem references social unity and the search for a mechanism whereby to guarantee it. That is, he adopts what might be considered a *statist* perspective. But in recent years, undertaken largely by Christian scholars employing a partial postmodern genealogical approach, a different reading of that story has developed. My purposes here is to give that reading a name and to demonstrate just how and why this reading of the emergence of liberalism inclines members of traditional Christian communities toward the rejection of liberalism's self-image and to reconfigure the story along a more politically problematic line. In brief, the counternarrative emerging at the hands of Christian scholars is an *ecclesiocentric* narrative that reads the emergence of the modern liberal state from the perspective of how that historical development has affected the Church.[43] The Church thus becomes the institutional instantiation of the membership-based perspective that I have been employing as the vantage point whereby to critique Rawlsian exclusionary liberalism. For from the ecclesiocentric perspective there is a sudden retelling of the emergence of liberalism and the modern state. William Cavanaugh discounts liberals like Rawls, Judith Shklar, and Jeffrey Stout who "would have us believe that the State stepped in like a scolding schoolteacher on the playground of doctrinal dispute to put fanatical religionists in their proper place." Rather, this standard liberal read must be stood on its head: "The 'Wars of Religion' were not the events which necessitated the birth of the modern State; they were in fact themselves the birthpangs of the State." Cavanaugh goes on the detail how the creation of the concept of "religion" was instrumental in the privatization of the Church and the correlative rise of the State. Focusing on the late fifteenth-century

Italian Renaissance thinker Marsilio Ficino, Cavanaugh locates the emergence of the idea of religion as a universal impulse, which thus interiorizes religion "and removed it from its ecclesial context."[44]

Religion, now cast in Rawlsian terms, became freestanding from a hitherto required institutional instantiation. Through Bodin, Hobbes, and Locke, there subsequently emerged the concept of religion as "domesticated belief systems" which are now to be "manipulated by the sovereign for the benefit of the State." Thus where the liberal statist perspective views toleration as the historical vindication of public reason and the hallmark of the enlightened society, the ecclesiocentric perspective reads toleration as "the tool through which the State divides and conquers the Church." Cavanaugh's conclusion rejects the "self-righteous clucking about the dangers of public faith" which liberals routinely invoke. With the concept of religion a creation of Western modernity by which to tame the Church, the liberal state has been freed to view itself as peacemaker. But its hands were bloodied from the beginning by fueling the so-called 'religious wars.' And "the wars of the nineteenth and twentieth centuries testify the transfer of ultimate loyalty to the liberal nation-state has not curbed the toll of war's atrocities."[45] The sword of the liberal (peacemaking!) state drips bloody red.

The ecclesiocentric perspective thus gives a more political and less "naturalistic" read to historical development. Rejecting the mystifications of modern liberal Whig-like readings of the key centuries of early modernity, John Milbank claims that proper understanding begins by recognizing "the positive institution of the secular", a conscious work of construction whereby "the secular as a domain had to be instituted or *imagined,* both in theory and, in practice."[46] The new science of politics we associate with Hobbes and others must be read not as culmination of historical development so much as conscious *act,* a will to power, if you will. Central to this new science of politics was its decoupling from theology. The "new science of politics both assumed and constructed for itself a new autonomous object—the political—defined as a field of pure power."[47] But in order to accomplish this, modern political science had to participate in and capture the reigning public discourse of Christian theology and its coin, biblical hermeneutics. It is curious that liberals routinely discount, ignore or consider insignificant great portions of the founding texts of modernity like *Leviathan* or Locke's *First Treatise on Government.* For it is in those neglected sections that Hobbes and Locke demonstrate their abilities as *political theologians* employing a particular hermeneutic.[48] Milbank captures this necessary project of modernity whereby it publicly displaced the Church and its reading of Scripture. He bears quotation at length:

The new, secular *dominium* could not, according to the totalizing logic of willful occupation which now mediated transcendence in the public realm, really tolerate a "political" Church as
a cohabitant. Nevertheless, the surviving presence of the authoritative text of the Scriptures within the new space of sovereign
power could not be denied. It was even essentially *required* by
this power, as the source of a positive divine reconfirmation of
the covenantal principle, and for the truth that God stood behind
the positive authority of nature. However, one use of the Bible
had to be prohibited. This was its truly Catholic use, which accorded interpretive authority to a *tradition* of reading. It was
therefore necessary for the new political science to "capture"
from Catholic Christianity the text of the Bible: to produce a
new Biblical hermeneutic. This is the reason why both Hobbes's *Leviathan* and Spinoza's *Tractatus Theological-Politicus*
comprise a political science and a Biblical hermeneutics bound
together in one volume. The hermeneutics, just like the politics, possesses both liberal and absolutist aspects which turn out
to be really identical. [49]

Liberal and absolutist. Exclusionism thus abides as a fixed part of the
permanent structure of liberal thought and practice. It is an additional
"fundamental commitment" in Hampton's "common faith of liberalism." [50]

Walking the Liberal Beat

It is part of the task of those Christian theologians and thinkers who
view the situation less problematically as set out here to seek for the
proper adjustments or accommodations between what is often called
"religion and democracy." Public theology is a thriving enterprise
among proponents of *sola* and *plus* perspectives, and such efforts have
their Catholic, Protestant, liberal and conservative adherents. [51] What
are we to make of this ongoing project of accommodation/adjustment?
From the ecclesiocentric perspective it is both doomed to failure and
acquired at too high a price. The reason lies in the fact of liberalism's
essential, necessary and ineliminable commitment to exclusionism; or,
in other words in liberalism's permanent fingering of the Church as
requiring scrutiny, surveillance and policing. Liberalism walks the beat,
and the Church is subject to a kind of "ecclesial profiling." Thus public
theologians who speak of "religion" play into the hands of the liberal
authorities. Cavanaugh in his critical survey of recent public theologies
argues that to speak of "public" and "religion" involves public theologians in "a game at which the Church will inevitably lose, precisely because the very distinction of the public and private is an instrument by

which the State domesticates the Church." Religion, as we have seen, is permitted entrance into the public discourse only after it has been properly bent. But such a discourse "is detached from its specific locus in disciplined eccesial practices so that it may be compatible with the modern Christian subjection to the discipline of the State." Religion, liberal civil religion, is the glue that holds the liberal regime together. So the new generation of liberal philosophers (which I discussed above) have finally gotten it, even albeit reluctantly Rawls. We must have religion, liberals now recognize, but "not the Church, for the Church must be separated entirely from the domain of power."[52]

Against the liberal self-image of the regime as the realm of full human emancipation and reason is arrayed the ecclesiocentric counterimage of the liberal regime as police state. As Barry Harvey puts it, "the notions of confinement, surveillance, and utilization accurately describes the fate, not only of certain individuals, but also of *nonliberal traditions and communities* within the disciplinary configurations of liberal cultures and institutions." Public theology unwittingly participates in what Harvey calls (following Foucault) the liberal "panoptic confinement" of religion, "the procedures of virtually every type of public theology perpetuate the social grammar of confinement, the pacification of Christian existence."[53] Indeed, following this line, there may well be truth in Chesterton's observation of America as a nation with the soul of a church, for that in effect is what modernity has tried to produce. The nation-state as the church. "The rationalized configurations of liberal democracy, in other words, are posited as the last best hope for humankind. What is this except a secularized version of *extra ecclesiam nulla salus?*"[54] The panoptic process involves three interrelated objectives according to Harvey:[55] (1) the assigning of "virtually all non-Western and pre-enlightenment traditions to the sphere of 'religion,' where it 'protects them as a 'private value,'" (2) the reinscription of this now privatized religion to the margins of a modern secular society, "where it is effectively precluded from being directly involved in, or interfering with, society's primary modes of discipline and supervision"; and, (3) the panoptic grant of permission that this "value" may be invoked at the public level whenever, as Rawls puts it, "a society is not well-ordered and there is a profound division about constitutional essentials." At such a moment "the nonpublic reason of certain Christian churches" may be employed to support "the clear conclusions of public reason."[56]

From the ecclesiocentric perspective, to do public theology is to sing the captor's song. But what the Church looks for is redemption and release.

Conclusion

Rawlsian liberalism will pass. Newer forms, versions, and accounts will arise with some more successful than others. But as long as it is liberal, exclusionism, or the panoptic policing of the Church, will be there as well. It is a curious thing when a child of darkness sees more clearly than a child of light what the game is really all about. But such was on display a few years ago in the pages of *First Things,* a neo-orthodox journal concerned with religion and the public square, and under the editorial leadership of Fr. Richard John Neuhaus. For there, Stanley Fish, no darkener of church doors, lays out in clear light (in chastising well-meaning religionists, like Neuhaus, who would play the game of liberalism) the "common faith of liberalism" as it pertains to the issues herein discussed:

> liberalism rests on the substantive judgment that the public sphere must be insulated from viewpoints that owe their allegiance not to its procedures—to the unfettered operation of the marketplace of ideas—but to the truths they work to establish. That is what neutrality means in the context of liberalism—a continual pushing away of orthodoxies, of beliefs not open to inquiry and correction—and that is why, in the name of neutrality, religious propositions must either be excluded from the marketplace or admitted only in ceremonial forms, in the firm, for example, of a prayer that opens a session of Congress in which the proposals of religion will not be given a serious hearing. [57]

Christian scholars are called to strengthen that which remains.

Notes

1. The literature here is vast already, but for helpful discussions on the "turn" itself, see Robert Alejandro, "What Is Political About Rawls's Political Liberalism?" *The Journal of Politics* 58, no. 1 (February 1996): 1-24; and Patrick Neal, "Does He Mean What He Says? (Mis)Understanding Rawls's Practical Turn," *Polity* 27, no. 1 (Fall 1994): 77-111.

2. Kelbley, "Political Liberalism," *International Philosophic Quarterly* 36, no. 1 (March 1996): 97.

3. Jean Hampton, "The Common Faith of Liberalism,"*Pacific Philosophical Quarterly* 75 (1994): 186-216. In this paper I am borrowing Hampton's term more than analysis.

4. Rawls, *Political Liberalism* (Columbia University Press, 1993): xvi.

5. Alejandro, "What Is Political About?" 7.

6. Alejandro, "What Is Political About?" 13—emphasis in the original.

7. Alejandro, "What Is Political About?" 21.

8. For a similar view that Rawls, rather than lessening his ambition in the shift from *Theory of Justice* to *Political Liberalism*, actually raises it, see Neal, "Does He Mean What He Says?" 109-11.

9. Rawls, *Political Liberalism*, 139.

10. William Galston, "Two Kinds of Liberalism," *Ethics* 105 (April 1995): 516-34.

11. Hampton, "Common Faith," 211.

12. The following is from Paul Weithman, "Rawlsian Liberalism and the Privatization of Religion," *Journal of Religious Ethics* 22, no. 1 (Spring, 1994): 3-28.

13. Rawls, *Political Liberalism*, 246.

14. See David Hollenbach, "Public Reason/Private Religion?" *Journal of Religious Ethics* 22, no.1 (Spring 1994): 39-46.

15. Rawls, *Political Liberalism*, xviii.

16. See Timothy Jackson, "Love in a Liberal Society," *Journal of Religious Ethics* 22, no.1 (Spring 1994): 29-38.

17. Rawls, *Political Liberalism*, 247-52.

18. The significance of Rawls's confession (found in *Political Liberalism*, footnote 36, at 247) of shifting from his original preference for "exclusion" to his acceptance of "inclusion" is itself a story to be considered. I think a partial explanation may be found in the situation I describe in Part II below.

19. Hampton, "Common Faith," 210.

20. It is interesting to note that members of other kinds of particularistic communities have a similar take on the effect of Rawlsian theory. For a feminist account of Rawlsian exclusionary liberalism, see Elizabeth Frazer and Nicola Lacey, "Politics and the Public in Rawls' Political Liberalism," *Political Studies* 43 (1995): 233-47.

21. The literature on the communitarian versus liberalism debate is too vast for comprehensive citation here. Two helpful volumes are Daniel Bell, *Communitarianism and its Critics* (New York: Oxford University Press, 1993), and *Communitarianism and Individualism*, ed. Shlomo Avineri and Avner de-Shalit (New York: Oxford University Press, 1992). For an early collection of the kind of reconsidering and reconceiving of proper justificatory strategies undertaken by philosophic defenders of liberalism, see *Liberals on Liberalism*, ed. Alfonso J. Damico (Lanham, Md.: Rowman & Littlefield, 1986).

22. Galston, "Defending Liberalism," *American Political Science Review* 76, no. 3 (1982): 621-29.

23. Perry, *Love & Power: The Role of Religion and Morality in American Politics* (New York: Oxford University Press, 1991): 138.

24. Moore, *Foundations of Liberalism* (New York: Oxford University Press, 1993): 193.

25. Galston, *Liberal Purposes: Goods, Virtues and Diversity in the Liberal State* (Cambridge, Mass.: Cambridge University Press, 1991): 292.

26. "Perfectionism" is the term used by Rawls to describe those moral/political theories which claim that the purpose of the regime is to accomplish some specific set of human excellences or virtues. For Rawls's discussion of and rejection of "perfectionism" see *Theory of Justice* 24-27, 325-32, and 414-16, and again at 527.

27. Galston, *Purposes*, 299.

28. Galston, *Purposes*, 89.

29. Galston, *Purposes*, 261.

30. Perry, *Morality, Politics & Law: A Bicentennial Essay* (New York: Oxford University Press, 1988): 270, 271, and 102.

31. Galston, *Purposes*, 278 and 258.

32. Galston, *Purposes*, 279.

33. Perry, *Love and Power*, 81 and 88.

34. Moore, *Foundations*, 155, emphasis in the original.

35. Galston, *Purposes*, 258, 293, and 294.

36. Macedo, *Liberal Virtues: Citizenship, Virtue, and Community in Liberal Constitutionalism* (New York: Oxford University Press, 1990): 40 and 46.

37. Macedo, *Liberal Virtues*, 52 and 63.

38. Macedo, "Liberal Civic Education and Religious Fundamentalism: The Case of God v. John Rawls?" *Ethics* 105 (April, 1995): 468-96; 496.

39. Perry, *Love and Power*, 106 and 100. It must be noted that Perry has become increasingly aware of and uncomfortable with the exclusionary nature of his earlier work. In both his *Religion in Politics* (Oxford, 1997) and his forthcoming *Under God: Democracy, Morality, Religion* (Oxford), Perry evinces real sympathy for the traditionalist voice. While I believe that ultimately his project will founder due to his liberal epistemic commitments, I both celebrate his earnestness in tackling this problem and am grateful for having been a part of the dialogue.

40. Moore, *Foundations*, 177 and 178.

41. Macedo, "God v. John Rawls," 485. In this fine and illuminating article, Macedo rules in the decision. God loses.

42. Rawls, *Political Liberalism*, xxiii-xxiv.

43. Yet another name for this Christian intellectual movement can be found in the special issue of the Fall 1998 volume of *Telos*. See, "Toward a Liturgical Critique of Modernity," *Telos*, no. 113 (Fall 1998): 3-134.

44. Cavanaugh, "'A Fire Strong Enough to Consume the House': The Wars of Religion and the Rise of the State," *Modern Theology* 11, no. 4 (October 1995): 397-420; here 398 and 404.

45. Cavanaugh, "'A Fire Strong Enough,'" 405, and 407-9.

46. John Milbank, *Theology & Social Theory: Beyond Secular Reason* (Cambridge, Mass.: Blackwell, 1990). Space prohibits me from mining but a few rich nuggets from Milbank. *Theology & Social Theory* is the key work in the emerging ecclesiocentric perspective. Milbank clears away the underbrush which makes it possible for the positive project of theory construction by Christian political philosophers to commence. If Milbank did not exist, we would have had to create him.

47. Milbank, *Theology & Social Theory*, 10.

48. For a fascinating re-reading of early modern political philosophy (and philosophers) as political theologians see Joshua Mitchell, *Not By Reason Alone: religion, history, and identity in early modern political thought* (Chicago: University of Chicago Press, 1993). See also *Piety and Humanity: Essays on Religion and Early Modern Political Philosophy*, ed. Douglas Kries (Lanham, Md.: Rowman & Littlefield, 1997).

49. Milbank, *Theology & Social Theory*, 17, all emphases in the original.

50. For Hampton's five fundamental commitments that constitute the core of the liberal faith, see "Common Faith," 191-93.

51. The literature of public theology is also vast. But a variety of names captures the point: Niebuhr , Murray, Thiemann, Neuhaus, Fiorenza, Tracy, Placher, West, and Benne.

52. Cavanaugh, "'A Fire Strong Enough,'" 409 and 411.

53. Barry Harvey, "Insanity, Theocracy, and the Public Realm: Public Theology, the Church, and the Politics of Liberal Democracy," *Modern Theology* 10, no. 1 (January 1994): 29-57; here, 30.

54. Harvey, "Insanity," 35.

55. For Harvey's three-fold account, see, "Insanity," 38.

56. Rawls, *Political Liberalism*, 249-50.

57 Fish, "Why We Can't Just All Get Along," *First Things*, no. 60 (February 1996): 22.

Chapter 4

Selves in Relation: Theories of Community and the *Imago Dei* Doctrine

Paul A. Brink

Over the past twenty years, "communitarianism" has emerged as one of the most significant critiques of liberalism this century. Thinkers as diverse as Alasdair MacIntyre, Benjamin Barber, Michael Sandel, Michael Walzer, and Charles Taylor have offered important criticisms of both liberal political practice and liberal political theory, especially as articulated by the philosopher John Rawls. Liberals, for their part, have been quick to rise to the challenge: whether through accommodation or counterattack, liberals have taken the communitarian criticisms seriously and have developed elaborate responses to them. Thus the liberal-communitarian debate has been a primary focus of attention among contemporary political theorists; indeed, it has been perhaps the foremost debate in the political theory of this generation. For all the discussion, however, what is particularly striking is that the results have been remarkably inconclusive, further increasing the polarization of the parties. Despite many differences among the communitarian critics, clear lines have been drawn between them and the liberals, and those theorists who would seek to mediate the great divide soon find themselves required to align themselves with one or the other of the contending schools.

Part of the reason for this lack of progress, I believe, is that definitions of community are too often merely asserted or assumed in each school, due in large part to poorly grounded assumptions concerning the nature of human identity or selfhood. Simply to note this deficiency, however, is insufficient; the greater challenge is to find reasons for it, and perhaps even provide suggestions for overcoming it. I consider here an ancient Christian doctrine that teaches that all human beings are created in the image of God—in the *imago Dei*. Historically, this doctrine has been an important resource for Christians who sought to answer questions concerning human selfhood. However, not only Christians and Christian theology have benefited from the doctrine and from the traditions of interpretation to which it has given rise. Variations on its theme, in fact, can be observed in many of the theories of human nature found in the philosophies of the western world. Indeed, traditions of thought concerning the *imago Dei* continue to shape the ways in which we think about human nature today, and, accordingly, how we understand ourselves as participants in community.

What I investigate is the possibility that our thinking in this regard has been shaped especially by one dominant "stream" of interpretation of the doctrine, at the expense of another, minority "stream," and that our theories have been weakened as a result. After briefly outlining the two streams, I suggest that by reconsidering our concepts of identity and selfhood within this minority tradition, we may be able to unearth new resources for developing and refining our theories of community, identity, and difference, as well as discover new possibilities for constructive dialogue—even in such long-running debates as that between liberals and communitarians.[1]

"... in the image of God he created them."

In her noted *Public Man, Private Woman*, a volume which reviews the place of women in past and present social and political thought, Jean Bethke Elshtain presents an argument that the appearance of Christianity in the world was nothing less than "a moral revolution" in thought, values, and political practice.[2] The classical Greek worldview had strictly delimited a priori the potential of a given entity, including persons, by noting the actualization of its inherent capacities already at the start.[3] In contrast, says Elshtain, "Christianity redeemed and sanctified both *each individual life*, as well as *everyday life*, especially the lives of society's victims, and granted each a new-found dignity—a *dignitatis*—previously reserved only to the highborn, the rich, or the powerful."[4]

Politically, this had dramatic implications. The pre-Christian individual had not been free to consider his or her selfhood except as a functional part of a hierarchy of social roles within the larger social order. While the person could, with Socrates, endorse the withdrawal of the soul from the body, that individual could not remove him- or herself from the group.[5] Christianity, however, challenged the primacy of the *polis*. The claims of the public world no longer had to remain unquestioned, as the possibility of principled resistance to secular power was introduced. The result was an opening up to all individuals of a whole range of duties, rights, and identities resulting from their newfound power before God, a power that reserved ultimate authority only for God, and challenged any pretender who claimed that authority for it—or himself.

Christianity brought this new conception of the individual about through its understanding of the human being as created in the image of God. Although there are references throughout the Bible to God's image in human beings, particularly in the New Testament,[6] two verses from the first chapter of the first book of the Bible have nearly always been a primary focus. Genesis 1:26-27, in fact, is seen to be at the very core of the doctrine, as these verses record the event of the creation of the human species:

> Then God said, "Let us make humankind in our image, according to our likeness; and let them have dominion over the fish of the sea, and over the birds of the air, and over the cattle, and over all the wild animals of the earth, and over every creeping thing that creeps upon the earth." So God created humankind in his image, in the image of God he created them; male and female he created them.[7]

Over time, these verses have come to stand for what Christians believe *should be* with regard to the human person, an "abbreviated way of referring to what Christians consider the original status and vocation of the human creature."[8]

Although these verses are seen to be central to a Christian understanding of what it means to be human, and, in terms of Elshtain's "moral revolution," their effect was dramatic, there yet existed and still exists great diversity concerning how precisely God's "image" is understood to be manifested in his human creation. Particularly damaging has been the strategy that saw the reference in Genesis as an occasion to engage in all sorts of speculation concerning the "essential nature" of selfhood. "As blissfully unconcerned with authorial intent as any post-structuralist critic," writes biblical scholar Richard Middleton, "most medieval and modern interpreters have typically asked not an exegetical, but a speculative, question: In what way are humans *like* God and *unlike* animals?"[9] The proposed answers to this question have included rationality, moral sensitivity and conscience, capacity for religious worship, immortality, spirituality, aesthetic sense, freedom, speech, and personhood. Other candidates continue to be proposed today.[10] The result of this departure from standard hermeneutical practice, believes Middleton, is that the speculative sources of choice for many interpreters have been whatever philosophical trend is current at the time, thus reading contemporaneous theories of human nature into the Genesis text.[11] Complains another theologian, "By studying how systematic theologies have poured meaning into Gen. 1:26, one could write a piece of Europe's cultural history."[12]

Rather than investigate each of the proposals in turn, however, as might be expected in a work of historical theology, I will depend in this essay on a generalization based on research already done in that field. First proposed by Paul Ramsey in his *Basic Christian Ethics*, this generalization makes a distinction between two broad "streams" of interpretation of the *imago Dei* doctrine.[13] Looking at this distinction may help clarify the debate between liberals and communitarians with respect to identity, for I believe that the theories of identity presupposed by both groups can be found to have their roots largely within only one of the two streams, and that by considering the second we may be able to find additional resources for dealing with problems in the liberal-communitarian debate.[14]

The first of these streams, and the one that has historically been dominant, is the "substantialist" approach, introduced above. It singles out something from *within the substantial form* of human nature as the "stamp" of the *imago Dei*, some characteristic or capacity or quality that human beings are said to share with the divine being, and that distinguishes them from physical nature and from animals. Every human person can then be said to share God's image insofar as he or she shares in that quality, while other creatures do not. Two qualities in particular are often singled out as distinguishing people from "lower" creatures: rationality and free will. Rationality is probably the more persistent and the more influential of the two and was the clear favorite of classical Christian scholars such as Irenaeus, Clement of Alexandria, Athanasius, and Augustine. Their influence has indeed been great; in the modern period, says theologian Douglas John Hall, western civilization has become so persuaded that human rationality is our greatest achievement that many automatically assume that this must be what the *imago Dei* reference is about.[15] Particularly important is the historical link between Irenaeus, who was the first major theologian to discuss the *imago Dei*, through Augustine to Thomas Aquinas, and, eventually through Thomas to the Roman Catholic Church.

Freedom of the will is the second most popular "substantialist" interpretation, although rational thought and free decision are of course closely related. This argument emphasizes that human beings, unlike animals, are capable of independent action, capable of self-agency, and thus can be considered responsible for their actions. After the Reformation and the relative decline of the Roman Catholic Church, freedom came to be emphasized to an even greater extent than rationality, due in part to the influence of humanist, antirationalist, and romantic philosophic movements. By the nineteenth century, it was often combined with such notions as "spiritual being," "human personality," and "moral capacity."[16]

In all these, we can note the influence of nonbiblical explanations of the image of God in humans. In fact, in many cases, it seems that interpreters simply understood the image to refer to qualities already highly valued in the societies in which they lived. This points to the danger involved in understanding the *imago Dei* to refer to something inherent in human beings, says Hall, in that Christians risk merely "baptizing" those qualities lauded by the dominant culture, thus sacrificing a uniquely Christian understanding of the doctrine upon which a real societal critique and theoretical account of identity could be based.[17] The danger is that the quality in question is subsumed under the religiously neutral realm of "nature," therefore not to be included in the realm of supernatural grace, and thus unaffected by sin and redemption. Critique of these qualities, and of their products, becomes neither necessary nor possible.

It is partly out of this concern that a second, minority stream of interpretation also appeared within orthodox Christianity. Based particularly on the writings of Martin Luther and John Calvin, it attempted to develop a substitute for the substantialist interpretation. More recently, the work of Emil Brunner and Karl Barth has focused attention on this tradition and on the view of scripture that it implies. This interpretation argues that the analogy between God and human life in the image is not properly one of substance, but of *relation*. Nothing *within* the composition of human beings, so the argument goes, has the form or power of being in the image of God. The image is rather to be understood as *a relationship within which persons sometimes stand*, whenever they obediently reflect God's will in action and in thought. Barth emphasizes in his interpretation that the biblical text itself makes "no reference at all to the peculiar intellectual and moral talents" of the human creation, suggesting that the strategy of looking for qualities unique to human beings is flawed.[18] Rather, the relational stream conceives of the image to be a consequence of the relationship between Creator and creature. As Hall succinctly puts it: "To be *imago Dei* does not mean to have something but to be and do something: to image God."[19]

Although Barth is a particularly clear exponent of this tradition, the break with substantialism actually began with Luther and Calvin. For Luther, *all* the primary categories of Christian faith are to be expressed in relational terms: grace, for instance, is not a substance, but a deed; faith, a response to grace, implying ongoing trust in God's promises. Sin is not quantifiable, something that can be balanced or bought or paid off, but rather signifies the end of a relationship.[20] Similarly, the image of God is not a substance or a quality that a creature either does or does not possess. On the contrary, for Luther, the image of God is "entirely determined by man's response to God."[21] Calvin, like Luther, also broke with the substantialist tradition, stating specifically in his *Institutes* that "we are God's offspring, but in quality, not in essence."[22] Thus, he too rejects any suggestion of an "ontic connectedness" between God and the human creature. On the contrary, for Calvin, the *imago Dei* has to do less with a human *essence*, and more with a human *vocation*, namely to mirror the divine glory from within creation.[23] And this is accomplished not by any skill or innate possession unique to human beings, but simply by turning to the Creator, thus reflecting (imaging) the Creator within creation, just as a mirror reflects light so long as it is turned to a light source.[24]

The fall into sin, in this conception, implies not a loss of reason or of any other substance or quality, but rather a loss of relationship.[25] While Luther and Calvin differ with regard to whether the sinful person still remains an image-bearer (according to Luther, not at all; for Calvin, as a "frightful deformity"), they are in agreement that the human state of estrangement from its source means humans are quite literally disoriented—turned toward what is not God and imaging what is not God, with tragic consequences for their humanity. The story of Christian redemption then, is how Christ, the fully human being, the perfect *imago Dei*, was able to bring about the restoration of the original status of those who image God. Significantly, while the picture of Christ presented in the Gospel is undoubtedly of a rational and free being, the model of selfhood he offered was totally out of character, as human character might be understood. The substantialist strategy that holds up what is most noble and distinguishable about human beings collapses when faced with the perfect and fully human being who "did not count equality with God as something to be exploited," but rather "emptied himself, taking the form of a slave," and "found in human form, he humbled himself and became obedient to point of death—even death on a cross."[26]

What this emphasis on relation suggests therefore is that there exists a twofold implication of the *imago Dei* doctrine. First is the immediate (ontological) statement that we are created to be in some form of relationship with the Creator. But if this is so, this carries the further (theological) implication that there should be some connection between the quality of that relationship and that of our personhood. And so the ontological statement that our humanity is characterized by relation gives way to an ethical statement regarding the quality of that relation,[27] or the "direction" in which that relation is turned.[28] In the Christian perspective, this ethical thrust is presented as the image of Christ as image of God, suggesting, in Hall's words, "an identity into which we are beckoned."[29] Thus, we have the link between the image of Christ as the source of the Christian "new self" and the *imago Dei* as a category of creation. This new identity, made possible through identification with Christ, is a "renewal"[30] of human creatureliness as it was originally intended.[31]

Obviously, the relational interpretation will make little sense from the substantialist perspective. For the latter, to suggest the image of God has been lost, or even distorted, is to suggest that humans have lost their mind or their freedom.[32] Since it seems manifestly clear that this is not the case, the redemption brought by Christ is seen to refer to some other aspect of human life, perhaps in the private sphere of individual salvation (grace), or as something that will perfect or complete already-existing—and religiously neutral—human qualities of reason or freedom (nature). Indeed, the differences between the two interpretations and between the philosophic traditions to which they have given rise are so great that communication between them has been nearly impossible. This lack of communication may help explain why the substantialist conception has by far been the more important in terms of its influence on our modern theories of human selfhood and community that figure so prominently in our philosophies, theologies, and political theories.

To consider how this development took place, we need to recall that just as the Christian revolution described by Elshtain occurred within an earlier (Greco-Roman) philosophic context, and therefore could hardly help but be influenced by it, the Enlightenment was very much a product of developments within Christian theology and philosophy, as well as of the larger European society that remained, at least initially, professedly Christian. What this implies is that modern philosophies, together with their theories of human nature, arose from within the traditions of Christianity, regardless of whether they did so out of zealous attachment to the church's teachings, or in conscious indifference to them, or in explicit denial and defiance of them.[33] For this reason, the significance of the substantialist interpretation of the *imago Dei* as the dominant understanding of how a civilization understood human nature can hardly be overemphasized. While it is of course possible that competing theories of the self and identity might have developed independently within such a context, it is far more likely that most philosophers and political theorists, steeped in a Christian worldview, educated in Christian schools, and thus possessing a Christian (substantialist) intellectual understanding of the human creature, began their work with the current "common-sense" understanding of who and what people are.

Key to this process was the fact that the substantialist interpretation could be secularized relatively easily into a modern doctrine of human nature. In the modern era, the divine could be identified as the image of the divine in humanity, thus diminishing any need for a distinctive Christian vision. God, in effect, could be brought down to earth and identified with humanity's greatest gifts, although human nonetheless: its rationality and its freedom.[34] Human beings were thus "set free" from any responsibility to the transcendent realm and could now see themselves as masters of their own fate. Consider how this development occurred with respect to Thomas's teaching, for example. In his interpretation, Thomas had identified a particular human quality—reason—as the image of God found by "nature" in all human beings. Faith, in contrast, which could be found to varying degrees in different people, clearly belonged to the realm of "supernatural" grace and not to "essential" humanity. For Thomas, therefore, there existed a strict separation between reason and faith, one that corresponded to the separation between nature and grace, or nature and "supernature." Thomas, like Christians before and after him, in this way marked off "nature" as an area of human life more or less independent of grace, an area basically unaffected by sin and redemption.[35] The image of God in human beings was, for Thomas, very much within the realm of nature—as we noted above, we move *beyond* the image of God when we enter the realm of grace.[36] The things of nature, he said, do not differ according to one's religion, and we can therefore assume that this realm is essentially religiously neutral. As an activity of "natural reason," philosophy fit into this arrangement well and was contrasted with theology, which is concerned with matters of faith and revelation.[37]

The fundamental weakness of this conception, however, is that it contained little that might prevent it from being adopted with relative ease by theorists who sought to move beyond the boundaries to reason that Thomas and the scholastics had believed faith implied. In their declaration that reason should be freed from every a priori restriction,[38] modern theorists proved quite willing to accept the medieval Christian theory of human nature that emphasized primarily the *capacity* to know and love God, rather than whether particular individuals actually did so or not.[39] Thus they could begin their work with a religiously neutral, autonomous, rational human nature, while jettisoning "supernature" as exactly such an arbitrary, a priori restriction, one irrelevant to a "true" or "essential" understanding of the human being. The result was that modern theorists so clearly identified the divine with what they believed to be divine in human beings that only the capacities so identified "made the cut" into the "new" substantialism.

The implications of this move were great indeed. In general, by idealizing certain dimensions of the human self, the "binary opposites" of many of these dimensions were demonized or otherwise diminished in value, with drastic results for those creatures that possessed or were perceived to possess these opposites. But this ranking system devalued not only that which was not human, but also those people who were not perceived to possess the required substance to a sufficient degree. As Hall notes, one could speculate endlessly on the amount of damage inflicted upon women, children, the mentally disabled, and the uneducated and illiterate, even upon the "religious," on account of what was once the "Christian" practice of identifying the highest and the best in human beings with rationality.[40] Similar consequences resulted from the idealization of human freedom. Benjamin Barber has argued that one of the effects of the Enlightenment and its focus on freedom was to have left "modern women and men to live in an era after virtue, after God, after nature, an era offering neither comfort nor certainty." While freedom from God may have been achieved—no longer need we be concerned with "mirroring" him—this freedom was won "by a ruthless severing of ties and an uprooting of human nature from its foundations in the natural, the historical, and the divine."[41] He suggests that many of the challenges to freedom in contemporary society may not stem from the traditional sources against which political liberalism originally reacted, but rather from the consequences of the modern preoccupation with individual freedom itself. His call, therefore, is for a renewed concern over the political consequences of the "reification" and idealization of the individual and the individual's capabilities.[42]

Unfortunately, however, the idealization that Barber describes also discouraged precisely the criticism or suspicion of human abilities for which he calls, especially with regards to reason. This loss of an effective basis for a prophetic critique of human initiative was perhaps the most serious consequence of this idealization.[43] In the modern era, whatever human reason can create is good ("divine"), because human reason itself is considered good ("divine"). Of course, reason is not the cause of all evil, and a blind antirationalism is hardly its corrective. Yet the failure to recognize its limits suggests a commitment to human reason that itself defies reasonable explanation. It is toward correcting this failure that the minority stream of interpretation of the *imago Dei* doctrine can be put to good use. This stream, as articulated above, does not deny the value of rationality or freedom, but recognizes that either of these, or any other aspect of created reality, can be idealized or demonized. According to this interpretation, the human being as *imago Dei* implies that people are primarily beings "in-relationship." In fact, people are created in such a way that part of the very definition of selfhood, of what it means to be human, is to relate to an "other." Of course, people have the freedom to direct these relations in any way they wish, although their choices will certainly have consequences. But while they have freedom with regard to the form and content of their relationship, they are not free *not* to respond.[44] For, according to this conception, to respond to the other, to be in relationship, is simply an aspect of what it is to be.[45]

We can appreciate even from daily experience the importance of our relatedness with regard to each other. Turned (as a mirror) toward each other, we engage in dialogue, and we can expect, as Charles Taylor notes in one of his descriptions of dialogue, to "stand on a different footing when we start talking."[46] On the other hand, when we turn from each other, and relationships are broken, we experience distrust and suspicion, loneliness and alienation. Indeed, who we are, or rather, *how* we are, is determined by how or to whom we engage in relation. This resonates well, of course, with Taylor's argument that identity is created *dialogically*, that is, in partnership with our relations:

> We define our identity always in dialogue with, sometimes in struggle against, the things our significant others want in us. Even after we outgrow some of these others—our parents, for instance—and they disappear from our lives, the conversation with them continues within us as long as we live. . . . Thus my discovering my own identity doesn't mean that I work it out in isolation, but that I negotiate it through dialogue, partly overt, partly internal, with others.[47]

Again, just as we noted above with regard to the relationship between God and human beings, the fact that our personal identities are moulded through our relationships with others leads directly to normative and ethical questions regarding how we ought to regulate and "direct" these relationships, for this relational understanding of human nature necessarily implies a connection between the quality of our primary relationships and that of our personhood in general. And while "relatedness" can be said to be a given of human nature, this structure can still either be fulfilled or distorted. Merely because human beings are relational does not imply that any relationship is a good relationship, or that any community is a good community. Making these distinctions, as we noted above, is precisely where the substantialist tradition runs into difficulty. It is this ability that can lend this interpretation of the *imago Dei* doctrine a somewhat subversive character, as it can function as a transcendent ground of criticism vis-à-vis the status quo.[48] Here, it implies that not all relationships or not all communities in which relationships occur are to be celebrated. In particular, those that require the total sacrifice of the self for the "greater good" of the relationship or the community must be considered destructive. But it also implies a more general critique. Indebted to the substantialist conception of the *imago Dei*, the dominant culture in the West tends to value particular qualities of the mind and personality rather than the relationships for which those qualities might be used. From the relational perspective, however, without these relations human beings are little more than hollow shells.[49] It leads directly, therefore, to a criticism of those cultural practices that assign particular human beings greater or lesser value according to their share in one valued quality or another.

The Liberal-Communitarian Debate

Precisely because the relational interpretation of the *imago Dei* doctrine is able to focus on questions and issues not normally considered within the substantialist tradition of interpretation, I want to consider how reframing the debate between liberals and communitarians within this second interpretation might bring to light alternative perspectives on the individual and community in politics, positions which thus far have largely been relegated from the mainstream discussion. After reviewing here the positions of representatives of each of the two schools, we consider below how a number of ambiguities or problems in the debate might be reconstructed within the relationalist tradition of interpretation.

The work of John Rawls, particularly *A Theory of Justice*, published in 1971, as well as *Political Liberalism*, a collection of essays published together in 1993, can be seen as perhaps the most successful recent attempt by liberalism to place itself on new and theoretically secure foundations. In contrast to any form of utilitarianism, says Rawls, certain individual rights, founded in justice, are so fundamental that they cannot be overridden even in the name of the common good, however it is conceived. The challenge faced by Rawls is to provide a justification for these rights by deriving principles of justice in such a way that they do not depend on any particular conception of the good. The strength of his contribution stems particularly from his apparent ability to develop the required framework of political liberties and rights (the "right"), while acknowledging the existence of a great variety of individual ends (the "good"). He claims to accomplish this by virtue of the neutrality of the "original position," a hypothetical construct in which free, rational persons participate in a situation of total equality. Its design, says Rawls, is such that it does not choose in advance among competing purposes and ends. Furthermore, a "veil of ignorance" is established; none of the participants know their own status, skills, or individual ends and goals. All, therefore, will behave in a purely self-interested and rational manner, as all are similarly alienated from their individual identities.

Rawls argues that behind this veil, participants will agree to two main principles of justice: (1) Each person is to have an equal right to the most extensive basic liberty compatible with a similar liberty for others; and (2) social and economic inequalities are to be arranged so that they are both reasonably expected to be to everyone's advantage and attached to positions and offices open to all.[50]

Perhaps the most important difference between the original position and reality is that behind the veil, knowledge of the "good" (whatever that might be) is not permitted. In Rawls's words, it "does not specify the good independently from the right, or does not interpret the right as maximizing the good."[51] The obvious advantage of this strategy is that the principles of justice can be derived without presupposing any particular conception of the good and, therefore, cannot be said to be in anyone's interest. The only concession the good must make is to conform to the requirements of the principles of justice; that is, the right does impose certain restrictions on permissible goods. For this reason, the right can be said to be *prior* to the good. The failure to recognize this priority, according to Rawls, is the fundamental weakness of "teleological" doctrines:

> [F]rom the start they relate the right and the good in the wrong way. We should not attempt to give form to our life by first looking to the good independently defined. It is not our aims that primarily reveal our nature but rather the principles that we would acknowledge to govern the background conditions under which these aims are to be formed and the manner in which they are to be pursued. For the self is prior to the ends which are affirmed by it.[52]

Note Rawls's explicit separation of the self and the ends that it pursues. These ends, he says, are not how our "nature" as free and equal moral persons is revealed,[53] and accordingly, cannot be seen to be so constitutive of the self that they might be permitted to have a role in the development of the principles of justice. In contrast, the parties in the original position "think of themselves as beings who can and do choose their final ends," and therefore seek to establish the conditions "for each to fashion his own unity."[54]

The success of Rawls's work played a crucial role in the broadening of the historical foundations of liberalism in the twenty-five years after the appearance of *A Theory of Justice*. Common to all members of this "procedural" family of liberalism are these distinctions between the right and the good and between the individual and his or her particular identity. They tend to consider society primarily as an association of free and rational individuals, each of whom has a particular conception of a good life and a corresponding life plan. Because the principle of equality would be breached if society itself espoused one or another of these conceptions, a liberal society should not be founded on any particular vision of the good life, it is argued. The ethic central to a liberal society must be an ethic of the right, rather than the good.[55] Liberals thus claim to be exponents of pluralism par excellence, as only a liberal society provides a setting in which each individual can pursue his or her own freely chosen life, in which each tolerates the other, each view is held in equal respect, where no view is imposed upon another, and where the state is neutral between all competing particular value claims.[56] The primacy of the right over the good, therefore, means that liberalism is concerned most with freedom and how it may be preserved, rather than with what people might be interested in doing with their freedom.

It is precisely this priority of the right over the good and of the self over its ends that Michael Sandel presents as the central communitarian targets in *Liberalism and the Limits of Justice*, published in 1982. The criticism from the communitarians is that liberal society has become atomistic and therefore needs to develop or restore its sense of community. Following Tocqueville, they perceive the liberal emphasis upon the abstract individual and upon autonomy and rights to have destroyed public discourse and created or magnified many social problems.[57] Communitarians respond that we cannot justify any sort of political arrangements without reference to our common purposes and ends, and in particular that we cannot conceive of our personhood without reference to our roles in society: as citizens and as participants in a common life.[58] The too-abstract account of the liberal individual, they say, must be seen as ultimately responsible for a general failure on the part of traditional liberal theory to account for difference within and between communities. This perceived inability to deal with diversity leads them to look away from liberalism to an account of human selfhood that will not similarly construe difference as disadvantage. Communitarianism, then, represents one such attempt, or set of attempts, seeking to develop a new democratic theory that will lead to a more truly democratic result, one where communities can justly be sustained within situations of human diversity.

Sandel's central contention is that Rawls's conception of the person can neither support his theory of justice nor plausibly account for human capacities for agency and self-reflection. Justice cannot be primary in the way Rawls requires, for "we cannot coherently regard ourselves as the sort of beings the deontological ethic requires us to be."[59] By subordinating the good to the right, says Sandel, Rawls ultimately has a "problematic, even impoverished" theory of the good. While Rawls informs us that the choice of our good is our own, something that is "too important" for the power of the state to become concerned about, we are left with a self that has no *grounds* for making its choice, no reason for preferring, for instance, a life of service to the poor to a life of counting blades of grass.[60] Sandel complains that this fails to develop a "critical standpoint" of fundamental values required to evaluate more immediate wants and desires.[61] In fact, Rawls never really considers the nature of these "systems of desires," what they involve, or how they may be ordered. This failure, says Sandel, must eventually call into question the account of the self that Rawls assumes, and ultimately also the right and its claim for priority. Because reflection concerning the good is not permitted to take as its object the self *qua* subject of desires, Rawls permits us to look inward in a sense, but not far enough, "not all the way in." The result is a very narrow account of the self, says Sandel, as deliberation concerning it must be restricted merely to assessing its desires, while the identity is assumed or assigned in advance.[62]

Rawls's portrait of the self is even more fundamentally flawed, says Sandel, in that it does not acknowledge the degree to which communal bonds are inseparable from moral character and obligation. In judging the nature of the individual to be fixed, forever prior to the good, the good is declared contingent, and human community is banished to a status of one among many possible contingent goods. Thus, one of the most damaging effects of the veil is that certain indispensable dimensions of the human self are ignored. Once the principles of justice are established, concerns such as family, friendship, faith, and community are all considered to be too shallow to be constitutive of identity and are banished from the public sphere. Only in private may our conceptions of the good be expressed, while in public, where the principles of justice prevail, all must participate as unencumbered individual selves in the exercise of their rights of citizenship.[63] And because these rights override community claims, the ability of a community to hold *any* non-liberal beliefs at all is undermined. In fact, the pluralism that liberalism envisages is a rather benign variety. Diversity is included, but only within very narrow confines, only after it has accepted the liberal rules of the game. So while the efforts of liberals to structure a society in which people of different commitments and identities can live alongside each other is admirable, the strategy of reducing identity to mere patterns of individual choice neither deals justly with the nature of community claims nor permits personal commitments to have any relevance to the larger society and public situation in which individuals find themselves. In effect, says Sandel, the self is put beyond the reach of politics and makes any human agency "a premise of politics rather than its precarious achievement." Politics itself is emptied of real content, sacrificing any possibility that we might achieve a "good in common that we cannot know alone."[64]

Liberals, of course, have not been slow to respond to the challenge of Sandel and the other communitarians. They have argued that liberal theory is quite capable of accommodating concerns about community, and that the criticisms rest upon a fundamental misreading of Rawls's position, particularly concerning what he suggests about the self. Furthermore, they have offered their own counterchallenges to the communitarians, demanding that they specify more precisely how a communitarian account could correct the alleged defects in the liberal conception. Finally, they argue that in spite of their attacks upon the liberal "unencumbered self," communitarians remain loath to abandon the historic achievements of liberalism in defending the self against certain of these "encumbrances" when they become severe or oppressive.

Rawls himself has also responded to the communitarian critique, going great lengths to demonstrate that his approach eschews philosophical justification. In what has been seen by many to be an implicit concession to the communitarian critique,[65] Rawls's article, "Justice as Fairness: Political not Metaphysical," written fourteen years after *A Theory of Justice*, specifically avoids any claims to truth, as well as claims about the essential nature and identity of persons.[66] Rather, Rawls claims as his warrant the fact that his theory is derived ("unfolded," he says in *Political Liberalism*[67]) from the shared political culture of society, and further supported by an "overlapping consensus," including all the opposing reasonable philosophical and religious doctrines present in democratic societies.[68] In this manner, he claims to depend on the community for a shared understanding of the nature of the self and of the shared principles of justice:

> We look, then, to our public political culture itself, including its main institutions and historical traditions of their interpretation, as the shared fund of implicitly recognized basic ideas and principles. The hope is that these ideas and principles can be formulated clearly enough to be combined into a conception of political justice congenial to our most firmly held convictions.[69]

Therefore, he says, the aim of his theory is practical, not metaphysical, and is concerned with agreement, not truth. The question of truth Rawls ignores because, in his words, truth is "too important" to be resolved politically.[70]

Rawls maintains that the original position was introduced only to determine which traditional conception of justice specifies the most appropriate principles for realizing the traditional values of liberty and equality. Moreover, he says, it presupposes no particular metaphysical conceptions of the self, "for example, that the essential nature of persons is independent of and prior to their contingent attributes, including their final ends and attachments, and indeed their conception of the good and character as a whole."[71] Rather, the original position must be seen as merely a device of representation, one that considers individuals to be "free" in only a political, not a metaphysical, sense.[72] People need accept his conception of themselves as citizens only when discussing questions of political justice; they need not be committed necessarily in other parts of their lives to liberal moral ideals such as autonomy and individuality.[73] These, acknowledges Rawls, are indeed conceptions of a good, articulated by figures such as Kant or Mill, about which there is likely to be disagreement. In fact, they are extended too far when presented as the only appropriate foundation for a constitutional regime. His own justice-as-fairness, however, in contrast to liberalism as a comprehensive moral doctrine, is simply rooted in the basic ideas found in the public culture of a constitutional democracy, ideas that are likely to be affirmed by each of the opposing moral doctrines. So understood, liberalism itself "becomes but another sectarian doctrine."[74]

What is perhaps most significant about these newer arguments, however, is that in his response to the communitarians, Rawls seems to move away from the strict Right-prior-to-Good justification he had earlier espoused, one which sought an absolutely neutral "Archimedean point" in the liberal individual for the justification or critique of political institutions, practices, and policies. Rawls's more recent efforts to appease his critics tend toward a Good-prior-to-Right justification, emphasizing that the principles of justice together with their conception of the human person can win the endorsement of underlying conceptions—or a range of conceptions—of the good. No longer is he claiming any form of independent metaphysical truth concerning the self, but only a conception that does not violate people's own considered judgments of what persons are. Rawls writes in 1985:

> [I]n such a consensus each of the comprehensive philosophical, religious, and moral doctrines accepts justice as fairness in its own way; that is, each comprehensive doctrine, from within its own point of view, is led to accept the public reasons of justice specified by justice as fairness. . . . For, in general, these concepts, principles, and virtues are accepted by each as belonging to a more comprehensive philosophical, religious, or moral doctrine.[75]

This represents a significant change in strategy. No longer is Rawls—perhaps the most significant liberal thinker of his generation—accepting the centuries-old liberal doctrine concerning the supposed autonomy of theoretical thought; rather, he acknowledges that to be successful, his theory—including its account of the self—must presuppose the authority of certain religious and philosophic doctrines. Rawls's main response, therefore, is not that he never presupposed controversial philosophical or religious doctrines, nor that he no longer does so, but rather that in *Political Liberalism*, none of these doctrines *in particular* is presupposed. Thus, in spite of the fact that justice as fairness is "expounded apart from, or without reference to, any . . . wider background" of moral doctrine, Rawls clearly expects people to have such a doctrine, perhaps even as part of a yet broader philosophic or religious view about the world as a whole.[76] So while the political principles and the account of the self it presupposes "have a justification by reference to one or more comprehensive doctrines, it is neither presented as, nor as derived from, such a doctrine applied to the basic structure of society, as if this structure were simply another subject to which that doctrine applied."[77] Rather,"citizens themselves, within the exercise of their liberty of thought and conscience, and looking to their comprehensive doctrines, view the political conception as derived from, or congruent with, or at least not in conflict with, their other values."[78] In this way, Rawls claims to have found a justification for his principles of justice and his conception of the human self that does not privilege certain conceptions of the good, but yet remains favored by them to the greatest extent possible.

Of course, communitarians note that Rawls is not going nearly far enough; most of Sandel's criticisms, for example, they believe remain unanswered. And to a great extent, their concerns are quite justified; what they see in their community-held "shared understandings" is quite different from what Rawls sees in his overlapping consensus. Liberals, for their part, still observe many of the same weaknesses in their communitarian opponents: a poorly articulated doctrine of community, including an inability to lay out criteria for distinguishing between good and bad communities, and a general reluctance to specify more precisely how a "communitarian politics" might look. Despite Rawls's revisions, little progress has been made in bringing the opponents closer together. This is particularly true concerning the nature of "identity" or "selfhood," perhaps the part of their theorizing where the line between theoretical argument and pretheoretical assumption becomes most unclear. Rawls's revisions, in fact, may even have compounded the problem, as the debate now includes the issue of the overlapping consensus: whom Rawls presumes to include, and whom he considers to be too "unreasonable." What Rawls's efforts *have* accomplished, however, is to move beyond the long-term liberal strategy of attempting to create a perfectly neutral political order, free from any metaphysical baggage. He is still seeking a conception as impartial as possible (the goal remains "agreement, not truth"), but recognizes that it requires the endorsement of the various reasonable comprehensive doctrines of the good circulating within society. Therefore, despite the continued intransigence between liberals and communitarians over the nature of the self, we might note the fact that neither of the schools now attempt to develop their theories "deontologically," but rather appeal to doctrines or understandings already present in society. The two have therefore moved closer to one another at least in this one respect. We might even say that the debate has moved to a new level or entered a different phase. Indeed, Thomas Spragens has remarked that liberals and communitarians are now less opponents than "rival hermeneuticists" working within the same tradition,[79] suggesting that the debate is no longer one between non-traditionalists and traditionalists or liberals and restorationists over who has the most philosophically superior account of human selfhood. Rather, it has become a debate over the proper appropriation of tradition itself.

Especially given this new similarity, I suggest that the difficulty communitarians and liberals experience in their struggles to "get through" to one another results not from radically different starting points from which they begin their political theorizing, but rather may lie in their efforts to appropriate the tradition that the two share. In the rest of this chapter, by focusing on several problems or ambiguities in the debate where the breakdown in communication with regards to the self seems particularly obvious, I suggest that this common debt is actually a limitation, one that compounds the difficulty of resolving some of their remaining differences with respect to the self. And, of course, I argue that this is precisely where the relational perspective may be helpful, as, in contrast to liberalism and communitarianism, it conceives of the nature of our identity in a rather different way.

One such ambiguity concerns how relations between persons are to be understood. Thomas Hobbes, perhaps the earliest liberal philosopher, argued that to understand human nature, one must look *inward*, and because of the "similitude of passions," all specificity will be reduced to insignificance, at least to the extent that politics is concerned.[80] His model of human selfhood therefore suppressed or subordinated every major source of human variation: ethnic identity, social orders and classes, individual temperament, religious faith were all considered by Hobbes to be nonconstitutive of human nature, and irrelevant to the formation and maintenance of the body politic.[81] We can see Rawls's debt to Hobbes in his conception of society as "a system of cooperation between free and equal persons."[82] Yet Hobbes had no philosophic basis for assuming that by looking "inward," one can discover the essential and universal human self, shorn of specificity, to be the only significant unit in the state of nature. And Rawls's basis is similarly weak for his assumption that those in the original position are individuals who speak only for themselves. These critical assumptions concerning identity are, in fact, quite arbitrary.

What I have argued, however, is that Rawls's imagination was aided in this respect by a several hundred year old tradition, evident also in Hobbes, that what is important about human beings are specific characteristics or aspects they possess, particularly freedom and rationality, which, for all intents and purposes, represent the "essential" human being. Other characteristics or aspects can generally be assumed to be less significant for the task at hand, particularly those that might undermine the "substantial" aspects of the human personality. Thus, human relations, or aspects or institutions created from these relations, such as religion or community or family, are downplayed and privatized. Rawls's views on identity, therefore, flow directly from a long tradition of philosophic and religious thought that understood human nature in individualistic terms.

As we have seen, communitarians are highly critical of the liberal position on precisely this point. Often, with regard to this conflict over self and "shared relations," both sides are stereotyped; communitarians are said to understand the self in terms of relations with the community and other selves, while liberals ignore these shared relations. A more nuanced distinction, however, would consider the difference in terms of the role that relations play with respect to the self. Liberals are inclined to consider relations between selves and with a community as *contingently* shared; that is, while the content of a person's beliefs and values are bound to be influenced by the community and the social relations within which that person participates, this larger context is not seen to penetrate the self to the extent that identity becomes constituted by the relation or the relations themselves. Communitarians, on the other hand, espouse *essentially* shared relations; interpersonal relations are so significant that they penetrate to the very identity of the person, such that the self is wholly or partially constituted by these relations.[83]

Where both sides seem to find themselves in curious agreement, however, is that both seem to agree that to hold a particular position on the role played by shared relations with respect to the self somehow also signifies a commitment to a corresponding view on particular political issues. As Charles Taylor points out, for example, while the principal point of Sandel's work is *ontological*—concerned with addressing the terms accepted as ultimate in the order of explanation—liberals are likely to respond to it as a work of *advocacy*—concerned with a society that would have close relations analogous to a family, and thus unconcerned with justice.[84] In fact, however, either position on shared relations can be combined with either position with respect to questions of political advocacy. This becomes most clear when we notice that there exist both morally desirable and undesirable varieties of each conception of relations in concrete practice. For instance, communitarians often use illustrations drawn from the sphere of the family. The institution of marriage can be viewed as a "union" or "sacred bond" in which the identities of two selves are redefined through their essentially shared relation such that there comes to be one shared self where there once was two. The advantage to the communitarians of this conception is that the marriage "contract" between separate selves understood within the model of contingently shared relations is rather uninspiring in comparison.[85] What communitarians often ignore, however, and what liberals also ignore, even as they defend themselves, is that the distinction between contingently and essentially shared relations is not necessarily a normative one, and that to espouse one or the other in each and every situation is arbitrary and philosophically unjustifiable. Rather, there exist specific instances of either conception that may be found morally admirable or repugnant. So, returning to the marriage example, just as two spouses may "essentially" share a relation of love and support "constitutive of the identity of each," two other spouses may "essentially" share a relation of hatred and loathing (or dependence and abuse) that is similarly "constitutive of the identity of each."[86]

What occurs in the debate is that each side holds up in support of its model of shared relations only those instances of their conception in practice about which practically everyone is likely to have similar feelings. A more constructive dialogue, however, one which could take place within the relational stream, would avoid making a judgment on the initial *structure* of relation, rather acknowledging the fact that we need in addition to take note of the *direction* of the relation, taking into consideration factors such as the character and context of the relation or community, the persons involved, and wider background issues of community and culture. We might want to know, for instance, whether authority is exercised democratically or despotically within a particular relationship, or whether membership is distributed equally or unequally, or how well the relationship is fulfilling the mandate originally assigned to it. All these, *as well as* whether the relation is essentially or contingently shared, are important for a judgment on the normativity of the relation and its implications for identity.

My larger argument is that when speaking generally, neither conception of shared relations is superior to the other, nor is one a more accurate depiction of reality. Rather, the variety of relationship and the degree to which it is formative on individual identity varies according to the relationship or community in question. Moreover, we ought to be able to make normative statements regarding which relationships, communities, or associations *ought* to be more important for our identity. (Parents, for instance, do this for their children all the time.) We can take this even one step further: not only ought we to declare which relationships or communities are more important for personal identity, we even need to make normative statements regarding what they do for our identities, that is, how they shape our selves, and in which direction they appear to be sending us.

Thus, in their attention only to the type of relation that seems to support their arguments, both liberals and communitarians miss the point. More than that, they abstract from the full range of human activity and human life only those relationships that they deem as important, while others are deemed insignificant or morally repugnant. In this, both remain within the substantialist conception, reducing the human being to one or two arbitrary "essences" upon which a political theory can be constructed. In reality, however, we are neither "apart from" the other, nor are we enmeshed "in" the other. We are not "essentially" individuals, but neither are we "essentially" social. Our human identities are formed through our relations, but our selves cannot be reduced to them. This reductionism helps explain some of the misunderstanding between liberals and communitarians with respect to identity. Each contains an element of truth, as in any particular situation one of the liberal and communitarian accounts is likely to appear more accurate. However, because this element of truth is only one element, and one that has been abstracted from reality, the liberal and communitarian positions have only limited applicability, and therefore will find themselves continually vulnerable to criticism. Moreover, their willingness to abstract certain aspects from the totality of human life also weakens their ability to make normative statements concerning the desirability of any set of shared relations in a particular community or relationship.

The relational tradition of human identity has an advantage over the substantialist tradition on both these fronts. One of its primary strengths is that statements of "structure" (i.e., this type of relation is essentially shared) lead directly to normative and ethical statements of "direction" (i.e., this relation is important for healthy human development; or, this normative principle should govern this relationship). A much more nuanced account of community, and of shared relations more generally, is therefore more easily developed within the relational stream. This account can set out criteria as to how different types of relations may be classified and, in particular, how the relations with which we believe it is important to identify might be distinguished from those that could have more destructive consequences if allowed to assume too great a role in the constitution of selfhood. The relational tradition has the theoretical tools to make progress in this regard because it is able to articulate what particular human relations may be *for*.

The relational tradition also can provide resources for another important problem in the liberal-communitarian debate. Reacting to what they see as a preoccupation with neutrality, communitarians have been careful to consider questions concerning human nature and the political order within a social and historical context. Communitarian theorists advocate, therefore, looking to community for shared understandings about the self or principles of justice. The approach many communitarian theorists employ, for instance, is to discover a latent tradition of shared norms within the community in which human freedom can be grounded. Inasmuch as Rawls in 1985 was claiming that his principles are "political, not metaphysical," he implicitly accepts the central thrust of this communitarian argument and minimizes appeals to potentially controversial conceptions of human identity and philosophical principles beyond what community traditions might support. We noted above the significance of this implicit acceptance on the part of Rawls that any theory, liberal or otherwise, necessarily assumes some view of the self in society. Indeed, Michael Perry suggests that the earlier strategy of Rawls—to achieve an absolutely neutral politics, one that does not privilege one or more conceptions of the human being and human well-being—has been discredited, and in fact, largely abandoned.[87]

There remains an important question, however, unanswered by Rawls, whether such an overlapping consensus is possible. Perry suggests, for instance, that the hope that there exists on the horizon a conception of justice that will enjoy the support of such an agreement seems somewhat wistful, and he believes that at least for the foreseeable future, pluralist politics may have to proceed without benefit of this consensus.[88] But curiously, the communitarian hope that there actually exist shared understandings that may provide grounds for a tolerant and just political theory may seem to some to be unrealistic, perhaps even dangerous. Given our pluralism, both liberals and communitarians, in fact, are unduly optimistic about the possibility of using "what we have in common" as a basis for a political order. Most likely, the result will be a rather abstract or general "lowest common denominator" consensus that is too shallow and indeterminate with respect to the actual political conflicts we face, or, if it is more determinate, it unjustly minimizes the real differences that divide people, excludes those who are different in significant ways, and thus can hardly be called consensual or shared. In other words, I suspect that people differ from each other so greatly that efforts to ignore these differences by appealing to their common human identity (either as part of a Rawlsian overlapping consensus or in a communitarian shared understanding) will fail, either by not possessing sufficient resources upon which a just political order might be established or by excluding those people who are so different that everyone else ought to be especially concerned that they be "brought on board."[89]

Apart from these questions concerning possibility, however, what both communitarians and liberals ignore is whether this is actually a worthwhile approach to the problem. Both liberals and communitarians, in fact, face a crisis of justification in that however accurately they represent an overlapping consensus or shared understanding, we are still left wondering why we should accept this view as justification for their claims, for, as Neal and Paris note, consensual agreements are not warranted arguments.[90] One might hope that in addition to arriving at an understanding of how conceptions of the self are understood in a community or a society, a further task of political theory is to develop arguments for what these shared understandings or overlapping consensuses *ought* to be. Yet by accepting only "political" justifications, this is precisely what Rawls seems unable to do. No longer can he depend upon a philosophical position that deontologically places the right before the good, except where this is the consensus of the community. In fact, in his conception, he can put forward *nothing but* the community consensus—and even more significantly, neither can anyone else. Similarly, by searching for shared understandings or latent meanings within communities, communitarians risk losing any ability to mount an effective critique of those shared understandings which they may find offensive. In this regard, both sides go too far in their quests: by claiming to set questions of truth to one side and instead basing theory on political beliefs that already exist within the community or society, social philosophy is "deprived of the resources essential to its success."[91] This does not mean to minimize the significance of this type of political discussion or the importance of achieving political agreement regarding what a society values as important. However, by slipping so easily from philosophical argument to political agreement, not only do the participants miss possibilities to resolve their underlying differences, they also run the risk of fundamentally misunderstanding each other in the world of politics as well, damaging the prospects for political agreement.

Significantly, we can see that even in their willingness to set aside the quest for truth in their search for overlapping consensuses and shared understandings, the parties remain solidly within the substantialist tradition. The goal remains one of seeking an "Archimedean point" that can function as the ultimate point of reference by which all else can be measured. Rawls clearly believes that such a point can be located in the rational, autonomous individual, that this conception of human selfhood can be found in the public political culture, and that the various comprehensive doctrines of the good can provide it support. Communitarians likewise search for a final point of reference within society, too quickly adopting "community" as the primary unit of which everything else, including human beings, is a part. Again we see both sides reducing human beings to only a single aspect of their identity, betraying their common commitment to an ideology of human autonomy, and differing only upon whether the individual or the community ought to be the bearer of that autonomy.

This commitment, we learn, remains strong, even if what are basically arbitrary accounts of human identity threaten to overwhelm our ability to develop real criticisms of the society influenced by them, or to question sufficiently beliefs and values held by the individuals and communities who participate within that society. This is perhaps the most destructive consequence of the substantialist tradition of understanding human identity. This is the argument E. A. Goerner makes, for instance, in regards to Rawlsian liberalism, suggesting that Rawls began with status quo liberal society and attempted to develop some sort of theoretical justification for it. Writes Goerner in a review of Rawls's *Political Liberalism*:

> Political philosophy as official public justification of the established regime restricts itself to minor, safe tinkering at the margins. . . . The pragmatic bent of Rawlsian political philosophy, ever aimed at getting agreement, abandons all of the questioning, wondering, and thus subversive material that has remained part of the tradition since it got Socrates killed. . . . *Political Liberalism* is tamer stuff, a company newsletter.[92]

Ironically, Goerner's complaint here is almost that Rawls is too "communitarian," although in a rather unique sense. The charge is that Rawls basically accepted the communitarian focus on shared understandings too uncritically. Liberals miss the point that while communitarians may be correct to direct liberal eyes from the isolated individual to embedded selves, community understandings, and societal agreements concerning political principles, there remains a need for radical arguments that go *against* community understandings and that challenge shared meanings and overlapping consensuses, not because these understandings are not shared enough or are not sufficiently democratic, but simply because they are wrong.

Nancy L. Rosenblum makes a similar observation concerning the communitarians, suggesting that in their search for latent meanings and shared norms, they do not really seem to come up with much that presents a real challenge to liberal society. Rather, she suggests they are simply looking for a justification for a basically liberal society in a community-held "latent tradition of shared meanings," but they discuss it in a way that suggests that nothing they discover is likely to be incompatible with the public values of liberalism.[93] Her implication is that communitarians select only certain traditions or meanings or understandings from what they discover, although they are unclear as to the criteria they use to make their selections. Liberals suspect communitarians use an essentially liberal set of criteria. I would suggest, however, that while the criteria may not be liberal, at the very least they are indebted to the substantialist stream of interpretation.

The danger, as Rosenblum points out with respect to the communitarians, but I believe applies equally well to the liberals, is the tendency for the search for latent meanings and overlapping consensuses to become essentially an activity of reaction or conservation, seeking to resurrect or preserve something that has been lost or is in danger of being lost.[94] Conservation is not a bad thing per se—much that is good is in danger of being lost, and the struggle to preserve it is certainly worthwhile. But I would suggest that both communitarians and liberals are not immune to what sociologist Jean Comaroff calls a "post-partum" depression (postmodernism, poststructuralism, post-Marxism), leaving them "bereft of old enclosing certainties, adrift in a decentred world,"[95] desperately attempting to develop a new substantialist foundation for philosophy and politics that provides the secure grounding once provided by human rationality and freedom, but that in contemporary times seems seriously under threat.

Note that by setting aside questions of truth, both liberals and communitarians indicate once again their unwillingness to deal with questions of a "directional" nature, instead hoping that these can be settled some other way. As I have argued, however, this continues to avoid the real problem. Both groups of theorists ignore the fact that the distinction between answers developed within community over time and tradition or as the product of political agreement resulting in an overlapping consensus and answers derived by an individual theorist working alone, apart from, or in spite of community is not in itself a normative distinction. Rather, just as we noted above with respect to shared relations, there will exist admirable or offensive instances of each. What is needed, in contrast, is a set of tools to outline how the admirable and the offensive may be distinguished, to determine whether a particular political principle will encourage the development of healthy communities and individuals—whether, in fact, it will result in justice in the political sphere. Merely to proclaim that a particular answer was derived by one method or another is not enough to convince that it is the right answer. We require a stronger justification for political principles than knowledge of their origins.

My argument is also that because of their commitments to human autonomy and to reason, providing this set of tools is precisely what liberalism and communitarianism are most unwilling—and largely unable—to do. The questions raised here, questions regarding the normativity of political principles, however these principles are derived, ultimately require answers that assume an encounter with what is believed to be the source or meaning of politics and of philosophy. The contrast with the relational interpretation of the *imago Dei* by now should be clear. Because this tradition considers the human person in the context of all his or her primary relationships and understands there to be a connection between the quality of these relationships and human personhood in general, it will be particularly interested in normative questions regarding how these are regulated and directed. Religion, therefore, has a crucial role to play, as questions as to the direction of particular structures are inevitably religious ones. The strategy of looking to the community for these answers, whether in an overlapping consensus or a shared understanding, merely postpones the encounter.[96]

In general, however, the substantialist tradition would simply prefer not to deal with the problem, and therefore it downplays questions of religion or faith; by definition, it is interested in questions of substance, not relation. For instance, Rawls's weakness in this respect I have already implied: he requires people to have weak religious beliefs, diminishing the status of religion, in spite of his proclamation that questions of the good "are too important" to be resolved politically. Religious beliefs, as it turns out, are so important that they are not permitted to have any input into the content of the principles of justice,[97] nor, following Rawls's "duty of civility," are believers permitted even to conduct political discussion or deliberations on any basis other than the shared consensus.[98] In effect, the demand is that people split their identities into separate components;[99] for those people who seek to maintain an integrated identity, however, the "reconciliation" of goods that Rawls claims to exist within his overlapping consensus may well be experienced as a *conversion* to his position, one which permits only its own version of public philosophy. Once we have acknowledged this situation, we can get on with what I would suggest is the more important task of political theory, namely, determining whether or not some other theoretical conception can provide a theory of politics that is not so exclusive of the diverse individuals and communities living in a plural society.

All this suggests again that the old distinction between "religious" and "secular" is not as secure as it once was thought to be. This also underlines the importance of contributions to public discourse made by citizens who not only recognize their own religious commitments (and who are able and willing to recognize the commitments of others, acknowledged or not), but who also believe that their religious commitments have implications for politics. Moreover, it makes clear not only how impossible it is to de-politicize religion, or to extract from religion its political significance, but also how it is similarly impossible to "de-religiousize" politics, or to extract from politics its religious significance. Religious faith is one of the crucial elements of human identity, and for that reason, belief and trust are fundamental for any political theory; most attempts to keep them apart for too long ultimately result in a failure to understand either—and to deal constructively with the political problems before us.[100]

Conclusion

Part of what makes questions of identity and selfhood so difficult, so complex, is that they are so personal. Our identity, our self-concept, is how we understand ourselves to be, and for that reason, we quite understandably insist that our political theories recognize what we mean when we refer to our selves. The problem, however, as Taylor notes in "The Politics of Recognition," is that this recognition is not as easy today as it was not so long ago. All human beings must be recognized and accorded the respect they deserve as human beings, we declare, and our political theories must begin with such a statement. At the same time, however, we assert that the ways we differ from each other also merit public recognition, and woe to the political philosophy that papers over these differences or pretends that they are irrelevant to our fundamental political questions.

I have argued in this paper that liberalism and communitarianism both experience great difficulties as they attempt to navigate between these two perspectives. And this difficulty is due not primarily to the fact that most people are of two minds with regard to their selfhood (although this may be true to a certain extent), nor that there is an ongoing battle between the politics of universalism and the politics of difference that neither liberalism nor communitarianism can resolve (which also may be true), but rather that the two schools' own accounts of human selfhood are deficient in important respects. This deficiency, I argue, consists in the fact that both commit an error in abstraction, one resulting from the fact that both developed within a context where a particular Christian understanding of human nature was widely accepted, so widely accepted, in fact, that it provided the "normal" account of what people believed to be essential human nature. This account focused on certain aspects of human identity—namely human reason and human freedom—that were believed to raise man above the status of animal to a plane only "a little lower than the angels." Liberalism and communitarianism followed within this tradition, I argue, eventually dropping the explicitly religious elements, but by and large equating human nature with human reason or human freedom. I have noted that this selection has little to favor it in terms of philosophical or theological argument, other than that philosophers and theologians seem to prefer it. In other words, this account of identity is basically an arbitrary one.

As part of an effort to overcome these weaknesses, I have proposed a consideration of an alternative tradition of thought on human identity, one also rooted within the Christian tradition, one also
beginning with the Christian doctrine of the *imago Dei*, but one that
I believe provides a fuller account of the human self, and that, in particular, includes the dimension of faith. Just as we need approaches to
the problems of a plural politics that avoid the reduction of politics
to either the individual or the community, we also need approaches
that avoid the reduction of human identity to reason or to autonomy.
The significance for our political debates then, is that they are certain to have religious dimensions, just as human identities have religious dimensions. This explains the emphasis within the relational
stream on the ability of people and communities to bring their non-
shared, nonoverlapping beliefs into the public sphere within a politics
of plurality. The way to political decision making or persuasion cannot lie clear if the very reasons people hold to the positions they do
are to remain unarticulated. Again, we must forego our quest for the
One (one identity, one civil discourse, one public reason, one "Archimedean point"), and seek rather diversity and plurality in the public square.

This may appear to be an inordinate risk: when compared to the
claims of unity, the claims of diversity and pluralism appear disor-
derly, perhaps even an invitation to anarchy. To some extent, we
should expect that a move from a tradition which has long emphasized or idealized reason and freedom is almost certain to be perceived
as surrender to the opposites of these qualities: irrational disorder and
anarchy. Admittedly, this is not a politics of neutrality, and it will
very likely lead to controversy. If we recall, however, that the search
for a completely neutral politics has largely been abandoned, any social theory must develop certain propositions with which not everyone will agree. What makes theories developed within the relationalist tradition compelling, however, is that the difference between *this*
"exclusion" and the exclusion that results from the substantialist
strategy of seeking some shared tradition or consensus is that, here,
the right to enter and participate in public society is not lost, even if
one's position on public discourse is very much one's own. The emphasis continually is on keeping conversations going between people
and between communities, to keep finding ways to persuade, to include. In fact, rejecting the preoccupation with the One implies that
we ought not to expect to find an ultimate human consensus *ever*,
which should suggest to us again that if we are to look for a final
point of reference and source of authority, it can only lie *beyond* society.[101]

Thus, because social unity cannot be considered in a thoroughly immanentistic manner, and because ultimate truth cannot be our final goal, dialogue remains the most fundamental way people can express their relatedness with each other, despite their differences. Dialogue alone, of course, is not a sufficient condition for the discovery of solutions to difficulties regarding identity and politics—in this regard, this project is incomplete. However, I would argue that it is a *necessary* condition, and that within the substantialist tradition, this necessary condition has too quickly been stifled. So it is not simply that we have to discuss things that are important to us, but rather that we must be *permitted* and *enabled* to speak of these things. Our efforts ought to be directed at contending for the truth from out of our positions of commitment, rather than ignoring them because they are not shared, or retreating into them as if each were merely one among many. Thus, our commitments can be considered part of the solution, as we draw on the insights of those who have unique roles or experiences or beliefs or identities. This strategy, therefore, believes to be a strength precisely what a theorist like Rawls seeks most to overcome.

The dynamic nature of this dialogue, however, suggests an additional element that is easy to overlook: its essential nonstatic character. Any description of politics that seeks to provide an account of individuals, communities, relationships, institutions, cultures, and religions participating in continual dialogue can hardly describe such dialogue as a static phenomenon. Bernard Crick suggests something of this dynamism in his description of politics as not "a grasping for an ideal," nor "the freezing of tradition," but rather "an activity—lively, adaptive, flexible, and conciliatory."[102] This suggests something of the importance and the necessity of a renewed focus to be placed on a politics of persuasion, on how we want to "be," rather than on the principle under which we all ought to operate. Perhaps not surprisingly, an approach such as this seems to come closer to how people normally talk with one another, about politics or about anything else (perhaps what we might describe as a "normal speech situation"). Once again we can see the importance of resisting the temptation to work toward, or perhaps wait for, absolute certainty, the final answer that in Freud's words, "leaves no question unanswered and no stone unturned."[103] Such certainty will never come, least of all in politics; indeed, were such an answer to appear, it would likely crush what most requires nurturing. In contrast, what are needed are voices rooted in personal visions of what is true and good and right and just, who can contribute to an ongoing dialogue concerning how we might begin to discover truth and goodness, righteousness and justice—together, in relation.

Notes

1. This substance of this chapter was first presented at the annual meeting of the American Political Science Association, Boston, Massachusetts, September 3-6, 1998. I am grateful to Katherine Fierlbeck for her comments and suggestions at earlier stages of this project.

2. Jean Bethke Elshtain, *Public Man, Private Woman: Women in Social and Political Thought* (Princeton, N.J.: Princeton University Press, 1981), 56.

3. We read, for example, in Aristotle's *Politics* (ed. and trans. Richard McKeon [New York: Modern Library, 1947]), "For what each thing is when fully developed, we call its nature, whether we are speaking of a man, a horse, or a family. Besides, the final cause and end of a thing is the best." (1252b32).

Not only does this mean that the capacities or potentialities of a thing, as a member of a particular category or species, can be defined in terms of its function or final cause (*telos*), it implies further that this potential can be known in advance by considering the final or fully complete form of that category or species. Potential is thereby "naturally" predetermined: the entity is destined to fulfill its essence, and its essence is what it alone can fulfill. For Aristotle, in the completion of a thing (or a person) one can read its potentiality.

4. Elshtain, *Public Man, Private Woman*, 58.

5. Jean Bethke Elshtain, "'In Common Together': Christianity and Democracy in America," in *Christianity and Democracy in Global Context*, ed. John Witte Jr. (Boulder, Colo.: Westview, 1993), 70.

6. Most notably, Genesis 5:1, 9:6, I Corinthians 11:7, Colossians 3:10, and James 3:9.

7. Scripture quotations taken from Holy Bible, New Revised Standard Version. Copyright © 1989 by the National Council of Churches.

8. Douglas John Hall, *Imaging God: Dominion as Stewardship* (Grand Rapids, Mich.: Wm. B. Eerdmans; New York: Friendship, 1986), 61.

9. J. Richard Middleton, "The Liberating Image? Interpreting the *Imago Dei* in Context," *Christian Scholar's Review* 24, no.1 (1994), 10.

10. Anthony A Hoekema, *Created in God's Image* (Grand Rapids, Mich.: Wm. B. Eerdmans, 1986), 70.

11. Middleton, "The Liberating Image," 9.

12. Hendrikus Berkhof, *Christian Faith: An Introduction to the Study of Faith*, trans. Sierd Woudstra (Grand Rapids, Mich.: Wm. B. Eerdmans, 1979), 5.

13. Paul Ramsey, *Basic Christian Ethics* (New York: Scribner's, 1950), 250.

14. Perhaps the most comprehensive discussion of the two streams of interpretation since Ramsey is presented by Douglas John Hall, *Imaging God*. Other authors who have noted and discussed the two streams include Emil Brunner, *Man in Revolt*, trans. Olive Wyon (London: Lutterworth, 1939); Fr. M.-J. de Beaurecueil, "L'homme image de Dieu selon saint Thomas d'Aquin," parts 1 and 2, *Etudes et Recherches* 8 (1952), 45-82 and 9 (1955), 37-97; Karl Barth, *Church Dogmatics*, trans. J. W. Edwards, et al. (Edinburgh: Clark, 1958); G. C. Berkouwer, *Man: The Image of God* (Grand Rapids, Mich.: Wm. B. Eerdmans, 1962); David Cairns, *The Image of God in Man* (London: Collins, 1973); Claus Westerman, *Creation*, trans. John J. Scullion (Philadelphia: Fortress, 1974); Hendrikus Berkhof, *Foundations of Dogmatics* (Grand Rapids, Mich.: Wm. B. Eerdmans, 1981); Anthony A. Hoekema, *Created in God's Image*; Alistair I. McFadyen, *The Call to Personhood: A Christian Theory of the Individual in Social Relationships* (Cambridge, U.K.: Cambridge University Press, 1990); and D. Juvenal Merriell, *To the Image of the Trinity: A*

Study in the Development of Aquinas' Teaching (Toronto: Pontifical Institute of Mediaeval Studies, 1990).

15. Hall, *Imaging God*, 92.

16. Hall, *Imaging God*, 94.

17. Hall, *Imaging God*, 92.

18. Barth, *Church Dogmatics*, 183.

19. Hall, *Imaging God*, 98. Note that the argument here is not that human relations are not at all considered in the substantialist tradition of interpretation. Certainly in the work of Thomas Aquinas, for example, persons created in the image of God still relate to their God, to their neighbor, and to the world around them. The point, however, is the significance of these relations with respect to the *imago Dei* as it appears in human beings. For Thomas, the relation with the divine is certainly of paramount significance, but Thomas sees the person moving beyond the image (beyond reason, into the realm of grace) as this relation is assumed (Merriell, *Image of the Trinity*, 225). The focus with respect to the image is more upon the rational capacity to know and love God and neighbor, and less upon whether the individual actually moves into this relation or not (Merriell, *Image of the Trinity*, 189-90; Thomas Aquinas, *Summa Theologica. Basic Writings of Thomas Aquinas*, ed. Anton C. Pegis [New York: Random, 1945], I, 93, 4).

The parallel with the liberal account of selfhood is too striking to ignore. Liberals commonly claim to deal fairly with "shared relations," such as community and other shared identities, and in important respects this claim may well be accurate. But with respect to the liberal conception of human identity, it is important to see that liberals understand people to be moving beyond their essential selves as these relations are assumed. Accordingly, these relations are not seen to penetrate to the essence of the self, such that they might even be considered constitutive of it. We return to this discussion below, where we note certain ambiguities concerning "shared relations" in the liberal-communitarian debate.

20. Hall, *Imaging God*, 99.

21. Cairns, *The Image of God*, 125.

22. John Calvin, *Institutes of the Christian Religion*, ed. John T. McNeill and trans. Ford Lewis Battles (Philadelphia: Westminster, 1960), I, xv, 5.

23. Calvin, *Institutes*, I, xv, 4.

24. Calvin's mirror metaphor is particularly apt because it precludes a substantialist conception of the image. For Calvin, to speak of the image apart from the act of reflecting is inappropriate, as it would imply going outside the bounds of scripture. In contrast, the image of God is to be found first in the human being's relation to God, responsibility to God, and the possibility of fellowship with God. Capacities such as reason or the will are only the means whereby the person can fulfill his or her true function, only the "organ" of the relation to God (Brunner, *Man in Revolt*, 102). The point of the mirror metaphor as it is used by Calvin and by others after him is not that image-bearers possess the same characteristics as God does (as might be reflected in a mirror) because it is only while the mirror actually reflects an object that it contains its image. The reflecting (imaging) depends upon the position of the mirror in relation to the object. Thus, the mirror continues to reflect images if it is turned away from God, but this image is no longer the *imago Dei*. In this way, the mirror metaphor emphasizes that the image of God "happens" as a consequence of this relationship (Hall, *Imaging God*, 98).

25. It should be noted that I present here a considerable degree of unity among the "relationalists," the existence of which is questionable in important respects. Hall, for instance, questions whether the *imago Dei* can in any sense be said to remain in human beings outside the state of grace. Theologian G. C. Berkhouwer makes

a similar argument. Other interpreters such as Barth, Brunner, and Herman Bavinck suggest that there still remains a secondary role for fallen man's "continuing humanity" in the image, but differ among themselves as to what it might be. All would maintain, however, in contrast to Thomas, for example, that whatever this "broader" image is, it is as fallen as the rest of the person. See Anthony A. Hoekema, *Created in God's Image*, for a thorough discussion of some of these debates.

26. Philippians 2:6-8.

27. McFadyen, *Personhood*, 18.

28. Albert M. Wolters, *Creation Regained: Biblical Basics for a Reformational Worldview* (Grand Rapids, Mich.: Wm. B. Eerdmans, 1985), 49.

29. Hall, *Imaging God*, 82.

30. Colossians 3:1-4, 10.

31. Hall, *Imaging God*, 82.

32. Hall, *Imaging God*, 100.

33. Albert M. Wolters, "Facing the Perplexing History of Philosophy," *Tydskrif vir Christelike Wetenskap* 17 (1981), 15-16.

34. This is what Taylor describes as "the politics of equal dignity," based on a notion, derived from Kant, that what is of value in each human being—what ought to command respect—is each person's status as a rational, autonomous agent, and each person's ability to determine for himself or herself a view of the good life (Charles Taylor, "The Politics of Recognition," in *Multiculturalism: Examining The Politics of Recognition*, ed. Amy Gutmann [Princeton, N.J.: Princeton University Press, 1994], 41, 57).

35. Roy A. Clouser, *The Myth of Religious Neutrality: An Essay on the Hidden Role of Religious Belief in Theories* (Notre Dame, Ind.: University of Notre Dame Press, 1991), 83.

36. Merriell, *Image of the Trinity*, 225.

37. Aquinas, *Summa Theologica*, I, qu. 1, art. 1; Wolters, "Facing," 8.

38. Clouser, *Religious Neutrality*, 89.

39. Aquinas, I, 93, 4.

40. Hall, *Imaging God*, 109.

41. Benjamin R. Barber, "Liberal Democracy and the Costs of Consent," in *Liberalism and the Moral Life*, ed. Nancy L. Rosenblum (Cambridge, Mass.: Harvard University Press, 1989), 56.

42. Barber, "Liberal Democracy," 60.

43. Hall, *Imaging God*, 48.

44. McFadyen, *Personhood*, 22.

45. A further implication is that if we truly wish to learn what it means to be human, we cannot consider the human self apart from the context of all his or her primary relationships. If we are, by nature, in relation, the other to whom we must relate is not God alone, but also the other whom God has created, and the fact that we relate to our neighbor and how we do so is also an important component of our identity. Thus, in Christ's summary of the Mosaic law (Mark 12:30-31), one's neighbor is included, as well as one's God, as a primary focus of relation.

46. Charles Taylor, "Cross-Purposes: The Liberal-Communitarian Debate," in Rosenblum, *Liberalism and the Moral Life*, 168.

47. Taylor, "Politics," 32-34.

48. Middleton, "The Liberating Image," 16.

49. Hall, *Imaging God*, 116.

50. John Rawls, *A Theory of Justice* (Cambridge, Mass.: Harvard University Press, 1971), 60.

51. Rawls, *Theory*, 30.

52. Rawls, *Theory*, 560.

53. Rawls, *Theory*, 565.

54. Rawls, *Theory*, 563.

55. Taylor, "Cross-Purposes," 164.

56. Paul Marshall, "Liberalism, Pluralism and Christianity," in *Political Theory and Christian Vision*, ed. Jonathan Chaplin and Paul Marshall (Lanham, Md.: University Press of America, 1994), 148.

57. Patrick Neal and David Paris, "Liberalism and the Communitarian Critique: A Guide to the Perplexed," *Canadian Journal of Political Science* 28 (1990), 420.

58. Michael Sandel, "Introduction," in *Liberalism and Its Critics*, ed. Michael Sandel (New York: New York University Press, 1984), 5.

59. Michael Sandel, *Liberalism and the Limits of Justice* (Cambridge, U.K.: Cambridge University Press, 1982), 65.

60. Rawls refuses to give such guidance because he does not want to be exclusive. He therefore uses "good" in a nonmoral sense. George is "good," for example, in that he possesses certain qualities he and I value in him, totally apart from his teleological aim. All goods are therefore optional (in spite of the tendency toward certain goods that he calls the Aristotelian principle [Rawls, *Theory*, 424]), so long as they remain within the bounds of the right. Rawls therefore has no grounds for ruling the grass-counter out of order, nor those who pursue what might seem to be even more objectionable "goods," for instance, someone who enjoys finding new and complex ways to torture animals. All he can say is that we do not all have to enjoy this good, and that these individuals cannot expect public support to maintain this good (but neither, however, can museums [Rawls, *Theory*, 282-83]).

61. Sandel, *Limits*, 165.

62. Sandel, *Limits*, 159.

63. Sandel, *Limits*, 182.

64. Sandel, *Limits*, 183.

65. Neal and Paris, "Liberalism and the Communitarian Critique," 430.

66. John Rawls, "Justice as Fairness: Political not Metaphysical," *Philosophy and Public Affairs* 14 (1985), 223-51. This article, together with others written by Rawls between 1978 and 1989, was republished in John Rawls, *Political Liberalism* (New York: Columbia University Press, 1993).

67. Rawls, *Political Liberalism*, 27.

68. Rawls, "Justice," 225.

69. Rawls, "Justice," 228.

70. Rawls, "Justice," 230.

71. Rawls, *Political Liberalism*, 27.

72. Rawls, "Justice," 238.

73. Rawls, "Justice," 246.

74. Rawls, "Justice," 246.

75. Rawls, "Justice," 495.

76. E. A. Goerner, "Rawls's Apolitical Political Turn," *Review of Politics* 53 (1993), 713.

77. Rawls, *Political Liberalism*, 12.

78. Rawls, *Political Liberalism*, 11.

79. Neal and Paris, "Liberalism and the Communitarian Critique," 420.

80. Thomas Hobbes, *Leviathan*, ed. Richard Tuck (Cambridge, U.K.: Cambridge University Press, 1991), 10.

81. Kenneth D. McRae, "The Plural Society and the Western Political Tradition," *Canadian Journal of Political Science* 12 (1979), 682.

82. Rawls, "Justice," 249.

83. Neal and Paris, "Liberalism and the Communitarian Critique," 425. The helpful distinction between "essentially" and "contingently" shared relations is described more thoroughly in Neal and Paris (425-30). In their discussion, the authors note that in the course of the liberal-communitarian debate, each side claims to account for the other's concerns with regard to the self, but each conveniently casts these concerns in its own terms. Communitarians, for instance, suggest that liberalism takes no account at all of the significance of shared relations for the formation of attitudes and behaviors, and thus observe in their opponents a hopelessly naïve and anomic conception of the abstract individual, missing—or ignoring—the more nuanced version, and thereby criticize a shallow interpretation of liberal individualism rather than the real thing. Meanwhile, liberals mistakenly understand communitarians to be making little more than the sociological argument that relations and identities are important for human development. Thus, they believe themselves able to provide an easy answer to communitarians regarding social relations, when actually the questions raised regarding the interaction of shared relations and identity are highly significant. In this manner, by considering nothing more than the most superficial of each other's arguments, liberals and communitarians both consider the other to have "missed the point," and thereby they confirm their own positions.

84. Taylor, "Cross-Purposes," 160-61.

85. Neal and Paris, "Liberalism and the Communitarian Critique," 427.

86. Neal and Paris, "Liberalism and the Communitarian Critique," 428. This is not to say that there may not be certain institutions (such as marriage) where a particular model of shared relations is more appropriate and even more "normative." The point, however, is that blanket statements as to the inherent worthiness of one conception or the other are unhelpful and inaccurate, and hinder constructive dialogue between the parties.

87. Michael J. Perry, "Neutral Politics," *Review of Politics* 51 (1989), 494.

88. Perry, "Neutral Politics," 498.

89. These difficulties also demonstrate the weakness of a strategy of establishing a consensus first and then dealing with difference later. A "shallow" consensus is unlikely to possess the tools to deal with difference—in fact, dealing with difference is often what breaks apart "consensuses" (as my own country, Canada, has come so close to discovering recently). Meanwhile, a "deeper" consensus is likely to exclude the different to begin with. And, of course, once the different are excluded, it is not so hard to deal with difference in what is left.

90. Neal and Paris, "Liberalism and the Communitarian Critique," 434.

91. William A. Galston, "Pluralism and Social Unity," *Ethics* 99 (1989), 712.

92. Goerner, "Rawls's Apolitical Political Turn," 718.

93. Nancy L. Rosenblum, "Pluralism and Self-Defense," in Rosenblum, *Liberalism and the Moral Life*, 217.

94. Feminist scholars, of course, have long been warning of something similar, criticizing both liberals and communitarians for their conservatism with regard to the family and the status of women (Susan Moller Okin, "Humanist Liberalism," in Rosenblum, *Liberalism and the Moral Life*, 48, 49).

95. Jean Comaroff, "Missionaries and Mechanical Clocks: An Essay on Religion and History in South Africa," *The Journal of Religion* 71 (1991), 6.

96. The alternative, of course, is for liberals or communitarians to make what is essentially a religious commitment to the process of articulating shared norms or overlapping consensuses from society. Indeed, there are perhaps some that might resort to this option, accepting whatever comes from this source as gospel truth. I would submit, however, that few would be willing to follow this path consistently, as it would seem to imply a total surrender of personal opinion to whatever the community declares or agrees upon, however offensive, however contradictory. Most,

therefore, remain broadly within the substantialist tradition of thought, committed in theory to the universality of certain "good" human qualities such as rationality and human freedom, but increasingly worried whether such qualities actually exist, unsure whether the values that accompany such qualities are morally praiseworthy, and uncomfortable where such a thoroughgoing commitment ultimately might lead.

97. Rawls, *Political Liberalism,* 141.

98. Rawls, *Political Liberalism,* 217-18.

99. I have been speaking here mainly about faith, but this is also likely true for gender, race, disability, sexual orientation, or any other aspect of identity that we might experience as politically significant.

100. Note that this problem is not identical with the difficulty that occurs when we discover that once our political community is established, its founding principles are not sufficient in themselves to generate the spirit and unity required in political community. This was a problem noted by Rousseau, who advocated introducing a form of civil religion to perform this task. My concern here, however, is not that we reintroduce religion afterward as a sort of "community spirit" to make up for deficiencies inherent in the original position. Such an effort, in effect, is too little, too late: whatever we would seek to introduce would be unacceptable to many individuals and communities who are important constituents of that political community (Galston, "Pluralism and Social Unity," 712). More constructive, it seems to me, would be to take seriously people's religious beliefs and other crucial dimensions of our identities from the beginning, as we consider the foundational principles of our political community (as Will Kymlicka begins to do with cultural identity, for example).

101. Bernard Zylstra, "The Bible, Justice and the State," *International Reformed Bulletin* 55 (1973), 13.

102. Bernard Crick, *In Defense of Politics* (Harmondsworth, U.K.: Penguin, 1982), 55.

103. Elshtain, *Public Man, Private Woman,* 300.

Chapter 5

Rehabilitating the State in America: Abraham Kuyper's Overlooked Contribution

Timothy Sherratt

From curing faction's mischiefs to balancing government's budgets, from checking and balancing to term limits, the 1990s have witnessed a steady undercurrent of experimentation with governmental design as an alternative to personal choice in the American political tradition. But this current has been so dammed and diverted as to become more and more a backwater. The Gingrich revolution is fascinating in many respects, not least for the tangled epistemology that reduces government in the name of personal freedom but simultaneously frees government from the impact of personal choice to operate as a machine that would run of itself. The main currents of American public discourse trap the state in negative images of abusive power and inefficient bureaucracy, inviting both an older language of rights against such government and a more recent, increasingly discredited, rhetoric of entitlements to its resources and power. These images, and the scholarship that has failed to lay them to rest, create a fragmented and contradictory theory of government's role, nowhere more so than in the courts where government must prove a compelling interest before it is permitted to place restrictions on fundamental rights but need only demonstrate a rational basis for expansionist social and economic programs—reasoning that has imposed considerable strain on the separation of powers. American public and scholarly discourse succeeds in being antistatist despite the presence of a large state apparatus. Lost in the shuffle, so to speak, is the state itself, its authority either defied or dissolved in notions of social contract and popular consent, its executive powers diluted in pluralist theory.

If Theodore Lowi is right, there is not even the consolation of success to smooth over the contradictions.[1] The American state has expanded despite the rhetoric of rights and the warnings about power, despite the separation of powers and the Bill of Rights. Its regulatory reach is pervasive but its real authority is qualified by the practice of democratizing administration of the majority's will. Thus, liberal leaders "do not wield the authority of democratic governments with the resoluteness born of confidence in the legitimacy of their positions, the integrity of their institutions, or the justness of the programs they serve."[2] This chapter will make considerable use of Lowi's well-received analysis and prescriptions; taken together, they lay important groundwork for the contribution neo-Calvinism might make to resolve the dilemma of the state in American politics and political science.

The rehabilitation of the American state appears to be linked to the disentangling of the institutionalist, republican tradition from the quasi-libertarian language of rights and minimalist government. The "overlooked contribution" of the writings of Abraham Kuyper in particular, and of neo-Calvinism in general, lies in its theory of the internal design of the state, its juxtaposition of the state to personal and group liberty, its religious view of life and resulting respect for religious liberty, and its embrace of pluralism. The neo-Calvinist state is limited in function but morally purposeful, responsible for sharing authority with differentiated societal institutions and for interpreting the relationship between those institutions and the persons who occupy them. While the neo-Calvinist state is to a degree contained both by American-style checks on its authority, the principal "checks and balances" are structural arguments asserting the irreducible grounds of that authority. Finally, the scholarly orientation reflected in the neo-Calvinist conception of the state finds questions of the positive state and of church-and-state closely connected, whereas American political science has typically kept them separated.

Theodore Lowi and the State in America

Although it conforms in most respects to the received view of the evolution of the state in the United States, Lowi's treatment of the subject is noteworthy for its development over some three decades. Indeed, the received view owes much to his scholarship, which has had a profound effect on the study of American government, from public policy analysis to the presidency to the state of the discipline itself.[3] But in singling out Lowi's analysis of the American state, I am in a sense also invoking several generation's worth of scholarship seeking to mobilize effective authority and administration within and in the service of liberal democracy, what Seidelman and Harpham term the "Third Tradition" in political science.[4] Lowi's contribution lies principally in his call for juridical democracy.[5] His insistence that the crisis of the republic under an uncontrolled interest-group liberalism should be met by attention to the basic internal design of the republic brings him into fruitful contact and even limited agreement with the Kuyperian view of the state. It does so in three respects. First, it applies a remedy where Kuyper had most to offer—not where he had least—for Kuyper identified the state's purpose and limits by laying alongside one another the roles, or divine callings, of the state, social institutions, and individuals rather than pursuing the Anglo-American emphasis on limited government as a corollary of presocial individual rights. Second, Lowi's remedy is in some respects much clearer than Kuyper's and sheds critical light on the latter; specifically, the principles Lowi recommends for checking the positive state operate with less ambiguity than the principles one must infer to justify state intervention in a Kuyperian polity. Third, however, Lowi's remedy reveals the weaknesses inherent in the general tendency within political science to consider the issues of the welfare state separately from questions of religious liberty and, indeed, innocent of the "religious" presuppositions that guide them. Here, the integral Kuyperian approach is demonstrably superior.

The Federal Constitution of 1787 established a central government with exclusive functions in the area of foreign policy making, and with control over subsidies, tariffs, public lands disposal, patents, and coinage domestically. These domestic powers had been hewn from the much larger set of functions held by state governments, which retained almost all regulatory functions like judicial and criminal procedure laws, public health laws, and banking and credit laws.[6] Left obscure in the Constitution was the federal-state balance of power and function in respect of commerce, because, while the Constitution granted Congress power to regulate interstate commerce, it did not accompany that grant with a corresponding prohibition on the states. The early federal state was a "patronage state" in Lowi's words. Though it was the largest institution in American society and its activities significantly influenced commercial development, investment, and productive population distribution, the Federal government in no sense coordinated a national policy—unless one credits Chief Justice Marshall with doing so. Instead, it brokered countless individual decisions and distributed its patronage in jobs and policies.

The patronage state was first supplemented by elements of a regulatory state in the late nineteenth century. At first the agitation for government regulation of industry barely touched the federal government, but the inability of states to tackle the whole problem precipitated national legislative action.[7] Supreme Court decisions restricting the reach of early federal regulations perhaps retarded national regulatory efforts, notably the decision in *Hammer v. Dagenhart* in 1918, so the patronage state survived as the dominant form into the 1930s. Indeed, Lowi regards this as a settled matter within the discipline: "There is no need to document for political scientists the contention that the American state until the 1930s was virtually an oxymoron. The level of national government activity was almost as low in 1932 as it had been in 1832."[8] The nationalization of political focus brought about by the Civil War and industrialization, by the mass media, and by social movements did, however, precipitate the emergence of a national state.

With the coming of the New Deal, the now-expanding patronage role was broadly supplemented by regulatory and redistributive functions, which respectively imposed obligations directly upon citizens and set up the programs that earn the redistributive function the title of "welfare" state. These developments were supported by the Supreme Court from 1937 (*NLRB v. Jones and Laughlin Steel Corp.*) and then given wholehearted encouragement in 1942 (*Wickard v. Filburn*). In Lowi's words, if Filburn (a small farmer growing wheat for private consumption in excess of his federally allotted quota) can be reached by congressional act, then "economic federalism is dead."[9]

For Lowi, the development and endorsement of the regulatory and welfare states constitute a revolution making the federal government responsible for citizens' well-being and steering popular expectations of good government away from its representativeness toward its capacity to deliver services. But crucial to the analysis is Lowi's charge that Court and Congress together perverted the framers' design for a separation-of-powers system and erected in place of the original balance a presidency equipped with unchecked, delegated powers of enormous reach. Despite the American tradition of individual rights and limited government and a rhetoric to match, America got a state that strained the definition of limited government and became the authoritative deliverer of rights as well as their natural enemy.

The new state, what Lowi terms the Second Republic of the United States, was a positive, interventionist state, centered on the executive branch; it began life having been granted unqualified validation by the Court concerning national economic power and the separation of powers; it controlled aspects of the electoral process traditionally left in private hands; it assumed these controls at the expense of the political parties; it rapidly acquired an autonomous bureaucracy; and its epistemology looked to economics rather than to law.[10] It is the breakdown of the rule of law and its replacement by bargaining that Lowi finds to be the distinguishing feature of the Second Republic and the focus of his proposals for reform.

Lowi's indictment of this American state is his familiar critique of interest-group liberalism. Liberal governments undermine popular decisions by democratizing their administration, decline to set standards, fall short of justice by failing to make policy on the basis of prior moral rule, and substitute bargaining for formal (legal) procedure. His response is to call for *juridical democracy*, in its simplest form a return to predictable and accountable government under the rule of law, a form rejected by the Supreme Court at the very moment the United States embraced a federal state in earnest. Under juridical democracy, governments would have to define policy goals with precision, that is they would have to write laws that leave minimal discretion to administrators. As Lowi had observed long before,[11] implementation of policy under loosely written laws involves not mere administrative rule-following but genuine decision-making power. Where that early work concentrated on analysis alone, *The End of Liberalism* was openly critical of the delegation of power, the broad discretion it gave bureaucracy, and the failure of the courts to contain delegation within a clear and workable principle conceived within the structural intent of the Constitution. The centerpiece of his remedy is a return to the rule of law.

When in the American republic a political scientist reaches for internal solutions of this kind rather than further external checks on the scope of governmental authority, and when the solutions reached for are principles to govern the distribution of power and functions among the branches of a system of separated powers, then we can move beyond the stale rhetoric of more versus less government that has cramped public discourse for decades back toward the language of America's internal design. And that is to move back toward the republican foundations behind liberal democracy. Here a Kuyperian approach has much to offer.

The State in the Political Theology of
Abraham Kuyper

Abraham Kuyper (1837-1920) was variously a pastor, newspaper editor, parliamentarian, founder of a university, and prime minister of The Netherlands. His political thought emerges from writings over a long period and reflects all of these roles, yet McKendree Langley cautions that Kuyper was "unable to articulate a systematic Christian theory of the state."[12] In place of such a theory, Kuyper seems to have worked out the main lines of a perspective having the virtue of ongoing application in his journalistic and political work. Kuyper's approach to the state may be understood as practical, with the proviso that his practicality's hallmark is its consistency with a Calvinist confession. That confession, and with it Kuyper's political thought, begins and ends with the sovereignty of God.

The Juridical State and Sphere Sovereignty

Kuyper defined sovereignty in juridical terms, as "authority that possesses the right and duty, and wields the power to break and punish all resistance to its will " And he appealed to the inner voice of conscience for the view that such a power can only be God's—intuitively we are to recognize limits on the exercise by human beings of this sort of power: "And does not an ineradicable conscience also speak within you, telling you that original, absolute sovereignty cannot reside in any creature, but must coincide with the majesty of God?"[13]

When human offices exercise an authority divine in its origins, they simultaneously gain legitimacy for that authority and acknowledge limitations to its exercise. Divine authority in human hands is limited authority both because its source is God and because its manifestation is multifaceted: there are sovereignties of state, society, and church. Not only does this threefold organization restrict the reach of each sphere into which it is organized, each of these is also subject in turn to internal qualifications. Sin, the fundamentally disintegrating force in the cosmos, thwarts the realization of world government, the polity befitting our human nature for we are all of "one blood." Nation-states therefore do not harmonize with our human nature. Their status is temporary, artificial. Unlike some contemporary Reformed thinkers who derive the authority of the state directly from the "cultural mandate," God's command to man in Genesis to subdue, cultivate, and replenish the created order,

Kuyper wrote somewhat ambivalently on this subject.[14] In his *Lectures on Calvinism,* he argues that the state may only derive authority directly from God, a strictly juridical authority that would be moot in a world without sin. Here the state is a state of enumerated rather than implied powers, as Augustinian as it is traditionally Calvinist, whose authority is both justified and exhausted in response to the disintegrating effects of sin: "When sin tears man apart, and when sin reveals itself in all manner of shame and unrighteousness, the glory of God demands that these horrors be bridled, that order return to this chaos, that a compulsory force, from without, assert itself to make human society a possibility (*Lectures on Calvinism*: 82).

The true picture appears somewhat more complex, however. In his writings on the doctrines of particular and common grace, Kuyper clearly, if implicitly, embraces the cultural mandate. Particular grace is the saving grace of God; common grace reflects God's willingness to sustain the creation. The two are both related and "antithetical." S. U. Zuidema[15] writes of them as polar in a magnetic sense, simultaneously attracting and repelling. Thus, common grace has to do with creation (that is, nature, because for Kuyper these were synonymous), particular grace with re-creation. Ipso, particular grace is superior and common grace is ultimately dependent upon it, for the creation itself is under judgment and awaits the fulfillment of God's purposes in history, purposes which cannot be reached through (fallen) nature: "By its inner nature (common grace) . . . aims at its own creaturely end, which as such has no real connection with the hereafter and no real connection with the mystic life of the souls that are saved."[16]

Kuyper always insisted that his was not an Anabaptist position[17] which wrote off creation and led to world-flight but one in which the very relationship of attraction and repulsion between particular and common grace clarified and underscored the distinct callings of social institutions and the church. Since the principles on which Kuyper's political theory rests invoke these callings and the requirement not to violate them, we can see that the particular/common grace distinction sharpens the role of the state. The state is an agency of common, not particular, grace. Thus its task is to sustain creation, not to redeem it. In Kuyper's biblical perspective, sustenance is not a neutral life-giving: sustaining a fallen creation is largely a matter of one act of correction after another—for unredeemed humanity abuses God's creation—and in *that* sense the state exercises an exclusively juridical authority. All the same, his position remains ambivalent for the cultural mandate suggests elements of sustenance other than correction. Perhaps Kuyper viewed other elements as exclusively the province of God. Whether he was right to claim that the common grace juridical calling of government has "no real connection" to redemption is a major point of theology that I will not attempt to take on.

A state that exercises only a derived, creational authority and exercises that authority especially on account of sin can claim none of the traditionally liberal or democratic foundations for exercising governmental power—consent, majority rule, social contract, and so forth, albeit democratic elections select a governing party. Indeed, Kuyper draws an explicit set of contrasts between the popular sovereignty of the French Revolution, which expressly rejected existing human and divine authorities in favor of popular sovereignty, and the state sovereignty of the German rulers, which claimed that the state embodies the most perfect relationship between man and man; and this theory of derivative sovereignty. He commends Calvinism for its "two-fold insight" into the state's dark side (a potential despotism) and its light side (the only alternative to a "veritable hell on earth"). Kuyper's formulation rejects both popular and state sovereignty but preserves the legitimacy of the state without discounting the threat governments pose to human freedom:" We have gratefully to receive from the hand of God, the institution of the state with its magistrates, as a means of preservation, now indeed indispensable. And on the other hand . . . we must ever watch against the danger which lurks, for our personal liberty, in the power of the State."[18]

The Kuyperian state is grounded in and bounded by three principles: only God possesses sovereign rights because God is the nations' creator, maintainer and ruler; sin has broken down God's direct rule, thus the exercise of authority has been vested in men for a mechanical remedy; and Man never possesses legitimate power over fellow man in any other way than by an authority which descends on him from the majesty of God. That this is a limited state is obvious in the first principle—no human being can claim the status of creator, maintainer, and ruler of the nations, even if the task assigned to her office is to participate in sustaining the creation. The second principle appears illogical on its face: if human disobedience has broken the personal rule of God, vesting authority in humans seems to be exactly the wrong response. Kuyper resolves the apparent contradiction by reasoning that the only kind of authority reconcilable with God's sovereignty is an authority that leaves little discretion in the human hands that will exercise it—it is a "mechanical" authority. The third principle Kuyper justifies on the grounds that any right to rule over a fellow man will become the right of the strongest.[19]

To justify the broad division of divine authority into spheres, Kuyper offers two sorts of arguments. The first is to maintain, as Herman

Dooyeweerd was to do later, that such a division is ontologically sound, deriving as it does from the ordinances of God. Kuyper argued that the independence of spheres was logically required to demonstrate that they have "nothing above themselves but God, and that the State cannot intrude here, and has nothing to command in their domain."[20] We have seen that Kuyper qualifies the common Calvinist justification that state authority derive from the cultural mandate by assigning it the principal task of counteracting the effects of sin. Accordingly, in his *Lectures*, Kuyper treats the state as a special kind of sphere, more mechanical than organic in character. The social spheres represent organic life; the family, for instance, is natural, innate, spontaneous, biological. Though sin intrudes into every area of life, its worst effects on the social spheres are blunted by common grace, the action of God that operates to benefit everyone, believer and nonbeliever alike, restraining sin and preserving the created order.

Kuyper described this central Calvinist dogma as God's intervention in the human condition to prevent the total annihilation of his own work, which would have led to a "total degeneracy of human life." Common grace arrests "the complete effectuation of sin . . . partly by breaking its power, partly by taming [man's] evil spirit, and partly by domesticating his nation or his family."[21] Common grace, Kuyper claims, lends coherence to history, flowering both in classical thought and modern scientific knowledge. By its action, all things are shown intuitively to be worthy of investigation.

By resorting to an argument from common grace for the organic and relatively unsullied character of the social spheres and contrasting this with the mechanical character of the state, Kuyper further buttresses his conception of limited government. Given the ontological status of the social spheres, the state never confers authority upon them or grants them freedom(s) but "merely recognizes" the unique authority that descends on each directly from God.

The second argument is less pejorative in regards to the state. Kuyper finds the distinction among the social spheres and between them and the state marked by two antithetical "sovereignty credos." The unbeliever separates faith and sovereignty and vests the latter exclusively in the state, which confers, or if it is weak allows, the social spheres to possess what freedom they enjoy. By contrast, the believer links the two, vesting human freedom in God and recognizing that the state is "marked by an authority derived from Him."[22] Yield the Christian revelation, Kuyper argues, and under whatever "hybrid theories" you hide it, Caesarism emerges: "Thus the ancient history of the world confronts us with the

ignominious drama of how, despite stubborn and sometimes heroic resistance, freedom within the various spheres dies out and the power of
the state triumphs, turning eventually into Caesarism."

Rights and the State

Kuyper deduces the rights and liberties of social life from the same
source from which the high authority of government flows, the "absolute
sovereignty of God." And if rights and state authority come from the
same source, "these two must therefore come to an understanding," for
"both have the same sacred obligation to maintain their God-given sovereign authority and to make it subservient to the majesty of God."[23]
This juxtaposing of rights and state authority as derivative sovereignties
will not allow their permanent situating in opposition to each
other—even though Kuyper recognizes that the "battle of the ages" is
the battle between authority and liberty—but points to a symbiosis by
which the assertion of the one or the other may be obligatory for the
good of all. Thus, Kuyper describes the struggle for liberty as "not only
. . . permissible, but is made a duty for each individual in his own sphere
. . . The very innate thirst for liberty . . . proved itself the God-ordained
means to bridle the authority [of the state] wheresoever it degenerated
into despotism."[24]

All political authority, then, whether in the hands of individual persons, social institutions or the state, is derivative authority. Nor is the divine grant of authority unconditional; what was ordained (Romans 13)
may be taken away by a God ever active in the affairs of humankind.
Under certain conditions God plants his sovereignty in the people,
Kuyper acknowledges, only to deny that this justifies an assertion of
popular sovereignty "as was atheistically proclaimed in Paris in 1789."
But, "(e)ven a Calvinist gratefully recognizes . . . the divine judgment
which at that time was executed in Paris." The point he seems to want to
make is that the right way to comprehend events like the French Revolution is through the lens of divine judgment, not the lens of natural
rights; and an occasion for divine judgment does not translate into a
grounds for popular sovereignty. Kuyper insists that the "desirable condition" of popular rule can be removed, or never bestowed, as a matter
of divine judgment "when a nation is unfit for it, or, by its sin, has ut-
terly forfeited the blessing."[25] What he fails to explain is how one recognizes such a bestowal or removal of sovereignty. When is a military
coup judgment, and thus legitimate in some limited fashion; when is it to
be resisted without any moral self-examination on the part of the people

or their democratically elected government? Can the legitimacy of the judgment be affirmed independently of Calvinist theology—a vital requirement for a pluralist polity, one would think? The theological point being made is much clearer than any practical principle to be derived from it.

The requirement that all human sovereignties derive from God appears to circumscribe the state rather more than it does the individual. When Kuyper describes the sphere of government as supplying a mechanical remedy, he asserts that state authority is both justified *and exhausted* in correcting the disintegrative effects of sin. By contrast, the social spheres are organic and innate, that is they enjoy the sustaining power of God (common grace) relatively unsullied by the debilitating effects of sin. The state is restricted by necessary deference to the "innate law of life" at work in the social spheres and by the limits of its own mandate:

> The sovereignty, by the grace of God, of the government is here set aside and limited, for God's sake, by another sovereignty, which is equally divine in origin. Neither the life of science nor of art, nor of agriculture, nor of industry, nor of commerce, nor of navigation, nor of the family, nor of human relationship may be coerced to suit itself to the grace of the government.[26]

I remarked above that the doctrine of vocations was the implicit ground on which Kuyper's political thinking rests, implicit enough at any rate to be largely unremarked in his treatment of politics in his *Lectures*. Contemporary neo-Calvinists allow the doctrine more force in their political theory. Discussing the doctrine of vocation as it appears in Calvin's *Institutes*, Hancock distinguishes the Calvinist official, a "conduit of the will of God, which he cannot possibly embody" from the Aristotelian aristocrat, whose virtue embodies what is good for man.[27] For Hancock, Calvinist calling depends directly on God's sovereignty. One might be called equally to service of the state as to ministry in the church, yet "equality under God's will binds men to their respective callings; it does not liberate them as political actors." Here is the mechanical character of office in an older, Calvinist guise.[28]

Contemporary neo-Calvinists sometimes write as though vocation does indeed liberate one as a political actor, or at least lend further validity to the view that the state possesses some independence from the social spheres. Zylstra, for instance, argues that the norm of justice "requires social space for human personality. By personality I mean the human self whose calling lies in love of God and love of neighbor." Zyl-stra lists the social spheres as valid domains for fulfilling one's vocation and includes public office along with them, without reference to the or-ganic/mechanical distinction by which Kuyper divides them. This is misleading on account of the individualist motives it allows to attach to the performance of governmental office, which for Calvin and Kuyper is not a sphere in which to practice *creative* individuality, but obedience to the cultural mandate. Indeed, Zylstra himself recognized public office as unique, divinely established to "maintain a public realm in which the rights of persons and institutions are recognized, protected, and guaran-teed."[29] On this reading, contemporary neo-Calvinism would seem to want to broaden the role of government to include a directive function along with the juridical function.[30]

A more far-reaching interpretation of Kuyper involves the marriage of sphere sovereignty with the concept of rights, which also emerges in Zylstra's writings, especially in respect of religious liberty. Such an in-terpretation is not without warrant, given that Kuyper asserts the rights of people to control their own purses and insists that law, not the magis-trate, must decide rights. But what is striking about Kuyper's treatment of rights is how sparse it is. Acknowledging that popular assemblies now protect rights, resisting the notion that any person possesses a right over any other, speculating on the need for a "corporative right of franchise," in Kuyper's treatment public justice depends to only a limited extent on individual rights. Perhaps the process of re-expressing Kuyper's political theory using conventional rights language robs it of its structural focus, turning Kuyperian political theory away from its continental center of gravity as a structural representation of state, individual and differenti-ated society in the direction of an Anglo-American scheme for limiting government in the name of individual liberty. This interpretation must be treated cautiously if it seeks to identify itself as Kuyperian, for Kuyper is never as individualist as he is personalist. At best it focuses on a secon-dary aspect of his political thought, at worst it distorts the latter's salient features.

The State as an Agent of Public Justice

Kuyper's juridical conception of government's essential functions did not permit him to legitimize a patronage state along the lines of Lowi's model of the first federal regime. Subsidizing private activity to achieve governmental aims would have been suspect, I think. Sphere sovereignty permits the state to intervene to enable the social spheres to do what they do best, to prevent violations of individual freedoms within these spheres, and to maintain parity between spheres, but such intervention could never be for "positive state" reasons. It is hard to imagine Homestead Acts and railroad land grants emerging from a Kuyperian state in that these did not represent neutral governmental encouragement of private enterprise for its own sake. Sphere sovereignty principles restrain government in this way chiefly to check imperialism or other manifestations of Caesarism, but they may also unintentionally thwart economic development. Only if state encouragement of economic development can be interpreted as an expression of public justice could such intervention be justified.

Kuyper contemplated the rise of the positive state, especially the development of direct cash welfare programs, and sharply criticized it. Writing in 1891, he insisted that state and society each possess its own sphere. The class strife brought on by the industrial revolution elicited from him a restatement of sphere sovereignty principles, not a new venture in public policy. Such ventures, he warned, were the mistaken undertakings of social democrats and state socialists, both of whom erased the distinction between state and society and forfeited the free society ordained by God. What Kuyper objected to in the positive state was a distortion of divine ordinances epitomized by the presumption that men had to design governmental solutions to the social problem de novo. "We do not have to organize society," he maintained, "we have only to develop the germ of organization that God himself has created."[31] Here, finally, Kuyper resorts explicitly to the cultural mandate. Man is to "preserve and cultivate" the natural world because barbarism will ensue when human society is left to nature without higher supervision. Kuyper acknowledges the general contribution of human governments to resisting barbarism while noting the unhealthy consequences of government action originating in false, that is, non-Christian, principles. Such governments permit the powerful to exploit the weak, or to coopt government offices and turn government's powers against the weak. By contrast, a Calvinist government is to move cautiously in the area of social experimentation, refusing "to erect any structure except one that rests on foundations laid by God."[32] Once again, as he was to do in more abstract terms in the Stone Lectures but here in an applied setting, Kuyper turns to the cautionary tale of social democracy and state socialism, the one allowing society to swallow the state, the other permitting the state to absorb society: "Against both of these, we as Christians must hold that state and society each has its own sphere, its own sovereignty, and that the social question cannot be resolved rightly unless we respect this duality and thus honor state authority as clearing the way for a free society."[33]

Although the terms and examples in which he expresses his reluctance to engage in social experimentation might mark Kuyper as a conservative pure and simple, they do lay the foundations for qualified intervention. Rejecting individualism on the basis of common human guilt and "the mystery of the reconciliation on Golgotha," Kuyper commends the "interconnected wholeness of our human society," rejects both an absolute property right as a violation of God's sovereignty and a community of possessions as a violation of the right of rule "in the context of the organic association of mankind," and identifies the problem of poverty as a clash *between* social spheres where government intervention is warranted.[34] The clash in question is, of course, the class struggle, the conflict between business and labor. Compelled by the ordinances of God to stay out of the social spheres but equally compelled to uphold justice equitably (which Kuyper extends to withstanding the physical superiority of the strong, presumably because this falsely advances a right to rule), the state must act evenhandedly. "A code for business . . . calls also for a code for labor."[35]

Coupled with cautious advice about direct cash payments to the poor or unemployed—he opposed them—Kuyper's prescription for the social crisis of his day is a strengthening of the structures of pluralism. The state and only the state is positioned to bring this about. Hence the principle of intervention to restore balance among the spheres. In other respects, however, the problem of poverty lies beyond its reach, for state intervention of any other kind risks sapping the natural resilience of the poor. Instead, Kuyper appeals to individual Calvinists to "place life eternal in the foreground of both rich and poor."

In conjunction with his other writings, *The Problem of Poverty* sheds especially clear light on the Kuyperian state. Unlike its Lockian-American protagonist in its libertarian guise, it is not minimalist or morally neutral; quite the contrary, its role vis-à-vis individuals and social institutions is irreducibly moral, stemming as it does from the ordinances of God. Unlike the Lockian-American state in its interest-group liberal guise, it is not a positive state. Moreover, the will of the people provides precious little grounds for justifying social or economic experimentation. Its center of gravity lies in divinely ordained structures, not in political goals. Henig, writing of a related Christian Democracy, remarks that it supplies "a framework for politics, not a set of objectives." He might have added, "nor a rule-based approach to guiding and limiting public policy."[36] His observation captures Kuyper's preoccupations with respect to the state well. The Kuyperian state stands over against the liberal state by virtue of the juridical calling to which it is confined and the new relationships among state, individuals, and social institutions that it formalizes. Its objectives turn out to be the protection of structures that secure public justice—an architectonic project in statecraft, not a prudential one in decision making.

The Problem of State Intervention

The society that emerged from Kuyper's theological wrestling with divine and human sovereignty is a community of communities and the state a special sphere in which divine authority is exercised to promote justice. However satisfying this juridical formulation may be structurally, it lacks an operationalized principle or set of principles which justify state intervention in a wide range of common situations. To put it somewhat crudely, differentiating state, society, and individuals is not the same thing as relating them. For example, it is well and good to argue for the protection of communities—families, schools, churches—from the coercive power of the state. But when is state intervention justified? Should parents be permitted, in the name of the state, to withhold essential medical treatment from children? What if schools inculcate hatred and undermine the state? In what body is that determination finally vested? What rules may courts reasonably develop for making these determinations?

Kuyper did not develop in detail the principles upon which state intervention must rest, apart from the equality principle discussed in *The Problem of Poverty* (see above), if we mean by principle the operationalizing of a value. The basic Kuyperian principle is, of course, for persons and offices to respect the substance and limits of their respective callings. It will be useful to refer parenthetically, therefore, to Herman Dooyeweerd who explored the "inner nature" or basic character of the state, albeit in rather abstract terms. I am relying heavily on R. D. Henderson's work *Illuminating Law* for the points that follow, a noteworthy contribution for its discussion of the dependence upon Kuyper that Dooyeweerd acknowledged.[37] Dooyeweerd agreed with Kuyper's distinction between the "organic" social spheres and the "mechanical" legal sphere, in large part because to depict the state as organic was to hinder it in its special task of doing justice. Organic views of the state lead to a form of state autonomy whereas Dooyeweerd insists that the state and its legal institutions must continually adapt themselves to development in other spheres. To render the state in anthropological or organic terms earns it loyalty derived from blood ties that place other spheres in a subordinate position to it. And to justify a "concrete legal system (positive legality) in terms of a goal (e.g., the general good or will of the people) negates its sovereignty as a distinct sphere."[38] Instead the "mechanical" character of the state directly reflects the character of legality itself. "Legality is characterized by a permanent principle, viz, the principle of retribution, taken in its most general and objective sense. . . . It is the essential reaction of the divine legal order against those who violate it in a way [that] demands punishment."[39]

The principle of retribution operates in two senses to limit the role of the state. First, it lays claim to an exclusive operation in its sphere. Thus, Dooyeweerd asserts, it is not a teleological, reform-oriented, or purposeful principle that would allow reform or deterrence to be proper considerations in law's administration. Liberal approaches to criminal justice are severely curtailed. Second, it operates in a mechanical fashion because it is constrained by the presence of ethics, a sovereignty grounded in love, from reflecting revenge. "Retribution should be carried out in connection with the violation of a distinctly *legal* and not a typically ethical norm.[40] Both these modes of operation of the retribution principle take on greater significance given that Dooyeweerd considered retribution not to be the operative principle of criminal law alone, but of all good laws.[41]

If Dooyeweerd can be said to clarify neo-Calvinist principles for state intervention, it must be concluded that the result is much more continental than it is American with respect to the mechanism that secures the intervention. As the inclusion of the Bill of Rights as a condition for ratification of the Constitution nicely illustrates, Americans have not been satisfied with the argument that the structure of government alone can guarantee liberty; they have insisted on listing their liberties (with the additional qualification of Ninth Amendments) to keep government at arms' length from their consciences, their houses and effects, and their persons. And surely, for reasons that have much in common with Protestant suspicions everywhere: you cannot trust people with power. If the principle determining when government may intervene is not to be appear abstractly lodged in the internal makeup of the state ("retribution is the meaning of the law sphere"), it must be situated in a discourse that treats the state as something other than the natural enemy of liberty (or the friend of the 'interests' for that matter). It must be possible to have confidence in a set of values underlying such a state and such a theory of state intervention. What must come into view alongside the suspicion of people with power is the confidence that there are common human commitments holding civil society together. These are not absent from the American political tradition as a reading of the framers makes only too plain. But from the triumph of the Federalists on, those common commitments have tended toward only nationalistic expression.[42] Right across the political spectrum in the 1990s the nationalistic tendency remains: even among those countering individualism, the collective nouns deployed are marked by nationalist overtones—'family' and 'community' are applied to the entire society. Neo-Calvinist discourse can help to remedy this situation by putting forward the language of differentiated society, a society of persons, families, churches, communities of various kinds, businesses, and voluntary organizations.

The Role of the State:
Kuyper and Lowi Compared

Can neo-Calvinism ever compete with liberalism in application of a rule of law? In an American context, probably not. The liberal setup of presocial rights ranged against government authority contained by consent is pretty straightforward when it comes to working out how you attain a balance between the rights of the individual and the authority of government. Rights generally limit government. Fundamental rights impose especially strict limits. Liberalism's post-Lockian focus on external checks on government yields more accessible principles and, therefore, rules for determining when government may intervene. By contrast, the continental preference for internal checks, while expressible in structures of government, is a good deal harder to express as a set of rules for resolving dilemmas. Kuyper's state will not take revenge or reform or deter by virtue of its calling, Dooyeweerd's by virtue of its structure—not because of a Bill of Rights. There is no equivalent to the relatively elegant liberal formula of fundamental right triggering strict scrutiny demanding evidence of compelling state interest—or nonfundamental rights resulting in milder standards of review permitting the legislature to satisfy the courts with only a rational basis for its laws.

But the crucial point here is that external checks are only as good as internal design. The two are mutually dependent in the American tradition. What liberal polities need to see, Lowi argues (though not in so many words) is that external checks alone are not enough. The United States got a state, positive, directive, relatively autonomous, and it got it *despite* a tradition of individual rights and limited government, despite simple rules and lucid logic! But rights themselves are flexible notions, as Glendon laments,[43] in an era dominated by the conversion of so many issues into rights talk. Once the legitimating force of right could be attached to economic status, the state could become rights' principal agent. The liberal polity failed for this reason to contain the state not because it did not possess external checks but because the mechanism of external checks turned out to be only as good as the definitions of its component parts. The industrial revolution wrenched rights out of their largely political context as restrictions on a government assumed to be liberty's chief foe and threw the burden of protection back toward internal design. If Lowi is right, virtually no one noticed that this had happened. Hence the resistance to Lowi's call to revive the rule of law to restore the internal design of the separation of powers (specifically the *Schechter* rule forbidding delegation of power from Congress to the President "without sufficiently defining the policy or criteria to guide the administrator").

Lowi is not as much interested in rolling back the positive state as he is in making liberal democracy a coherent form of government, however. It is actually far from clear that Lowi's juridical democracy would greatly clarify the role of the state though it would equip it with greater authority within a more limited scope. A clearly defined rule of law would, it is true, encourage a new public philosophy, a new climate for politics and policy. By way of example, Lowi cites the *Dagenhart* decision as chilling new federal regulatory initiatives in the 1920s on the grounds that members of Congress then assumed such national economic powers would be unconstitutional. His call for revival of the *Schechter* rule could create a similarly chastened climate in respect of delegation of powers. But isn't the point of *The End of Liberalism* the revival of liberalism? And are not the accompaniments to liberalism in America a thin atmosphere in which the rich web of civil society dissolves in the acid of nominalism? We must go beyond liberalism to reclaim proper relationships between state, individual, and society, and thereby to clarify the proper functions of government.[44] Lowi's juridical democracy is juridical in a *procedural* sense only. Structurally, the building blocks of the positive, liberal state remain in place. At best, a course correction, albeit a very welcome one, would result from implementation of Lowi's procedural recommendations. Success, however, would be defined as a liberal government that *could* plan and could exercise meaningful authority, a government that could achieve the justice that democracies can best deliver— public policy reflective of public opinion within the framework of individual rights. The positive state would be reined in, not subjected to rethinking of the presuppositions on which it rests. In Seidelman and Harpham's observation, Lowi's research is a lengthy discovery that liberal hopes must be dashed because his formalist remedies for liberalism's contradictions are impossible to attain within liberalism.[45] Or to put it more bluntly, in the words of Paul Kahn, "[t]he break between contemporary [constitutional] theory and practice is a consequence of the ultimate impossibility of uniting self-government and the historical state."[46] Lowi's juridical democracy falls short, then. Because he will not transcend the liberal state, his prescriptions remain contained by its rhetoric.

Return to the State: The Role of Religious Presuppositions

Oddly enough in view of the foregoing, no one more than Lowi has grasped the extent of the interrelationship between political science and the state, and no one has expressed greater concern that the relationship has made political science flaccid and public discourse toxic.[47] The discipline has undergone in recent years a soul-searching transformation from behavioral hegemony toward a quasipluralism of method and ideology.[48] In that kind of atmosphere, the neo-Calvinist perspective can emerge from the marginalized obscurity[49] that has shrouded evangelical scholarship for decades. A rapprochement unthinkable in the behavioral era is now a possibility.

Despite the gulf that now appears to separate political scientists in the liberal progressive "third tradition" of Wilson, Ward, Beard, Merriam, Easton, Truman, Lowi, et al. from Reformed evangelicals critical of liberalism, they share a concern for articulating a theory of the state in democratic polities.[50] As Seidelman and Harpham point out and as I have attempted to describe in reference to Lowi's magnum opus, the Third Tradition has met severe obstacles in its attempts to defend the administrative state against charges that it threatens the liberal tradition. Neo-Calvinist (Reformed) scholarship is equally concerned that a theory of the state be constructed, and with its emphasis on a limited (but not morally minimalist) state, structural (and confessional) pluralism, and consociational democracy, may be better placed than the Third Tradition to defend it.[51] Paradoxically, the gulf between Lowi and Kuyper, though narrowed by the conviction that one must articulate a theory of the state, also widens, for each brings radically different presuppositions to bear on the problem. If one can speak of religious presuppositions in Lowi's case, these do not transcend a Lockian view of humans as reasonable, socially inclined utility maximizers. Lowi's prescription for what ails the liberal state is not, on this account, radical, for the problems of the liberal state may not be laid at the feet of sinful man. As a result, Lowi seems willing to place all his eggs in the one basket of a return to the rule of law.

There can be no pretence that a Kuyperian attempt to reconcile America's institutionalist and radical democratic traditions would leave either intact and would simply discover a hitherto undiscovered unity between them. I have already noted that the more one pursues neo-Calvinism to its roots, the more it emerges in continental European guise in its view of state and society, in its qualified treatment of rights, in its defense of the legitimate authority of the state, an authority independent of popular consent. I am perhaps less confident than some of my neo-Calvinist colleagues that a Kuyperian interpretation of the American political tradition would point to anything less than wholesale transformation of that tradition. As I have observed elsewhere,[52] a Kuyperian approach to the American situation has some things in common with anti-federalism in its regard for a differentiated civil society built on common values. But there's the rub. The civil society reached for by anti-federalists and sought after again by neo-Calvinists, Catholics, and others with like sympathies today did not capture the American imagination nor dominate its rhetoric as does the curious mix of Madison and Locke. One may argue that American discourse generally is as satisfied as Lowi in particular with their "religious" presuppositions and has not seen the problems of liberal democracy as calling for their radical reexamination.

For precisely this reason, one must be cautious about the prospect of neo-Calvinist presuppositions receiving a warm welcome in America. Short of a wholesale transformation, the Kuyperian orientation may make its most salient contribution by disentangling republicanism from the Lockian view of society in which rights are located outside the state, which is denied an independent foundation in common values or natural law. The republican tradition, even Madisonian republicanism with its accommodation of individualism and its ambiguity with respect to the public interest, is starved in the thin Lockian air. Elshtain puts it this way:

> [T]he empirical reality of American democracy, in [Tocqueville's] view, even as it frees individuals from the constraints of older, undemocratic structures and obligations, also unleashes atomism, individualism, and privatization. . . . The lure of private acquisitiveness spawns political apathy and invites democratic despotism. All social webs that once held persons intact having disintegrated, the individual finds himself isolated and impotent, exposed and unprotected. Into this

power vacuum moves "the organizing force of the government," the centralized state.[53]

Elshtain's argument takes us beyond Lowi's prescription of juridical democracy to the disintegrative forces that would nullify that procedural cure. These are the forces neo-Calvinism addresses. Neo-Calvinism gives the republican tradition a second chance, so to speak. In its treatment of the state and no less in its treatment of rights, it brings that tradition back into view. It allows us to see again that the ratification of the Constitution represents continuity with republican thought at least as much as it represents disjunction and a new beginning. The religious character of Kuyper's thought is itself an aid to this end. "Kuyperian presuppositionalism," writes Marsden, "is a style of Christian thought that emphasizes that crucial to the differences that separate Christian worldviews from non-Christian ones are disagreements about pretheoretical first principles, presuppositions, first commitments, or basic beliefs."[54] Law and politics stem from these basic beliefs, irrespective of the deity that is worshiped. In this foundational sense Skillen writes that "religion . . . is inescapable for human beings."[55]

This treatment of man as a religious being lends further clarity to the functions and limits of the Kuyperian state described above. Not only is the state seen as deriving its authority from God's ordinances (a view dependent on a *particular*, Calvinist, religious orientation), but, by extension, the state itself is also viewed from a perspective that holds all fundamental human commitments in high regard because they stem from basic beliefs. Giving these commitments their due requires sharing of authority in the interests of the general welfare; and it requires freedom for a plurality of such commitments to find expression politically. Here is an emphasis entirely missing from Lowi's analysis and prescriptions.

The contemporary neo-Calvinist perspective thus affirms that the theory of the state is interdependent with the theory of church and state, and it is critical of the separationalist approach to the latter that still holds sway on the Supreme Court. For from the neo-Calvinist perspective, full religious freedom is not to be secured by reaffirming the freedom to worship in churches of one's choice and it is positively affronted by walling off religion from the public square. On the contrary, the foundational character of religious commitment necessitates its recognition and protection in multiple domains: in churches and families, naturally, but also in schools and social service agencies, in and out of the public square. Rights are grounded in the religious character of humankind for no right turns out to be as important as a broadly construed right of free exercise; or, to put it another way, the concept of free exercise takes on dimensions undreamed of by the founders protecting the cerebral, low-intensity Protestantism of the "Gentlemen" of the late eighteenth century, a religious outlook and practice presumably needing precious little protection! Among contemporary neo-Calvinists, this enlarged and nuanced view of religion has manifested itself in calls for pluralism in education, health, and welfare and for a system of proportional representation to replace the present electoral system.[56]

In sum, the neo-Calvinist perspective could rescue the American state from the theoretical obscurity it wallows in and the disdain in which its post-1930s manifestation is held. Should the present welfare state be comprehensively dismantled, the state's juridical functions would still need clarification of the kind neo-Calvinists can offer, for Kuyper shows us the need for justice within and between the various spheres of social life, in addition to criminal justice and a policy of national defense. Given the upsurge in ethnic and religious sensitivities and the troubled awareness of multiple cultures within the American nation-state, Kuyper's high view of religion as a way of life no less than the particular insights of his Calvinism takes on a new significance. It is hard to see how Lowi or the Third Tradition might articulate such issues distinctively.

Conclusion

From at least the Populists to the New Left, the American state either represented the people against the interests (taming them by regulation) or it sided with those interests against the people, indicting itself by "democratic" standards. The legitimacy of governmental authority rested on these mutually exclusive options, which built both statist reality and antistatist feeling on their Lockian foundations. Where a quasi-Lockian discourse pits state and individual against each other and largely overlooks the intermediary institutions of civil society, neo-Calvinist discourse, a religious discourse on reality with a high view of religious freedom, situates the state in a three-way relationship with individuals and societal institutions that multiplies the roles and stances of the state: in partnership with the individual to protect civil rights when a family, school, club, or business would deny these; in deference to churches in their exercise of ecclesiastical law with respect to church members; in retributive relationship with convicted criminals; in cooperation with faith-based social service providers, and so forth. Since a differentiated society is the locus of most citizen freedom (people live out their lives in a web of institutional "memberships"), the integrity of these institutions emerges as a proper object of governmental concern and protection. If the larger number of relationships just described do not simplify the work of courts (as I allude to in my discussion of neo-Calvinism's articulation problems in regard to state intervention), it does foster a richer public discourse, one less circumscribed by artificial and typically reductionist treatment of people and their multifaceted relationships and obligations. One could put this another way, following Walzer who observed that the truncated discourse of American politics could be viewed either as bad (invoking a highly restricted view of persons and societal relationships) or simply wrong.[57] Neo-Calvinists may rightly maintain that the three-way relationships I have just described constitute a better description of *existing* relationships in which the American state is involved than the conventional terms for discussing the state offers—existing relationships denied visibility in law and political culture.[58] The situating of the state in relation to persons and differentiated social institutions takes us away from the nominalist categories of American discourse and allows the state to emerge from its hiding place behind a Lockian social contract formula, a formula that hoodwinked us into believing that popular consent dissolved the problem of political authority. With Kuyper's help, to put it simply, Christians may challenge and change public discourse. The importance of such challenges lies in the prevalence of the utilitarian, materialist, and reductionist views of human life that have flourished in American political culture.

We are left with an interesting dilemma. If I am right, then the particular contribution the neo-Calvinist writings can make is to the reshaping of what Lowi, following Walter Lippmann, called the "public philosophy." But it lacks a practical, rule-based theory of state intervention to give practical effect to its biblically based principle of fidelity to calling, a deficiency compounded by the elegant formulas of liberal democracy. It cultivates a biblical sensibility to politics but suggests only in general terms the outlines of public-legal arrangements. These features limit its appeal in the American context. Here, the features recognized as most attractive may be limited government and the priority for protecting religious liberty, but to speak of a religious view of all of life is more likely to invoke New Age than Christianity!

Circumstance, rather than theory, may situate American discourse in a reconsideration of the state, as the promises attached to government downsizing are held up to the light of actual experience. Moreover, as more is learned about the actual relationship between government and private agencies, along the lines of the work being done by Monsma[59] and the Center for Public Justice, a richer understanding of government's empirical role can emerge to replace overly simplistic separationist logic. This research points to complex, cooperative interaction between government and religious agencies, a reality that stretches the separationist dogmas of the Supreme Court and the volunteerist/limited government dogmas of conservatives to their respective limits. In that climate, the Kuyperian juxtaposition of society, persons, and the state may inform the subsequent debate. For, despite the beating it has taken, the Madisonian tradition of confidence in internal design may have seen its time come again, although, curiously, its recent revival owes more to quasilibertarians bent on shrinking the state than civic republicans willing to describe it afresh and affirm its necessary functions in democratic society.

Notes

1. Theodore Lowi, *The End of Liberalism: The Second Republic of the United States*, 2d ed. (New York: W.W. Norton, 1979), Part III, 167-270.

2. Lowi, *The End of Liberalism*, 295.

3. Along with *The End of Liberalism*, the principal works are: "American Business, Public Policy, Case Studies, and Political Theory," *World Politics*, vol. 16 (1964), 677-715; *The Personal President: Power Invested, Promise Unfulfilled* (Ithaca, N.Y.: Cornell University Press, 1985); and "The State in Political Science: How We Become What We Study," *American Political Science Review*, 86 (1992): 1-7.

4. Raymond Seidelman and Edward Harpham, *Disenchanted Realists: Political Science and the American Crisis, 1884-1984* (Albany: State University of New York Press, 1985), 1-18.

The first tradition is the institutional tradition of the Constitution that achieved order by regulating, not suppressing, society's factions. The second tradition is democratic, in the spirit of Paine and the Antifederalists and also of the Populists and muckraking. Viewed from within either tradition, the other appeared in conflict with it. But the third tradition insisted on their compatibility, on the possibility of combining the two into a single political science. See Seidelman and Harpham, *Disenchanted Realists*.

5. Lowi, *The End of Liberalism*, 295-313.

6. Lowi, *Personal President*, 24.

7. Lowi, *Personal President*, 42.

8. Lowi, "The State in Political Science," 1.

9. Lowi, *The End of Liberalism*, 50.

10. Lowi, "The State in Political Science," 2-3. Specifically, Lowi associates the Second Republic with a new emphasis on science, with statistics leading the way and flowering as the public opinion subfield. As he recognizes, developments of this kind were anticipated in the field of Constitutional law at least as early as *Lochner v. New York* (1905), in which an social science asserted an independent authority distinct from the republican political science of the founders. See Paul W. Kahn, *Legitimacy and His-*

tory: Self-Government in American Constitutional Theory (New Haven, Conn.: Yale University Press, 1995).

11. Lowi, "American Business," 690-715.

12. McKendree R. Langley, *The Practice of Political Spirituality: Episodes from the Public Career of Abraham Kuyper, 1879-1918* (Jordan Station, Ontario: Paideia Press, 1984), 151.

13. Abraham Kuyper, *Sphere Sovereignty (Souvereiniteit in Eigen Kring)* (Kampen: J. H. Kok, 1930 [1880]), 3.

14. See for example, Brain Walsh and Richard Middleton, *The Transforming Vision* (Downers Grove, Ill.: InterVarsity Press. 1984).

15. S. U. Zuidema, *Communication and Confrontation* (Toronto: Wedge Publishing, 1971).

16. Quoted in Zuidema, *Communication and Confrontation*, 69.

17. Just as creation and regeneration are related and disconnected at the same time, so the church is not natural (creational) but supernatural (regenerational). Kuyper does not allow the church to seek to construct the kingdom of heaven on earth for this reason—an error of the radical Anabaptists in his opinion (See Zuidema, *Communication and Confrontation*, 71-74).

18. Abraham Kuyper, *Lectures on Calvinism* (Grand Rapids, Mich.: Wm. B. Eerdmans, 1970 [c1931]), 81.

19. Kuyper, *Lectures*, 82.

20. Kuyper, *Lectures*, 91. The spheres in question are identified in quasi-functionalist fashion, for each links a function, its matching institutions, and the requisite authority to give effect to both. Kuyper first distinguishes the social spheres from the sphere of government. The distinctions between spheres and institutions becomes somewhat blurred but the social spheres include the social, where differential personalities prevail, the corporate (universities, guilds, associations, churches), the domestic (the family, married life), and "communal autonomy." But in a use of the term that does not entirely fit with this, art is described as a sphere where "genius is a sovereign power." In other uses, commerce is a sphere, as is labor. Benevolence and philanthropy are described as a "field," and so on. Despite these inconsistencies, a view of society as differentiated by organic function and personal vocation and talent emerges quite clearly. Kuyper found little equality in the social spheres, but this did not concern him, for though "dominion is exercised everywhere . . . it is a dominion which works organically; not by virtue of a State-investiture, but from life's sovereignty itself" (*Lectures*, 95). For example, the extraordinary competence of the mathematical genius is not a threat to society but a positive benefit. Citing approvingly "the dominion" of Aristotle, Plato, Lombard, Thomas Aquinas, Luther, Calvin, Kant and Darwin, Kuyper asserted that such is "a gift of God, possessed only by His grace. It is subject to no one and is responsible to Him alone Who granted it this ascendancy" (*Lectures*, 95)

21. Kuyper, *Lectures*, 124.

22. Kuyper, *Sphere Sovereignty*, 7.

23. Kuyper, *Lectures*, 98.

24. Kuyper, *Lectures*, 80.

25. Kuyper, *Lectures*, 84.

26. Kuyper, *Lectures*, 96.

27. Ralph C. Hancock, *Calvin and the Foundations of Modern Politics* (Ithaca, N.Y.: Cornell University Press. 1989), 68.

28. Hancock, *Calvin*, 70.

29. Bernard J. Zylstra, "The United States Constitution and the Rights of Religion," in *Political Order and the Plural Structure of Society*, ed. James W. Skillen and Rockne

M. McCarthy (Atlanta: Scholars Press, 1991), 321.

30. Zylstra's "departure" from Kuyper does appear more marked if one takes the "mechanical" view of the state prominent in the *Lectures* as the point of that departure. Conversely, the implicit embrace of the cultural mandate discussed by Zuidema in his discussion of Kuyper's views on common and particular grace may allow for such a role as an aspect of the organic, and thus changing, nature of creation itself. As I pointed out, however, and as Zuidema acknowledges, Kuyper became too preoccupied by the magnitude of the abuses of common grace, of creation's rich potential, to allow government much of a long leash in this respect.

31. Abraham Kuyper, *The Problem of Poverty*, ed. J. W. Skillen (Grand Rapids, Mich.: Baker Book House, 1991 [1881]), 69.

32. Kuyper, *The Problem of Poverty*, 64.

33. Kuyper, *The Problem of Poverty*, 65.

34. And warranted as much for the employer as the employee when the circumstances demanded it. When a railroad strike threatened to disrupt the national economy in 1903, Kuyper as prime minister provided strong support for the railroad company, condemning the strike as an illegitimate severance of contract. Subsequently he introduced bills to prevent such strikes in the future, to explore criminal wrongdoing by the strikers, and to establish a state commission to investigate the grievances of railroad personnel (Langley, *Political Spirituality*, 91-101).

35. Langley, *The Practice of Political Spirituality*, 71.

36. Stanley Henig, ed., *European Political Parties* (New York: Praeger, 1970), n. p.

37. R. D. Henderson, *Illuminating Law: The Construction of Herman Dooyeweerd's Philosophy* (Amsterdam: Free University Press, 1994), 166-69.

38. Henderson, *Illuminating Law*, 169.

39. Henderson, *Illuminating Law*, 167.

40. Henderson, *Illuminating Law*, 168.

41. Henderson, *Illuminating Law*, 169.

42. Jean B. Elshtain, "Citizenship and Armed Civic Virtue: Some Critical Questions on the Commitment to Public Life," in *Community in America: The Challenge*, ed. Charles H. Reynolds and Ralph V. Norman (Berkeley: University of California Press, 1988), 47-55.

43. Mary Ann Glendon, *Rights Talk: The Impoverishment of Political Discourse* (New York: Free Press, 1991).

44. See, for example, James Skillen, "Going beyond Liberalism to Christian Social Philosophy," *Christian Scholars Review*, 19 (1990): 220-30, in which the author argues that only a profound rethinking of the individualistic assumptions of modern, philosophic liberalism holds any prospect of transcending those assumptions.

45. Seidelman and Hapham, *Disenchanted Realists*, 200-213.

46. Kahn, *Legitimacy and History*, x.

47. Lowi, "The State in Political Science," 3-6.

48. Gabriel A. Almond, "The Return to the State," *American Political Science Review* 82, no. 3 (1988): 853-901; Seidelman and Harpham, *Disenchanted Realists*; David M. Ricci, *The Tragedy of Political Science: Politics, Scholarship, and Democracy*. New Haven, Conn.: Yale University Press, 1984); David Easton, *The Political System: An Inquiry into the State of Political Science* (Chicago: University of Chicago Press, 1981).

49. Donald Tewksbury's classic study of American higher education showed how dominant were denominational colleges in the United States prior to the Civil war—in effect, they postponed a movement to establish "revolutionary" colleges on a Jeffersonian model for the better part of a century (Donald Tewksbury, *The Founding of American Colleges and Universities before the Civil War* [New York: Archon Books, 1965]).

The emergence of political science as a distinct discipline had to await this development (Anna Haddow, *Political Science in American Colleges and Universities, 1636-1900* [New York: Octagon Books, 1969 [1939]]), but the rise of political science in the new state universities and certain private colleges then proceeded to bypass the denominational colleges altogether. When communities of faith came to political science, then, they encountered a fully formed discipline (organization, bureaucracy, body of knowledge). The collapse of evangelical academia in the United States was not only a function of this eventual supplanting by the Jeffersonian model, however. It resulted also from internal intellectual weakness (George Marsden, "The Collapse of American Evangelical Academia," in *Faith and Rationality,* ed. Alvin Plantinga and Nicholas Wolterstorff [Notre Dame: University of Notre Dame Press, 1983]), and from fragmentation in the Protestant community itself. Evangelicals and liberals had preserved a coalition on social and political, if not theological questions as late as the First World War (George Marsden, "The State of Evangelical Christian Scholarship," *Christian Scholar's Review,* 17, no. 4 (1988): 347-60). Splitting first over questions of patriotism, the supposed impact of German theology on German culture, and the rise of premillenialist writings in the wartime atmosphere, they polarized decisively—and permanently—over evolution and modernism, disputes that culminated in the Scopes trial of 1925. Thereafter, fundamentalism, and by association evangelicalism more generally, was well and truly rusticated by liberal Protestantism and the secular academy. Denominational identity itself was downplayed, especially in higher education (Marsden, "Christian Scholarship," 184-95; see also James Burtchaell, "The Decline and Fall of the Christian College," *First Things,* 12 (1991), 16-29.

50. If neo-Calvinist political inquiry does break new ground with respect to a theory of state and society, the widely noticed "return to the state" in the discipline at large does not promise to make this common ground (see Dryszek and Leonard, 1988, 1245-1260). For Lowi, as for Almond, the return to the state offers no fresh examination of the normative questions linking state, individual and society, but rather a new awareness of government as a variable. I agree. What is needed is not to make the state a variable, "but to make political science, through a new and higher level of discourse, a discipline worthy of constitutional democracy—scientific, theoretic, historical, and critical (Lowi, "Reply to Almond: Return to the State," 891). If there is nothing more to the movement than a course correction away from the Almond/Easton-inspired language of the political system (see Bernard Susser, *Approaches to the Study of Politics* [New York: Macmillan, 1992]), then we cannot expect a convergence with the normative concerns of neo-Calvinist thought. Such, for the present, appears to be the case.

51. The superficial affinities between branches of evangelicalism and traditions in political science are as follows: Reformed evangelicalism is hermeneutically sympathetic to the Institutionalist tradition—"the dominant mode of American governmental organization and political thought in the late eighteenth and nineteenth centuries" (Seidelman and Harpham, *Disenchanted Realists,* 4; see also James Farr, "Francis Lieber and the Interpretation of American Political Science," *Journal of Politics* 52 (1990), 1027-49, on the prehistory of political science as a form of hermeneutics). To evangelicals who trace their roots to the radical Reformation, to Anabaptists and quietist sects, radical democracy with its built-in antipathy to structures and institutions, its spontaneity, and its suspicion of the powers that be, is inherently appealing. As for the Progressive liberal Third Tradition, it has attracted evangelical realists in the tradition of Reinhold Niebuhr, who argue for prudence—a composite of factual knowledge and discernment—in translating biblical principles into policy. Adaptability to changing and interim circumstances is perhaps the hallmark of both the Third Tradition (one thinks of Herbert Croly's harnessing of Hamiltonian means to Jeffersonian ends) and this Christian Realist orientation.

148 *Timothy Sherratt*

52. Timothy R. Sherratt and Ronald P. Mahurin, *Saints as Citizens: A Guide to Public Responsibilities for Christians* (Grand Rapids, Mich.: Baker Book House, 1995).

53. Elshtain, "Citizenship and Armed Civic Virtue," 48.

54. Marsden, "State of Evangelical Christian Scholarship," 355.

55. James W Skillen, *Recharging the American Experiment: Principled Pluralism for Genuine Civic Community* (Grand Rapids, Mich.: Baker Book House with the Center for Public Justice, 1995), 35.

56. Stephen Monsma, *When Sacred and Secular Mix: Religious Non-Profit Organizations and Public Money* (Lanham, Md: Rowman & Littlefield, 1996); Stanley W. Carlson-Thies and James W. Skillen eds., *Welfare in America: Christian Perspectives on a Policy in Crisis* (Grand Rapids, Mich.: Wm. B. Eerdmans, 1995); James W. Skillen, ed., *The School-Choice Controversy: What Is Constitutional?* (Grand Rapids, Mich.: Baker Book House, with the Center for Public Justice, 1993); Rockne M. McCarthy, James W. Skillen, and William A. Harper, *Disestablishment a Second Time: Genuine Pluralism for American Schools* (Grand Rapids, Mich.: Wm. B. Eerdmans, 1982); Bernard J. Zylstra, "The Bible, Justice, and the State," in *Confessing Christ and Doing Politics*, ed. James W. Skillen (Washington, D.C.: Association for Public Justice, 1982); James W Skillen, *Recharging the American Experiment*, 137-55.

57. Michael Walzer, "The Communitarian Critique of Liberalism," *Political Theory*, 18 (1990): 6-23.

58. Stephen Monsma (*When Sacred and Secular Mix*) has documented highly interdependent relationships between faith-based social service providers and state and federal governments—although in the solitary modern-era case addressing this relationship the Supreme Court's reasoning maintains a contorted separationalist logic, requiring that the agencies not be pervasively sectarian and that the funds go for exclusively secular purposes (*Bowen v. Kendrick*, 1988).

59. Monsma, *When Sacred and Secular Mix*.

Chapter 6

Deliberation or Agony? Toward a Post-liberal Christian Democratic Theory

Ashley Woodiwiss

James Tully has aptly described our contemporary theoretical situation as one of "strange multiplicity."[1] Where the domain of political theory throughout the 1970s and 1980s could be characterized as chiefly defined by the theory of liberalism (and responses to it), by most accounts we now inhabit a post-liberal theoretical context. Liberalism continues, of course. However, our day is marked by the flourishing of a "strange multiplicity" of voices and perspectives many of which take for granted that liberalism's theoretical hegemony has been eclipsed. Consequently, the decade of the 1990s has witnessed an impressive development in the literature of political theory. One specific discourse within political thought that has flourished throughout this decade has been that of democratic theory, no doubt in part due to the events of 1989-1990 and the ensuing third wave of democratization. Thus a key development within political theory after liberalism has been the self-conscious effort to distinguish democratic theory from that of liberal thought. There is no clearer expression of this theoretical move than in the literature of what is called "deliberative democracy." Here I set out what might be called the "common faith" of deliberative democrats.[2] Focusing primarily on the work of Habermas and Benhabib, I show how deliberative democrats in general hold to the hope that their model will "enrich and improve democratic practice and overcome the many obstacles to the public use of reason in contemporary political life."[3] As such, deliberative democracy carries forward the emancipatory project of modernity.

149

I then move to consider the rhetorical and political limitations of the deliberative model as disclosed by the perspective of *agonistic pluralism* (focusing primarily on the work of Chantal Mouffe). Agonism reveals deliberative democracy as inextricably involved in an exclusionary project similar to the liberalism it claims to have overcome. Next, I suggest that agonistic pluralism helps to re-situate the Christian theorist and her task. For Christian theorists working in the post-Christian, post-liberal agonistic context, our thinking about the possibilities and limits of liberal democracy cashes out in nurturing what Nancy Fraser has called "subaltern counterpublics." The task for Christian political theory is cultivating Christian citizenship for contemporary agonistic democracy.

Deliberative Democracy Ascending

Two events occurred in 1989 that had direct and substantive impact upon the development of the deliberative model of democracy. First, that year witnessed the outbreak of public democratic movements in China and Eastern Europe which re-energized democratic aspirations and thought in the older liberal democracies of the West. Meanwhile, in the same year and in the more out-of-the way venue of the professional academy, MIT Press published the English version of Jurgen Habermas's *The Structural Transformation of the Public Sphere.* A conference given to the theoretical analysis of Habermas's text was held later that same year and culminated (in 1992) in the first major systematic effort to give the model of deliberative democracy theoretical and analytical clarity.[4] Now at the end of our present decade, the literature on deliberative democracy has grown in substance and importance.[5]

What characterizes this literature? Macedo in his recent volume rightly notes that "the phrase 'deliberative democracy' does not signify a creed with a simple set of core claims" and that "those who seek to advance the cause of democratic deliberation do not altogether agree about what the democratic ideal is or how it should be fostered."[6] Nevertheless I do believe it possible to point to some major themes or idioms that are found in the literature of deliberative democracy and which are here relevant for my purposes. Let me mention three: (1) deliberative democrats view themselves as articulating a conceptual alternative to that of liberalism (and specifically to the preeminent form of liberal thought; that is, that set out by John Rawls); (2) they rest their conceptual apparatus for the most part on (or in response to) the insights of discourse theory as set forth by Habermas.[7] Deliberation for these democrats is situated within the context of specified *procedures* and *canons of rationality* that both demarcate and inform a particular conception of *public space*; and, (3) deliberative democrats view their model as "the only one that is compatible both with the general social trends of our societies and with the emancipatory aspirations of new social movements."[8] Taken together these three characteristics form a post-liberal (anti-Rawlsian) emancipatory model of democracy.

The deliberative democrats pick up the critique of liberalism where the communitarians of the 1980s left off. The democrats focus not on the "metaphysical" Rawls of *A Theory of Justice* (1971)—the central target in the communitarian critique—but the "political" Rawls of *Political Liberalism* (1993). Specifically they distinguish their model from Rawls's concept of "public reason." Seyla Benhabib acknowledges that both Rawlsian liberalism's concern for public dialogue and the democratic emphasis on public deliberation hold in common the view that "the legitimation of political power and the examination of the justice of institutions to be a public process, open to all citizens to partake in." However, Benhabib addresses three differences that exist between the rival liberal and the deliberative conception of the *public* as well as the nature of speech that goes on there. For Benhabib, Rawlsian public reason involves a "restricted agenda" (limiting the subject matter for public deliberation), a "regulative principle" (imposing limits upon how individuals, institutions, and agencies ought to reason about public matters), and a statist location (within an undue emphasis on the legal/juridical domain).[9] In distinction, the deliberative model purports to be more inclusive with respect to the agenda, less regulative discursively, and more broadly situated, encompassing non-statist locales of/for public deliberation. Macedo, in acknowledging the antagonism which many democrats possess to liberal "public reason," notes how "[d]eliberative democratic ideals respond to many of these disparate sources of complaint by arguing for a more wide-open and inclusive model of democratic discourse."[10]

What precisely is it that deliberative democrats believe occurs when citizens participate discursively about politics? I have earlier suggested that deliberative democrats view themselves as extending the emancipatory trajectory of modernity. In what terms does the model reflect emancipation? As a postliberal project, deliberative democracy seeks to emancipate individuals qua citizens from the liberal view of the individual as a private utility maximizer. That is, the deliberative model is set forth as transformative, reconfiguring the self-identity of individuals. More precisely, democratic deliberation transforms the preferences of citizens by orienting them away from private interest and toward the public good, a project, to use Habermasian terminology, of democratic will-formation. And so, the model is publicist, working to forge strong bonds of solidarity for late twentieth-century inchoate liberal societies. Finally, by participation in the various sites of democratic deliberation, citizens experience rational reflexivity. The process of articulating good reasons in public leads to what Arendt called an "enlarged mentality" wherein one escapes the ghetto of parochial particularistic thought and approaches a more universalistic view. Unlike liberal reflexivity, which urges the individual to view herself in a decontextual universalistic way or republican/communitarian reflexivity which situates the individual in thick communities of teleological particularism, democratic reflexivity situates the individual as a civic deliberative fellow participant in the "decentered society" of late capitalistic multicultural pluralism. Emancipation then is defined as the publicly orienting work of rational reflexivity. Iris Marion Young sets forth the ideal of deliberative democracy as "a process that creates a public, citizens coming together to talk about collective problems, goals, ideals, and actions."[11] What might be called the "common faith of deliberative democracy" then rests upon the belief, as Benhabib describes it, that "the institutions and culture of liberal democracies are sufficiently complex, supple, and de-centered so as to allow the expression of difference without fracturing the identity of the body politic or subverting existing forms of political sovereignty."[12] At the end of the day, the proper procedures for democratic public talk as governed by the norms of communicative rationality offer hope for the satisfactory and peaceable negotiation between (democratic) identity and difference. Or, as the Beatles put it, we can work it out.

Why We Can't Just All Get Along

Not surprisingly, the deliberative model has received strong criticism from a number of different vantage points.[13] But I want here to consider the account I take to be most helpful in figuring out what direction Christian theoretical work ought to take in our post-liberal world. Specifically, I am interested in that account that I think best captures the actual existing condition of the *public sphere* in contemporary liberal pluralist societies.

Benhabib acknowledges that deliberative democrats face a strong critical challenge from what she calls "the agonistic model of democratic politics."[14] The agonistic critique of deliberative democracy draws upon a number of different sources, such as poststructuralism, postmodernism, and postfeminist strands of thought. Taken as whole the literature of agonistic democracy unmasks the *political* problems involved in the deliberative model and posits, in its place, an alternative model of democracy that embraces "the ineluctability of antagonism." Agonism affirms "the existence of the political in all its complexity."[15]

Simply put, agonism reveals the asymmetrical exclusionary nature of deliberative theory. The model's proceduralism, canons of rationality, and teleological consensualism repeat (now in democratic tones) similar themes of exclusion as found in liberal and republican models. As such, deliberative democracy though postliberal, holds onto the hidden exclusionary nature of modern political thought. It is a model that works to "reward" certain forms of discourse (and the groups who possess them), and to marginalize others. While friendly critics of Habermas have revised his model on a number of different fronts,[16] the agonists are inclined to reject the *model* of deliberative democracy altogether. Why is this the case?

Agonistic democrats question the very legitimacy of attempting such a project as undertaken by the deliberative democrats. The effort to *theorize* the public realm as a space amenable to procedural and discursive regulation, culminating in some kind of consensual universal democratic will-formation hides from public view how this "objective of unanimity and homogeneity is always revealed as fictitious and based on acts of exclusion." As Mouffe concludes, with deliberative democracy "relations of power and antagonisms are erased, and we are left with the typical liberal illusion of a pluralism without antagonism." Such an evasion of the political "is to remain blind to the relations of power."[17]

Iris Marion Young, points to two forms of exclusion that are at work within the model. She notes how the model's "tendency to restrict democratic discussion to argument carries implicit cultural biases that can lead to exclusions in practice. [And] its assumption that unity is either a starting point or goal of democratic discussion, moreover, may also have exclusionary consequences." Deliberativists tend to assume that deliberation, once political and economic power have been bracketed, "is both culturally neutral and universal."[18] This move ignores how forms and styles of speech are culturally freighted.[19] Rather, the model of discursive rationality privileges the culturally specific qualities of speech associated with communicative practices of the historically emergent social power/position of white, middle-class, highly educated (that is bourgeois,) males.[20] As Young notes, the various norms of deliberation (formal and general speech, assertiveness, combativeness, dispassionate, disembodied, literalness, etc.) work to silence those forms of communication, style, and expression located in the otherness of women and minority voices. Young also faults the assumption of unity found in deliberative literature. She notes that democratic proceduralists tend to either invoke a form of consensual unity as standing prior to the deliberative process (through the invocations of "shared understand-ings"), while others, perhaps sensitive to the problems with the former, locate unity at the end of the process; the outcome of the process rightly working. But for Young, both are problematic. The former is empirically weak (just how much shared understanding and to what de-gree is there in contemporary multicultural, pluralistic societies?) and only thinly transformative (if we all share understandings in common, how much revision and reflexivity is really required?). Meanwhile the latter, unity as outcome, works to privilege some groups conception of the common good over others: "When discussion participants aim at unity, the appeal to a common good in which they are all supposed to leave behind their particular experience and interests, the perspectives of the privileged are likely to dominate the definition of the common good."[21] More recently, Young, though sympathetic to the Gutmann-Thompson model, nevertheless continues to chide deliberative democ-rats for not taking the problematic nature of exclusion seriously enough: "Democrats frequently act as though one can promote inclusion by simply forbidding active and explicit exclusion. More is needed, how-ever, to counteract the "passive" exclusion that often occur in contem-porary democracies. Designers of deliberative processes should worry about the timing, location, and structure of deliberative events with an eye to maximizing social voices."[22]

To see how exclusion works when deliberativists get practical, con-sider this example from Seyla Benhabib. Can the deliberative model work in the face of some groups whose commitments and/or beliefs ap-pear to reject the model all together? Benhabib points to "religious sects living within the boundaries of the liberal-democratic constitutional state" such as Orthodox Jews in Israel, Orthodox Muslims living in some European states, and Christian Scientists in the United States. Military service is at issue in the first, public education of women in the second, and health care for a sick child in the last. While she acknowledges that it is arguable whether discourse ethics may "presuppose too strong a model of agreement" she nevertheless holds that "a form of deliberative proceduralism is the most viable normative answer."[23] She then pro-ceeds to work out the knotty theoretical/political problems that such groups pose. What's most instructive here is not so much what Ben-habib concludes—Orthodox Jews should not be forced to serve, Muslim women should be forced to attend public school but permitted to wear their *chador* (head scarves), and Christian Scientist parents ought to be forced to provide medical attention to their sick children—but *how* these conclusions are reached and, indeed, that she even concludes *at all*. For in doing so, she exhibits some of the very qualities that the agonists claim reside hidden from view within the deliberative model. In adjudi-cating (for this is precisely the tone her comments take) these tough cases, Benhabib invokes several juridical concepts (like separation of church and state), couching her comments in the language of rights and what is or is not required as "constitutional minimums" for living within the jurisdiction of the liberal-constitutional state. Thus "deliberative proceduralism" evaporates in her account, being replaced by juridical concepts and the stipulated (though undiscussed) norm of "respect and equality" that serves to trump the interest of the Christian Science and the Muslim parents. Deliberative democracy in her hands becomes juridical not political. But the fact that Benhabib "rules" in these cases at all, indicates that "deliberative proceduralism"carries with it a necessary though hidden "managerial elite" who preside over the process, guiding it and steering it to politically satisfactory outcomes.[24] As her comments seem to clearly indicate, procedures in fact *cannot* be neatly distinguished from substantive commitments. Indeed as Stanley Fish has indicated,

> The problem is that the distinction between what is procedural and what is substantive is itself a substantive one, and therefore in whatever form it is enacted, it will engender the very conflicts it was designed to mitigate, as those who would have enacted it differently or not enacted it at all all cry foul,or error, or blasphemy. When this happens (as it always will), the would-be engineers of peace and stability always respond in the same way, by calling the malcontents unreasonable, or fanatical, or insufficiently respectful of difference, or some other name that dismisses their concerns by placing them beyond appeal whose boundaries they continue to claim, have been drawn by nature or by reason.[25]

This is directly in line with the agonistic critique. As Mouffe puts is, both liberalism and deliberative democracy "generally start by stressing what they call 'the fact of pluralism' and then proceed to find procedures to deal with differences whose objective is actually to make those differences irrelevant and to relegate pluralism to the sphere of the private."[26] Deliberative unity is reached at the expense of difference.

For agonistic pluralists, the problem is not that exclusion is part and parcel of the deliberative model. The problem is that the model purports to be inclusionary and only covertly smuggles exclusion back into its practices and putative outcomes. So Ian Shapiro illustrates how in the Gutmann and Thompson model, religious fundamentalists are invited to the deliberative table, and even to make religious appeals, only so long as these premises do not require taking the Bible literally, for such claims are held by Gutmann and Thompson to be rationally implausible.

For Shapiro this is nothing more than gatekeeping and for the fundamentalist "it would look as though she were being told that it is fine to
be a fundamentalist so long as she abandons her fundamentalism. . . .
The Gutmann/Thompson model works only for those fundamentalists
who also count themselves fallibilist democrats."[27] The necessary but
hidden dimensions of exclusion in the deliberative model proves "em-
barrassing because they point to an act of power, of premptory exclusion and dismissal, that cannot be acknowledged as such lest the liberal
program of renouncing power and exclusion be exposed for the fiction
it surely is."[28] For agonists, true ("radical") democracy accepts up front
the reality and ineliminable nature of exclusion in democratic politics.
All efforts (whether liberal "neutralism" or democratic "proceduralism")
to theorize the "place of the universal, to fix its final meaning through
rationality must be rejected since the recognition of undecidability is the
condition of existence of democratic politics."[29] Rawlsian "public reason," Habermasian "communicative rationality," and democratic proceduralism all posit the well-ordered society as "a society from which politics has been eliminated."[30] As Fish puts it, politics cannot be freeze-
framed "at the moment its wheel of fortune delivers an outcome you
favor." But such "end of politics" models are (political-rhetorical) efforts to do just that. However, "there are no different reasons or
stronger reasons than policy reasons and the announcement of a formula (high-order impartiality, mutual respect, the judgment of all mankind) that supposedly outflanks politics or limits its sphere by establishing a space free from its incursions will be nothing more or less than
politics by another name."[31]

For agonists, the *political*—the realm of intractable power and antagonism—returns to theoretical primacy through the rejection of those
liberal and democratic models that are informed by a rationalistic
framework. Rather, real democracy "rejects the very possibility of a
nonexclusive public sphere of rational argument where a non-coercive
consensus could be attained." Suspicious as they are, "of any attempt to
impose a univocal model of democratic discussion," agonists accept that
democratic politics cannot eradicate power and antagonism and remain
true to itself. In the end, there cannot be a rational definite solution to
the question of justice in a democratic society. Any effort "to reach a
final destination can only lead to the elimination of the political and to
the destruction of democracy."[32]

Christian Postliberal Democratic Theory

How does this particular discourse in contemporary democratic theory
assist Christian theoretical work in our postliberal context? Agonistic

democracy most closely approaches a similar (and recently developing) Christian perspective on the modern liberal regime. I would like to suggest that to understand politics agonistically is to re-situate the Christian theorist and her work. It is to make her work at once more political but also more chastened. If, following the poststructuralist and postmodernist critique, we understand modernity as a project to end politics by means of a regulative model of unity, and, further, if in following this line we also understand the political as ineliminably agonistic and all about power and antagonism, then we are better situated to critically assess the historical emergence of modernity as a specific political act with its own exclusionary agenda. As John Milbank states at the beginning of his *Theology & Social Theory*: "Once, there was no 'secular.' And the secular was not latent, waiting to fill more space with the steam of the 'purely human,' when the pressure of the sacred was relaxed. Instead there was the single community of Christendom, with its dual aspects of *sacerdotium* and *regnum*. The secular as a domain had to be instituted or *imagined*, both in theory and in practice."[33] This forcible evacuation of the Christian construal of the properly constituted public—what Oliver O'Donovan calls the *Christendom idea*—has resulted in the historical emergence of the modern secular emancipatory public sphere.[34] But of course, this evacuation could neither be totally clean nor totally successful. So a trace, a haunting of the original construal (or perhaps better, the situation *just prior* to the original construal) has continued to plague modernity, serving as the nightmarish Other in constant need of policing and surveillance, and selectively co-opted lest its disruptive powers break out once more and return us to that (pre-) original chaos, the state of nature. And for liberal modernity, that Other is the public political Church. "The new, secular *dominium* could not, according to the logic of willful occupation which now mediated transcendence in the public realm, really tolerate a 'political' Church as a cohabitant."[35]

Such an agonistic re-description of the historical emergence and nature of the modern regime requires that Christian theorists, first, re-visit their theological concepts to critically examine how far and to what degree they have been and continue to be complicitous in theologically justifying the modern regime of asymmetrical exclusion, and then, second, they must be about the articulation of a positive alternative. With respect to the first requirement, I would argue that our post-liberal context necessitates the development of a suitable post-Christendom political theology (a project that as documented here is already well under way).[36] I am not sure that continued evocations of natural law, sphere sovereignty, common grace, justice, and/or common good have any public purchase, or that we ought to support any contemporary regime in which they did. Those traditional theological constructs all have the net effect of establishing a form of dependent relationship whereby the Church identifies her own well-being with that of the flourishing of the nation-state. And certain practical policies and advantages at law under-taken by the nation-state on behalf of the Church have materially ce-mented that dependency. The net effect has been what Stanley Hauer-was calls, "the democratic policing of Christianity."[37]

With respect to the second requirement, I think a fruitful beginning may be found in Nancy Fraser's idea of the *subaltern counterpublic*, a concept she employs both to re-describe the modern liberal public realm as in fact constituted by many publics, and to locate the place of spe-cific communities of identity within it. And where her concern is pri-marily with feminist communities, I think we can fruitfully extend this analysis to communities of traditional faith.

Fraser commences her "rethinking the public sphere" with the claim that "the general idea of the public sphere is indispensable to critical theory although the specific form in which Habermas has elaborated this idea is not wholly satisfactory."[38] Her own effort is to critically inter-rogate and reconstruct Habermas's project in order to project an alter-native model of democracy, one capable "of theorizing the limits of actually existing democracy." In doing so, Fraser is drawn to the insights of certain strands of feminist thought which alert us to how deliberation "can serve as a mask for domination." Indeed, such domination can "extend beyond gender to other kinds of unequal relations, like those based upon class or ethnicity."[39] Even in the absence of formal exclu-sions, particular forms of social inequalities can privilege some, victim-ize others. Fraser also criticizes deliberative democrats for stressing the singularity of the public sphere with the consequent view that whenever other publics emerge it signals a breakdown of that regulative ideal. "This narrative . . . then is informed by an underlying evaluative as-sumption, namely, that the institutional confinement of public life to a single, over-arching public sphere is a positive and desirable state of affairs, whereas the proliferation of a multiplicity of publics represents a departure from, rather than an advance toward, democracy."[40] Against this modern univocal model, Fraser pits an alternative model of multiple publics. In making her argument that "a plurality of competing publics better promotes the ideal of participatory parity than does a single, comprehensive, overarching public," Fraser points to revisionist historiography which records how "members of subordinated groups—women, workers, peoples of color, and gays and lesbians—have repeatedly found it advantageous to constitute alternative publics." Then follows Fraser's conceptualizing of this pattern: "I propose to call these *subaltern counterpublics* in order to signal that they are parallel discursive arenas where members of subordinated social groups invent and circulate counterdiscourses to formulate oppositional interpretations of their identities, interests, and needs." Her chief empirical example of this phenomenon is the late-twentieth-century U.S. feminist subaltern counterpublic, which has witnessed the creation of a particularistic space sustained in part by "its variegated array of journals, bookstores, publishing companies, film and video distribution networks, lecture series, research centers, academic programs, conferences, conventions, festivals, and local meeting places." In this sphere, feminists have re-described social reality, and with their particularist language they have recast their needs and identities. Rejecting the charges of separatism that might be implied in her account, Fraser argues that ultimately her model is publicist in its orientation, that counterpublics "are by definition not enclaves, which is not to deny that they are often involuntarily *enclaved.*" Rather, subaltern counterpublics have a dual character: "On the one hand, they function as spaces of withdrawal and regroupment; on the other hand, they also function as bases and training grounds for agitational activities directed toward wider publics. It is precisely in the dialectic between these two functions that their emancipatory potential resides."[41]

I find Fraser's idea of subaltern counterpublic an empirically accurate description of precisely what has developed within the Christian community in the past half-century. Christians have in fact already established their own form of a subaltern counterpublic. But while this empirical situation has been achieved, Christian theoretical reflection has lagged behind. Perhaps due to our continued Constantinian aspirations, our contemporary political theologies and political theories are still for the most part informed more by univocal Christendom assumptions (or by their univocal "Anabaptist" rejection) than by the contemporary realities of our advanced capitalist, late modern pluralistic multicultural democracies.[42] Rather than continue in this situation, I would argue that Christian postliberal political theory accept this empirical reality as the starting point of theoretical reflection, relocate the Christian narrative as being but one voice in Tully's "strange multiplicity," and develop political theories consistent with that location. There has indeed been a structural transformation of the public sphere. And a Christian postliberal democratic theory ought to reflect that fact. My suggestion then, is that contemporary Christian political theory address the question: What is politics for the subaltern Christian counterpublic?

The Task of Christian Political Theory: Cultivating Christian Citizens for an Agonistic Democracy

To be authentically Christian, a postmodern Augustinian theory must recover from within the Christian theological tradition the conceptual resources whereby to image what it means to think politically within an agonistic context. Milbank has noted the same need for theology itself:

> Theology has frequently sought to borrow from elsewhere a fundamental account of society or history, and then to see what theological insights will cohere with it. But it has been shown that no such fundamental account, in the sense of something neutral, rational and universal, is really available. It is theology itself that will have to provide its own account of the final causes at work in human history, on the basis of its own particular, and historically specific faith. [43]

Christian political theory is but a mode of Christian (political) theology. Oliver O'Donovan has captured this nicely when he argues that Christian thinking about the *political* "is not a question of adapting to alien requirements or subscribing to external agenda, but of letting theology be true to its task."[44]

So then, what is the task? In the space that remains, I would like to trace out some conceptual *replacements* that Christian political thought must accomplish if we are to embark upon the project of cultivating Christian citizens for an agonistic democracy. Together these replacements portray the Christian citizen as neither conqueror nor passive victim. It is a project of will-formation, but not Habermasian democratic will-formation. Rather, contemporary Christian will formation is located in the practice of *peaceableness* and *self-restraint*. This turn requires Christian political theory to take its marking not from the needs and requirement of the modern state, but rather from the needs and requirements of the Church. It is to make Christian political thought ecclesiocentric.[45]

What then does it mean to argue that Christians ought to be *more* political and *less* Constantinian? It is to argue that Christians must *reconceive* their political context, their political ends, and the Christian civic virtues (intellectual and moral) necessary for both.

Establishing the first requirement has, of course, been the burden of this paper. Life in late-modern multicultural pluralist societies along with the postmodern agonism that most accurately captures this condition forces the Christian to relocate herself in a post-Christendom context. This necessitates the acceptance of the inevitable contingency of Christian political reflection that hitherto had been lost to view as long as the universalist presumptions of modernity could continue to serve as well as the carrier of Christendom political theologies. But now, situated as one among diverse and contending subaltern counterpublics, Christian communities must understand themselves as occupying a space between: its narrative no longer ruling, *but at the same time* also not powerless in the world. In the context of Fraser's "plurality of competing publics" Christian reflection should give definition to this new context, developing an account that can assist the Christian counterpublic to be about the task whereby Christians (as a subordinated social group) can "invent and circulate counterdiscourses to formulate oppositional interpretations of their identities, interests, and needs" (Fraser). We might call this task the cultivation of virtues internal to the community; that is, the cultivation of those virtues essential for the recognition, in our present context, of Christian identity, interests, and needs. This task has as its second moment, the cultivation of those virtues for relating the Christian subaltern counterpublics to other communities similarly situated. These are virtues necessary for proper negotiation. Taken together, the Christian theoretical task is a project of *identity-formation* and *negotiation*.

To accept the ineliminably contingent nature of our theorizing as well as the ever open nature of democratic politics (despite the best conceptual efforts to close it!) is to return *political judgment* to theoretical primacy and to see it as the key intellectual virtue required for our situation.[46] Just because democracy and disagreement are inextricably woven together, Christian political judgment is required to discover precisely the boundaries of subaltern Christian identity and the legitimate boundaries of its negotiations and relations with the others of many such counterpublics. In the absence of comforting universals and a consensual univocal public, the answers to the questions of *whither?* and *what?* cannot be given before hand but only emerge in the engagement with concrete particulars in concrete situations. It is to undertake what Mary Dietz has called "methodical thinking"; that is, a concrete form of political thought (inspired by Simone Weil) that is "(1) problem-oriented, (2) directed toward enacting a plan or method (solutions) in response to problems identified, (3) attuned to intelligent mastery (not domination) and (4) purposeful but not driven by a single end or success."[47] While Dietz ultimately succumbs to the temptation to see in methodical thinking a key for the modernist "project of emancipation," she has nevertheless seized upon a perspective that, if it cannot deliver her misplaced hopes, can provide the perspective whereby the Christian counterpublic discovers its identity and its politics through its open engagement with the concrete particulars of the lived ecclesial life situated among many other counterpublics. As Miroslav Volf puts it, "Whether the borders will be opened or closed will depend on the specific character of both the self and the other at a given juncture in their relation. The only advice possible is to seek supple wisdom rather than stable rules."[48] That is, specific qualities of Christian citizenship in an agonistic democracy will be disclosed through the exercise of Christian political judgment in the negotiation of concrete particulars. From this view, there is no common good per se (how can there be in the contemporary context of difference?), but only contingent localized and time-bounded common goods for the here-and-now and which may (or may not) emerge through subaltern negotiations. Only as Christian bodies think of themselves as subaltern counterpublics, out of power but not powerless, will they reorient their political identities, practices, and expectations.

What then might we reasonably expect the play of such judgment to produce? I would like to suggest that Christian political judgment well done will have as its ethical effect the cultivation of *peaceableness* and *self-restraint*. The former can be understood as the chief characteristic virtue of the Christian understanding of the *political* as understood from within its own tradition. That is, over and against the agonistic construal of the political and its late modern practical institutionalization there exists what Milbank has described as the *altera civitas* of the ecclesial community. As democratic politics agonizes in its perpetual pursuit of power, exclusion, and (always to some degree) violence, the Christian community comes to the negotiation of concrete situations as *embodying* an alternative, the politics of harmonic difference.[49] Rather than being subsumed or coded by the terms of power and interest that is the inevitable condition of all other subaltern communities locked into the Hobbesian paradigm of agonism, the Christian counterpublic exhibits—in thought, word, and deed—a peaceable alternative. In this recognition of agonism and in the corresponding cultivation of a counter-peaceableness lies the secret of the power that the Christian communities possess. Peaceableness, as the willing renunciation of the practices and tools of manipulation, coercion, and domination and, rather, the expression of the very way of Christ in the world who came "to serve and not be served" will find *neighborly affinity* (to borrow from Gadamer) with those other out-of-power subaltern communities who struggle to preserve identity. Peaceableness, thus, becomes the characteristic virtue marking the Christian citizen in agonistic democracy. It is the Christian civic virtue cultivated within the *altera civitae* of churches as the practical embodiment of Christian identity. It becomes the posture of relation to and negotiation with the other.

Peaceableness as the fruit of accepting the in-between status of the Christian narrative in the contemporary context (out-of-power but not powerless) leads to a second and even more other-directed civic virtue, *self-restraint*. Just because of the agonistic nature of the contemporary public, and just because democratic politics cannot without extreme violence ever be closed off, the Christian community informed by the narrative of peace must necessarily exercise self-restraint, and not seek its will as the will for all *even if it has the means to do so*. In the contemporary world haunted by, but now empty of, the "Christendom idea," there cannot be any other way for the Church to be and still be the *altera civitas*. One might suggest that in Christendom, the Church embodied the fullness of Christ's kingship and lordship over the earth. But in our post-Christendom context the Church embodies His way of peace, suffering, and powerlessness. This is not to locate self-restraint in the requirements for the maintenance of Rawlsian public reason or Habermasian deliberation, nor even in the empirical conditions of Christian political differences as some have done,[50] but rather in the very logic of the Church in today's world. Self-restraint, here, does not entail the abandonment of the sphere of the *political* or the public square (indeed such is impossible for both historical and theological reasons). Rather, self-restraint, as informed by Christian political judgment is a response to the agonistic nature of the modern public sphere. Self-restraint manifests itself in the rejection of totalizing stratagems and rhetorics that seek in thought, word, or deed to either revive what has been irretrievably lost or to continue to "baptize" exclusionary modernity. It reflects a will-formation oriented, following Volf, toward embrace not exclusion.[51] Caught in an agonistic context, inextricably committed to public life and yet possessing no sovereignty over it, the Christian community (or communities) must struggle to make sense of the requirements that this context dictates both for the preservation of its identity and for its relations with the other. Self-restraint works its way into a number of related (civic) virtues such as humility, hospitality, neighborliness, openness, etc. But my concern here is to image self-restraint as a fundamental political-ethical requirement for Christian communities in their subaltern status.

As Stanley Hauerwas puts it: "Our task is about surviving and not ruling."[52] Political judgment, governed by and informing the virtues of peaceableness and self-restraint, situates the Christian citizen in contemporary agonistic democracy as neither ruler nor victim, but as diplomat, negotiating the what and whither of subaltern dialogues concerning identity and otherness. Perhaps in the end we can work it out, but it will be a long and winding road.

Notes

1. James Tully, *Strange Multiplicity* (New York: Cambridge University Press, 1995).

2. Jean Hampton, "The Common Faith of Liberalism,"*Pacific Philosophical Quarterly* 75 (1994): 186-216.

3. James Bohman and William Rehg, eds., *Deliberative Democracy* (Cambridge, Mass.: MIT Press, 1997): xxvii.

4. See Craig Calhoun, ed., *Habermas and the Public Sphere* (Cambridge, Mass.: MIT Press, 1992).

5. Besides the Calhoun and the Bohman and Rehg volumes, see further examples such as *Democracy and Difference*, ed. Seyla Benhabib (Princeton, N.J.: Princeton University Press, 1996) and *Deliberative Politics*, ed. Stephen Macedo (Oxford: Oxford University Press, 1999). The idea of deliberative democracy attained a more widespread and public visibility with the publication of Amy Gutmann and Dennis Thompson's *Democracy and Disagreement* (Cambridge, Mass.: Harvard University Press, 1996). The Macedo volume is a collection of essays responding to Gutmann and Thompson.

6. Macedo, *Deliberative Politics*, 4.

7. See chiefly his "Discourse Ethics" in *Moral Consciousness and Communicative Action* (Cambridge, Mass.: MIT Press, 1993); "Remarks on Discourse Ethics" in *Justification and Application* (Cambridge,Mass.: MIT Press, 1993); "Three Normative Models of Democracy" *Constellations* 1, (April, 1994): 1-10; and *Between Facts and Norms* (Cambridge, Mass.: MIT Press, 1996). Indeed Gutmann and Thompson (relying more on Rawls) seek clearly to distinguish their model as different from and superior to the discourse theory of Habermas; see their *Democracy and Disagreement*, 17-18, and accompanying notes. But for an examination of their claims, see Jack Knight, "Constitutionalism and Deliberative Democracy," in *Deliberative Politics*, ed. Macedo, 162-63.

8. Benhabib, "Models of Public Space: Hannah Arendt, the Liberal Tradition, and Jurgen Habermas," in *Habermas and the Public Sphere*, ed. Calhoun, 95.

9. Benhabib, "Models," 74-75.

10. Macedo, *Deliberative Democracy*, 4.

11. Iris Marion Young, "Communication and the Other: Beyond Deliberative Democracy," in *Democracy and Difference*, ed. Benhabib, 121.

12. Benhabib, "Introduction: The Democratic Moment and the Problem of Difference," in *Democracy and Difference*, ed. Benhabib, 5.

13. For examples of critiques undertaken from perspectives other than the agonist I discuss above see Femia (1997) who rejects the model of empirical and conceptual grounds. For some additional critical sources see, Remer (1999), Dietz (1998), Sanders (1997), and Villa (1992). Macedo includes a number of critiques specific to the Gutmann and Thompson model of deliberative democracy in the first part of his volume.

14. Benhabib, "Introduction," 7.

15. Chantal Mouffe, *The Return of the Political* (London: Verso, 1993): 7.

16. For example, see Ivie (1998), Cohen (1996, 1997).

17. Mouffe, "Democracy, Power, and the 'Political,'" in *Democracy and Difference*, ed. Benhabib, 247.

18. Young, "Communication and the Other," 120-35.

19. So William Simon in setting out "Three Limitations to Deliberative Democracy," notes how "the rhetorical equality of the deliberative style can leave unabated a psychological inequality that distorts a subordinated group's sense of its interests

and capacities." See Simon, "Three Limitations" in *Deliberative Politics*, ed. Macedo, 51.

20. So Russell Hardin: "It is hard to avoid the suspicion that deliberative democracy is the 'democracy' of elite intellectuals. It is virtually impossible to avoid the suspicion that deliberation will work, if at all, only in parlor room discourse or in the small salons of academic conferences. Far too much of real politics is about winning and losing for the participants to miss opportunities for scoring against potential opponents." Russell Hardin, "Method, Not Theory" in *Deliberative Politics*, ed. Macedo, 112.

21. Young, "Communication and the Other," 126.

22. Young, "Justice, Inclusion, and Deliberative Democracy," in *Deliberative Politics*, ed. Macedo, 156.

23. The following is found at footnote number 14, in Benhabib, "Toward a Deliberative Model of Democratic Legitimacy," *Democracy and Difference*, ed. Benhabib, 89-90.

24. Indeed Daniel Bell has called on deliberative democrats to come clean on this issue: "Defenders of deliberation, however, need to be more explicit about the need to involve (relatively) capable and virtuous elites as a precondition for constructive deliberations concerning complex moral controversies with national (and international) implications." See Bell, "Democratic Deliberation: The Problem of Implementation," in *Deliberative Politics*, ed. Macedo, 82. (Bell, in fact, thinks that such conditions are sorely lacking in the United States but are present in much greater extent in some East Asian countries.)

25. Fish, "Mutual Respect as a Device of Exclusion," in *Deliberative Politics*, ed. Macedo, 99.

26. Mouffe, "Democracy, Power, " 246.

27. Shapiro, "Enough of Deliberation," in *Deliberative Politics*, ed. Macedo, 30-31.

28. Fish, "Mutual Respect," 95-96.

29. Mouffe, "Democracy, Power," 254.

30. Mouffe, "Democracy, Power," 252.

31. Fish, "Mutual Respect," 98-99.

32. . Mouffe, "Democracy, Power," 255.

33. John Milbank, *Theology & Social Theory: Beyond Secular Reason* (Oxford: Blackwell Publishers, 1990): 9.

34. See Oliver O'Donovan, *The Desire of the Nations: Rediscovering the Roots of Political Theology* (Cambridge, Mass.: Cambridge University Press, 1996).

35. Milbank, *Theology & Social Theory*, 17.

36. For further examples, consider Barry Harvey, *Another City: An Ecclesiological Primer for a Post-Christian World* (Trinity Press, 1999); and David Toole, *Waiting for Godot in Sarajevo: Theological Reflections on Tragedy, Nihilism, and Apocalypse* (Westport, Conn.: Westview Press, 1998).

37. See Hauerwas, "The Democratic Policing of Christianity," *Pro Ecclesia III*, no. 2 (Spring 1994), 215-31. For an historical account of how nineteenth-century American Christian bodies learned to police themselves, see Nathan Hatch, *The Democratization of American Christianity* (New Haven, Conn.: Yale University Press, 1989).

38. Fraser, "Rethinking the Public Sphere," in *Habermas and the Public Sphere*, ed. Calhoun, 111.

39. Fraser, "Rethinking," 119.

40. Fraser, "Rethinking," 122.

41. Fraser, "Rethinking," 122-24.

42. So, for example, Miroslav Volf shows how modern theology, in translating the doctrine of the Trinity to social ethics, has construed the options as either "copying God in all respects" or "not copying God at all." Volf maintains that a grasp of creaturely contingency as well as the marring effects of sin ought to incline us to view Christian social ethics as "copying God in some respects." See Volf, "'The Trinity Is Our Social Program': The Doctrine of the Trinity and the Shape of Social Engagement," *Modern Theology* 14, no.3 (July 1998): 405. Such chastened thinking is precisely in line with my idea that Christian political thought be both more political but less Constantinian at the same time.

43. Milbank, *Theology & Social Theory*, 380.

44. See O'Donovan, *Desire of the Nations*, 3. I think O'Donovan's subtitle telling in that it suggests that too much of modern Christian political thought has lost sight of its proper theological moorings.

45. I have set out the case for ecclesiocentrism at greater length in "Ecclesiocentrism: New Directions in Christian Political Thought," paper presented at the American Political Science Association meeting, Boston, Mass., September 1998.

46. For a longer elaboration on this theme, see my "The City of God as Narrated Peace: Augustine and Political Judgment," paper presented at the International Society for the Study of European Ideas, Haifa, Israel, August 1998 and the literature cited therein.

47. See Mary Dietz, "'The Slow Boring of Hard Boards': Methodical Thinking and the Work of Politics," *American Political Science Review* 88, no. 4 (December 1994): 873-86, at 880.

48. Volf, "'The Trinity is our Social Program'," 411.

49. See Milbank, *Theology & Social Theory*, 427-34.

50. Here I think of Michael Perry whose forthcoming *One Nation, Under God: Democracy, Morality and Religion* (Oxford University) just does locate Christian political self-restraint in the empirical condition of controversy and disagreement within Christian denominations over such contentious policy issues as same-sex marriages. He argues that such divisions ought to restrain those Christians who would rely on their beliefs about what the Bible teaches as a ground for opposing legal recognition of same-sex marriage. I am deeply indebted to Michael and our fellow interlocutor, Chris Eberle, for lengthy spirited exchanges over the conditions and reasons for Christian political self-restraint. To sum it all too quickly, at the end of the day Michael and I emerge at roughly similar political conclusions. However, while Michael gets there through the modern rhetorical device of epistemic fallibilism, I arrive there theologically, by arguing for the logic of the Christian narrative in the postmodern, post-Christendom context.

51. See Miroslav Volf, *Exclusion & Embrace: A Theological Exploration of Identity, Otherness, and Reconciliation* (Nashville: Abingdon, 1996).

52. Stanley, Hauerwas, *In Good Company: The Church as Polis* (Notre Dame, Ind: University of Notre Dame Press, 1995): 234-35.

Part Three

New Thinking in Policy

Chapter 7

Taking Ecclesiology Seriously: Catholicism, Religious Institutions, and Health Care Policy

Clarke E. Cochran

Introduction

It is now a truism, at least in some circles, that American institutions are deeply troubled.[1] The family comes to mind first, followed closely by civil society. Both receive frequent attention and recommendations from social commentators, public officials, and scholars. But these are not all. The American health care system, including its iconic institutions, the hospital and the physician's office, now experience profound dislocation. The freestanding community hospital is a relic; medical groups swallow the physician's practice. The same is true of social services to the poor. The 1996 federal welfare reform wrought decisive change in the structure of national and state policy, producing wholesale alteration in the public and private local organizations that determine eligibility, counsel clients, and contract for employment, parenting skills, child care, and the host of services linked to receipt of public assistance.

In the midst of these developments, there is another truism, at least in some circles. Religious institutions must take the lead in repairing the American family and healing civic, medical, and social service institutions. The only competitor in scholarly and public imagination, though a major competitor, is the market. Market models dominate the debate over school choice and health care, and they grow in significance in the welfare arena. Although religious institutions are not antithetical to the market, they are essentially nonmarket organizations (despite the contentions of much recent sociology of religion). Therefore, if religion is to play a role in institution building, it must demonstrate the resources needed to re-create effective institutions for social service. Different church traditions contain very different sets of internal resources to meet this challenge.

Yet the religious institutions designated to respond suffer considerable stress themselves. The religiously affiliated hospitals and social service agencies presently providing health and welfare services were created in the nineteenth and twentieth centuries with a clear focus, principally (though by no means exclusively) service to co-religionists. By the end of the twentieth century, client populations are more mobile, more religiously diverse. Moreover, these institutions must negotiate funding, personnel issues, and missions not simply with donors and denominational bodies, but also with secular charities, other denominations, and with federal, state, and local government officials. How will it be possible to design new service institutions without spending excessive time and resources in fund-raising, coordination, and record keeping, with fewer resources remaining for direct service? A directly related concern is the *identity* of religious institutions, such as hospitals and child care facilities. In what ways, if any, are Catholic or Baptist or Methodist hospitals different from secular counterparts? Do they have a distinctive mission, apart from chapels, a scattering of religious symbols, and a few phrases in old charters?

The key is to think in terms of religious *institutions*. Most research in political science involves theologies or attitudes and beliefs held by religious actors, whether clergy or lay. Scholars have identified particular "social theologies" that connect fundamental religious beliefs with political agendas.[2] Though not denying the importance of social theology, this chapter asserts the importance of the organizational forms, the ecclesial structures, that are part of the history of institutions within particular denominations or churches.[3] The claim is that the church qua church matters for politics and public policy. More than this, this chapter argues that significance resides in the *different ways* that churches organize themselves. Some ecclesiologies are better suited to meet challenges of identity, changing political environment, and changing social settings than others.

Health care institutions, more particularly Catholic health care organizations, test this argument. Although Protestants outnumber Catholics in the general population about two and a half to one, Catholic presence in the health care sector belies this ratio. There are, roughly speaking, twice as many Catholic as Protestant hospitals in the United States. Other traditions, notably Seventh-Day Adventist, are also "over represented," but constitute a far smaller portion of the health care system than Catholic institutions. This chapter explores the implications of this strong Catholic presence. It contends that Catholic social theory and Catholic practice possess distinctive resources as they bear upon health care delivery and health care politics. In particular, "ecclesiology," that is, the church's self-understanding as church, makes it distinctive. If these contentions are true, then ecclesiology may represent a potentially significant concept for thinking about the institutional and policy challenges of the next century and for understanding the behavior of religious groups in policy and politics.

There are two dimensions to these arguments. First, political thinking and political science can profit from attention to ecclesiology. Second, the Catholic tradition is fertile ground for making clear the importance of ecclesiology and its political implications.

Consider the first dimension. The dominant topics in the study of religion in politics in America are voting patterns of religious traditions, believer's attitudes toward policy issues, and the effect of the New Religious Right during the last two decades.[4] Interest group activity, especially in Washington, has received attention, most notably from Hertzke, Moen, and Hofrenning.[5] None gives attention to health policy activities. Most focus on issue positions and lobby effectiveness, finding that these are related less to denominational structure than to whether the group employs insider or outsider strategies. Hofrenning does suggest the paradox that the more hierarchical Catholic Church is in better synchronization with member policy attitudes than many of the Protestant denominations.[6]

Political scientists interested in the role of churches and other religious organizations might well consider the ways in which such entities think of themselves as churches. The differences may partly explain variations in their approaches to policy arenas. That is, in addition to the theological and philosophical dimensions (constitutive of social attitudes) of the way in which different churches approach (for example) medicine, the ways in which lay persons, clergy, and social activists view (and operate) church itself can influence health care policy behavior.[7]

Consider now the second point. There are clear differences in ecclesiology between Catholics, mainline Protestants, Evangelicals, Jews, and so forth. These differences say quite a bit about how they behave politically. "Public church" traditions, such as the Catholic, will produce a politics different from those of more inwardly focused ecclesiastical traditions.[8] To illustrate: a voluntaristic conception of church polity might incline evangelical Christians to establish medical missions in urban neighborhoods, but a sacramental and hierarchical conception among Catholics might produce hospitals. The kinds of institutions that evolve from contrasting church polities then place the two church types in separate spheres of interest when it comes to health care policy reform. This chapter attends to the Catholic tradition directly, but includes a brief, comparative discussion of Protestant ecclesiology. This angle of vision highlights the unique resources that the Catholic tradition brings to the institutional challenges of health care.

The Meaning of Ecclesiology

Importance

A variety of terms are roughly synonymous: ecclesiology, religious tradition, church organization, church polity, church authority, and structure. "Ecclesiology" can be considered broadly and normatively, as well as narrowly and descriptively. Literally, the term refers either to the study of or to the theory of the church. Since churches include beliefs, doctrines, rituals, customs, and organizational structures, ecclesiology broadly includes the mission of the church, membership, the functions of the church, and institutional structures. To deal fully with ecclesiology, therefore, would be to do fundamental theology; that is, to consider every facet of the life and theology of "church." This study reduces the wide-angle lens, "study of the church," to narrow the focus on the *structures and governance* of the church. For example, if the Catholic Church understands itself sacramentally, then it will organize itself in certain ways for action in history. It will develop structures and forms of governance different from those of Christian churches with less sacramental self-understandings. In short, its *organizational life* or its *"church polity"* will create highly structured, visible, and tangible institutions to manifest clearly its presence in the world. Moreover, as the church's self-understanding changes, its institutional form should change.

Health care and health care policy furnish a field of action upon which to observe such changes and through which to understand (partially) how it comes to be that Catholic institutional health care presence far outstrips the Catholic Church's proportion of citizenry. The ways in which Catholic institutions meet (or fail to meet) the challenge of maintaining identity and mission reveal not simply *differences* from Protestant approaches, but *strengths* from the Christian perspective. This way of looking at the ability of the Catholic Church to respond creatively in healthcare may suggest analogous resources for meeting demands in public assistance and civil society institution building.

There is no way to "prove" such contentions here or even to probe many of their dimensions. The intention is to explore the terrain. The importance of church polity is relatively neglected in social science. Neither the most recent study of Catholic philanthropy, nor the most recent study of the history of Catholic health care devotes more than peripheral and suggestive attention to issues of church organization, power, or authority.[9] Moreover, the *reciprocal* influence of church organization and policy arena constitutes what is important. It is not enough to point out the organizational features of the Catholic Church, for example. One must also explore the features of particular arenas of social life to see how they might interact with church life. Think of the analogy of viruses and human cells. Apparently, individual viruses have "hooks" that fit the receptors of certain cells but not others. Similarly, one characteristic of a church's life might tap into a particular area of social policy, while another grips a different area.[10] Thus a double thesis: (1) Catholic ecclesiology (church life) is distinctive and contains significant policy implications; (2) health care institutions today produce changes that call for the creation of new institutional forms. The Catholic Church may be better positioned to respond to these challenges precisely because of its ecclesiological commitments.

Catholic Ecclesiology

Catholic polity does not stand on its own. It flows from more basic theological commitments. The theological bloodline runs something like this: Social Life of the Trinity > Incarnation > Sacramental vision > Ecclesiology > Church institutions > Organizational ethics.[11] According to the doctrine of the Trinity, the life of God is relational. Because humans are made in the image of God, Catholic political thought and church life stress the relational character of human life. Equally they stress the Incarnation. Catholicism believes that, because God became human in Jesus, the church itself must, as it were, take on human flesh. The Catholic Church is, therefore, sacramental; God's most significant contact with humanity occurs in tangible signs and symbols. "No theological principle or focus is more characteristic of Catholicism or more central to its identity than the principle of *sacramentality*."[12] In healing, for example, "sacrament" refers to the unfolding mystery of God's love in the encounter between the sick person and living, breathing, tangible care givers. Thus, "sacrament" refers not only to the traditional Catholic sacrament of the "anointing of the sick,"[13] but also to the vital importance of tangible agents of God's love. The spirituality is incarnational. As St. Vincent de Paul (1581-1660) told the nursing nuns of the order he founded, the Daughters of Charity, "When you leave your prayers for the bedside of a patient, you are leaving God for God. Looking after the sick is praying."[14]

Structurally, this means *institutions*. Organized structures are not accidents of history. Catholics build institutions that become embedded in the world, human history, and culture quite intentionally. Institutions with authority structures, buildings, rules, and rituals are important to Catholics because they mediate God's incarnational contact with humanity.[15] Partly for this reason, Catholicism does not flee the world. The Catholic style is never to deny the world, but to engage it with a certain moral and spiritual vision. With respect to policy, therefore, the Catholic Church is often already institutionally located in the social world where problems arise.[16] These institutions then interact with the political, social, economic, and cultural environment to generate particular decisions, missions, ethical and political stances, and organizational cultures that instantiate the institution's links back to the generating theological commitments.

Such an orientation is different from a more "Protestant" ecclesiology, particularly an evangelical understanding of church, where the important thing is *not* to become institutionalized. Because institutions are easily corrupted, evangelical Protestants prefer to witness to the world through the word. The Christian may work *within* institutions, but may not work *through* them.[17] These differences are important politically.

It is no secret that the Catholic Church is hierarchical. Men with titles like pope, cardinal, archbishop, bishop, and pastor exercise various degrees of independent and delegated authority within particular jurisdictions. The Pope has his Curia, an old and a large bureaucratic structure for administering worldwide ecclesial operations. Bishops have their chanceries and staffs. A legal system (canon law) sets out the rights and duties of the persons in these offices, as well as the rights and obligations of the laity, the proper administration of sacraments, and other matters.

This hierarchical, institutional, and bureaucratic structure often is perceived (by those within and without the church) as rigid and inflexible, which indeed it can be. The institutional grid suggests prison bars. The sacramental/incarnational character of these structures and the degree of flexibility and adaptability that exist within them are easily missed. In these respects, the institutional grid suggests a trellis. For such a church, organization is not an afterthought or an unfortunately needed development; rather, in Theologian Richard McBrien's words, "order is *constitutive* of the Church rather than merely functional."[18] Other churches, in which institutions are only functionally required, will not (1) develop an institutional life and structure as fully articulated or central to the believer's life as the Catholic Church, and (2) will not interact with the political/policy system in the same way. These suggestions cannot be tested comparatively here, but the implications of Catholic institutional structure for health care policy can be illustrated.

The Catholic church's ecclesiology has always been plural. Definite ideas have dominated in particular periods, but no one "model" of the church rules. Although it is true that an institutional, hierarchial understanding of the church characterized the early decades of the twentieth century, it never stood alone. This became especially true after the Second Vatican Council ("Vatican II," 1962-1965), which legitimated a variety of "ecclesiologies."[19] Vatican II devoted two of its most important documents to the church's self-understanding (*The Dogmatic Constitution on the Church* and *The Church in the Modern World*), and many other documents contained important implications for ecclesiology.[20] The Council opened the church to the world, regarding it as essential to "read the signs of the times." The Council also emphasized service to the world, renewal of the sacramental life of the church, and the essential role of lay persons in the church itself and in the secular world.

Vatican II also made significant structural changes. As well as fortifying the independent role of lay persons, especially in service and in political activity, the Council saw the "universal church" as a communion of churches. Local dioceses and parishes received more autonomy in carrying out the church's mission in local circumstances. Tied to this notion was renewed emphasis on the "collegial" exercise of authority, partially institutionalized in synods of bishops that meet periodically in Rome to discuss and advise on matters of concern to the entire church or to geographic regions and partially institutionalized in various national councils of bishops that meet to discuss and make recommendations on matters pertaining to church life in particular nations. The National Council of Catholic Bishops has used this opportunity to engage a wide variety of political, policy, and social topics in the United States.[21]

These developments lie in the realm of the church's self-understanding. The reality of actual church life, both before and after Vatican II, evinces greater flexibility and adaptability than is obvious on first glance at Catholic polity.

The most clearly hierarchical feature of the church is the relationship of pastor to bishop to pope. Yet, in actual fact, pastors enjoy a good deal of autonomy in their administration of parishes, and bishops enjoy even greater autonomy in their dioceses, thus creating multiple centers of initiative for policy action. Although parishes have not been involved substantially in health care, they have been important in local politics and in policy areas such as education. Dioceses have been prominent in the development of Catholic health care institutions in America.

Although Vatican II gave new attention to national councils of bishops, American bishops met formally and informally throughout the nineteenth and twentieth centuries, spoke frequently on politics, and made decisions on issues of public concern. What one bishop in his own diocese may not be able to say effectively regarding policy, bishops as a collective body may address.

Religious orders of men and women (popularly "brothers" and "sisters" or "nuns") have considerable independence in developing ministries and in the institutions they establish. Although each order has a "superior," who is responsible for periodic accounting to the Vatican on the life of the order, many orders in practice have been democratic and collaborative, even before Vatican II. Moreover, and most significantly, religious orders are not part of the hierarchy. They are not directly responsible to local bishops or pastors. Although they need the permission of these officials to establish ministries in parish or diocese, they are not required to "report" to them (though prudence may advise it) unless employed by parish or diocese. Moreover, bishops often in practice find it difficult to refuse giving permission to religious orders when such orders desire to establish a ministry, thus giving them a high degree of institutional autonomy. Religious orders of women are integral to Catholic health care ministry in the United States and vocal in health policy advocacy.[22]

Lay societies, formal and informal, can attain relatively high degrees of autonomy without being considered in any way "out" of the church. Indeed, they often draw material and moral resources from the hierarchical church. Many of these societies deliver goods and services, accept contracts from governments, and engage in lobbying and other forms of political activity. Examples are the Catholic Worker movement, the Knights of Columbus, Diocesan Councils of Catholic Women, and Catholic Charities agencies. These are often incorporated separately from parish or diocese and not directly answerable to them. Other structures, for example Opus Dei as a "personal prelature," exist outside the lines above.

To summarize: from its trinitarian, incarnational, and sacramental commitments, the Catholic Church developed a strong ecclesiological orientation and complex institutional life. There are multiple players in Catholic life, with cross-cutting relationships and authority struc-

tures. This means that they can often draw upon one another's resources without being bound to their authority. Although all manifest
the institutional nature of Catholic ecclesiology, they do so in ways
that make these institutions highly flexible. (The diversity and relative autonomy also produce tensions and conflict within the church.)
This flexible institutional structure makes the Catholic presence in
political and policy life different from other churches.

Catholic Presence in Health Care

If the general points about ecclesiology's importance are valid,
Catholic presence in health care delivery and in health care policy
advocacy should reflect an institutional inclination and multiple centers of action and should be different from the Protestant presence in
these arenas. As this argument is exploratory, it focuses principally
on the Catholic side and draws only tentative conclusions. The discussion is in two parts: the contemporary presence of the Catholic
Church in health care delivery and the historical and theological
background of that presence.

Catholic Health Care at Present

The kinds of ecclesial orientations described above and the history of
medicine in the United States combined to produce a strong Catholic
presence in both health care delivery and in policy advocacy. Because
there are so many different kinds of church-related health care facilities and so many types, and because there is no unified or centralized
system of reporting, it is difficult to determine precise figures. Nevertheless, the available numbers portray the Catholic commitment to
health care in institutional terms and the basis for Catholic policy advocacy.

Church-related *hospitals* are the most prominent and easily
counted sign of religious presence in the most technologically advanced and visible part of the medical system. Often these hospitals
are associated with private or public medical schools, including
Catholic universities such as Georgetown. Because of the Church's
relatively hierarchical structure and the decades-long efforts of the
Catholic Health Association, the best data are available for Catholic
hospitals and other Catholic institutions. Some data, however, help to
assess Catholic size and impact relative to hospitals affiliated with
various Protestant denominations.[23]

In 1995, there were 5,194 community hospitals, of which 3,092 (or 60 percent) were operated by nongovernment, nonprofit entities, the category that includes church-affiliated hospitals. The nonprofits were larger than the average public and private, for-profit hospital, and they accounted for 70 percent of all community hospital beds (610,000), 73 percent of expenses ($210 billion), and 73 percent of full-time equivalent hospital employees (2.7 million). Data for Catholic hospitals reveals a substantial impact on the system. Hospitals affiliated with CHA (542 in 1998) accounted for about 10 percent of the nation's community hospitals, 15 percent of hospital beds, 16 percent of all admissions, and $44 billion in expenses in 1995. There are approximately 300 Protestant hospitals (roughly 5 percent of the total). If we add Catholic and Protestant together (and assume that Protestant hospitals are roughly the same size as Catholic), then Christian hospitals would account for close to one-third of all nonprofit hospital admissions and one-quarter of the admissions to general community hospitals.

Catholic institutions are larger and more complex than their Protestant or Jewish counterparts. In 1997, four of the nation's ten largest integrated health care systems were Catholic, and six of the ten largest nonprofit systems were Catholic. The *tenth largest* Catholic system had more beds than the *largest* non-Catholic religious health care system. Although data are hard to determine and methods of counting much disputed, these hospitals also account for a substantial volume of care for the poor, although less than the public hospital sector, which has explicit legal requirements for charity care. The Catholic Health Association reports a figure for Catholic hospitals of 14 percent of revenues (counting bad debt plus charity care and Medicaid's failure to cover costs).

It is difficult to get a fix on religiously affiliated nursing homes, but it is clear that their proportion of the total is far lower than the proportion of religious hospitals. The vast majority are private, for-profit institutions. In 1995, there were 16,700 nursing homes with nearly 2 million beds. Of these institutions, 11,000 were proprietary. Only slightly more than 4,300 were nonprofit (26 percent). It is not clear how many of these are religiously affiliated. CHA reports about 700 Catholic long-term care facilities with approximately 100,000 long-term beds (about 5 percent of the national total). Data are subject to many inaccuracies, as ownership is highly decentralized and some facilities are difficult to classify according to long-term or intermediate care. Whatever the numbers, however, it is clear that the number of Catholic long-term care facilities is large, but that the church's proportion of such facilities is small.

The number of home health agencies, hospices, mental health facilities, and neighborhood clinics is large, but the decentralized nature of these facilities, their rapid openings, mergers, and closings, and their often financially precarious position makes them difficult to count. Even more difficult to assess is the religious presence within them, although that presence is clearly important. Among these miscellaneous organizations, the percentages of church-related organizations is unclear. Voluntary nonprofits of all sponsorships own only 37 percent of home health agencies, but 90 percent of all hospices. It is not clear how many mental retardation or mental health facilities are nonprofit, let alone how many are church-related generally or Catholic specifically.

In 1992 CHA reported 115 religious institutes sponsoring noninstitutional health care ministries, but gave no indication of the total number of ministry sites or much detail about their activities.[24] The interdenominational Parish Nurse Resource Center reports approximately 2,500 parish nurses in the United States, but does not have data on how many are full-time or on the number or denomination of congregations with such a program. The Christian Community Health Fellowship is an interdenominational, mostly Protestant, network of health care professionals who have devoted their professional lives to health care ministry among the poor in the United States and the world. Data on the total number of such persons is not available.

The most visible national institution is the Catholic Health Association (formerly Catholic Hospital Association).[25] CHA represents and assists its members, who are primarily Catholic hospitals, health care systems, nursing homes, dioceses that sponsor health care facilities, and sponsoring religious congregations. There are also a few hundred individual members. It publishes a bimonthly journal, *Health Progress*, and a semimonthly newspaper, *Catholic Health World*, as well as occasional monographs on particular healthcare issues. CHA assists its members with ethical and legal consultations, networking, leadership training, and advice and information about changes in the national health care environment. It also keeps track of policy changes in Washington and the states and represents its members' interests in legislative testimony and proposals.[26]

Individual Catholic (as well as Protestant and other religiously affiliated) health care institutions are deeply enmeshed in public policy. They receive federal and state money from Medicare, Medicaid, and other programs that reimburse for direct patient care, as well as state programs funding the uninsured. They benefit from property tax exemptions and other tax benefits linked to their not-for-profit status. Religiously affiliated health care institutions train physicians and other health professionals, receiving federal and state support for these costs. Federal and state laws regulate staffing, quality of care, services provided, relationships with physicians and other health care providers, as well as occupational health and safety of workers. Naturally, when issues of health care reform, financing, organization, or regulation appear in federal or state legislatures, Catholic institutions and their representatives take a keen interest, often through action alerts disseminated by CHA.

The History and Ecclesiology of Catholic Health Care

The present position of Catholic health care organizations flows from characteristics of their pasts. Their histories reveal considerable adaptability to changing circumstances, multiple centers of initiative, and considerable differences from comparable Protestant health care structures.

Adaptability

The history of Catholic health care in the United States is characterized by "the adaptability of Catholic tradition."[27] From the very beginning Catholic health care adjusted to its public presence in a pluralistic, largely Protestant religious culture, featuring democratic political institutions at variance with Catholic hierarchical organization.[28] Religious orders were founded for the express purpose of staffing Catholic and, sometimes, public or private hospitals. Although most hospitals founded in the nineteenth or early twentieth centuries were established to care for the physical and spiritual needs of poor Catholics, including newly arrived immigrant groups, such hospitals were almost universally open to all persons without regard to religious affiliation or ability to pay.

Although not without a struggle, the hospitals and the religious orders that staffed them also successfully acclimated to medicine's change from comfort care and simple healing procedures to modern, curative, scientific medicine in the middle decades of the twentieth century. Religious orders adapted to new forms of nursing, standardized medical procedures, working with lay nurses, and new medical technologies. Sometimes these changes took considerable prodding from the clergy and national organizations such as CHA.[29]

Centers of Initiative

Multiple centers of initiative characterized philanthropy generally and health care specifically during the nineteenth and early twentieth centuries. The bishops' authority in dogma, discipline, and sacrament had to bend to agendas of the laity who provided support for charity. Similarly, laity and religious orders needed episcopal endorsement for official status. Religious orders of women struggled for independence, founded institutions, and developed health care ministries that were not always the first choices of local bishops. Ethnic societies used forms of fundraising different from more wealthy Catholics and were not always subject to effective control by bishop or pastor.[30] Because health care institutions were most often owned by religious orders, they had more independence from parish and bishop than other Catholic charities; but they also had special needs for endowment to support charity beds, which made their fundraising different as well.[31]

Catholic/Protestant Differences

A comparative perspective confirms that different ways of thinking about church matter for health care. During the nineteenth century, Protestant forms of benevolence more than Catholic focused on boards and foundations of wealthy donors. They often had national scope. Catholics, being more recent immigrants and lower in social and economic status, depended upon fairs and volunteer service, and the dedication, endowments, and (sometimes) begging of religious orders. An anti-Catholic, anti-immigrant animosity sometimes stimulated separate Catholic institutions as well. These differences, however, were not simply matters of status, but also of organization. "Sisterhoods were soon the most commented upon feature of Catholic charity organization, and indeed they represented an original development in American philanthropy more generally."[32]

Over the course of the nineteenth century, laity, religious, and clergy had worked in partnership to develop a large and diverse system of charities marked by considerable lay control and disproportionate reliance on female initiative and management. These features were certainly extraordinary in the society of the day, and particularly noteworthy in a hierarchical church.[33]

Although the distinction is not complete, Catholic hospitals tended to be founded either by bishops or religious orders, rather than philanthropists or physicians as among Protestants.[34] These differences stemmed from the Protestant theological emphasis on the individual conscience's direct relation to God and on the tendency to-

ward a more congregational ecclesiology,[35] as compared with the
more institutional and sacramental perspective in Catholicism.
Marvin R. O'Connell captures the spirit early after the Catholic-
Protestant break: "Extreme unction, therefore, as the council
[Trent] defined it, shared in the sacramental principle, in an incarna-
tional theology that stressed divine immanence in the human situa-
tion and was thus in marked contrast to that keystone of all classical
Protestant teaching, the notion of the transcendence of God."[36]

According to Kaufman, in nineteenth-century America:

> Protestants were equally concerned with the physical and pas-
> toral care of the sick, to whom they brought the comforting
> words of scripture. The Catholic response was made by per-
> sons committed to the vowed religious life with its evangeli-
> cal counsels of poverty, chastity, and obedience. Catholic
> rituals, symbols, and prayer mediated the religious experience
> inherent in critical illness.[37]

The rituals and symbols reflect the sacramental and incarnational
emphasis of Catholic theology, while the vowed religious reflect its
institutional uniqueness. "American Catholics revealed a striking
ability to institutionalize and organize, and, most visible of all, to express their ethos in bricks and mortar."[38]

Illustrating the characteristic Protestant orientation, H. R. Niebuhr can casually state that Christianity is a movement, not institutions, and report: "The institutional church was required to give way
to the living word of God. . . ."[39] He too agrees that the Catholic idea
of the Kingdom is mediated, where the Protestant idea is immediate
and direct. Similarly, a recent and very sensitive look at health and
religious institutions reflects the Protestant neglect of institutions
larger than the congregation.[40] Two of the better studies of the
health care system from Protestant perspectives focus on covenant[41]
and on justice and freedom.[42] The Protestant traditions in Numbers
and Amundsen's survey stress, predominantly, the individual soul, social transformation, and congregational ministry.[43]

When a Protestant religious tradition does get deeply into the institutional health care business, as for example, the Seventh-Day Adventist,[44] it typically reflects a distinctive theological and ecclesiological orientation, rather than merely unique historical or social
circumstances.[45]

Catholic Policy Advocacy

Although this point cannot be developed here, inseparable from health care delivery motivated and established along the historical and ecclesiological lines summarized, Catholic organizations advocate on a wide variety of health care policies. Policy advocacy takes place in the context of fundamental Catholic social principles such as human dignity and rights, human solidarity and the common good, option for the poor, social justice, and stewardship.[46] But it also takes place within a view of church that includes both health care ministry and political action as essential features.

Despite objections by some Catholic and non-Catholic commentators about the inappropriateness of bishops meddling in public policy, the Catholic tradition strongly supports the prudential application of general principles to practical politics. Vatican II stated that religious freedom includes the right of religious *organizations* as well as faithful *individuals* to bring their understanding to bear on law and policy. The 1971 Synod of Bishops stated, in what has become something of a mantra among Catholic justice activists, that social justice is "a constitutive dimension" of the church's mission. Pope John Paul II in his 1995 encyclical, *The Gospel of Life,* spoke specifically of the role of religious insight for policy.[47] Although some, for example Brian Benestad,[48] argue that the bishops have emphasized specific policy statements to the detriment of their role as evangelizers and teachers of the faithful, the bishops and the CHA contend that the location of Catholic institutions in the midst of the health care system (and the social service sector generally) gives the Church a unique ability and responsibility to speak to law-makers.

The American bishops and health care groups such as the Catholic Health Association appeal to these principles in their health care ministry and policy pronouncements. The American bishops and the CHA, as well as Catholic scholars and policy advocates, have been willing to be quite specific in such pronouncements. Their unique institutional location and strong organization give warrant and weight to Catholic health care lobbying.[49]

Yet, because Catholic institutions are so deeply established in the health care system, most proposals reflect a tension between principle and institutional interest. For example, the National Conference of Catholic Bishops' statement on health care reform acknowledges the status of the Church as a major employer and, therefore, a purchaser of health care and health insurance.[50] Despite the American health care system's over-reliance on technology and its tendency to raise false hopes and expectations, the CHA proposal placed strong emphasis on continued adequate flow of dollars into technology and research and development. Moreover, the proposal failed to include any measures to change the culture of medicine or to reduce unreasonable expectations. Indeed, the requirement that the proposed uniform benefit package be acceptable to all Americans worked toward even more deeply entrenching such expectations.[51] All of these proposals reflected the institutional interests of Catholic health care.

The Future:
Health Care Challenges to Ecclesiology

The future relationship between health care and church polity is uncertain in the face of temptations to neglect or compromise identity.[52] The challenge of this uncertainty flows from changes in both the health care system and in the church. According to Loren Mead, "We are being called to invent or reinvent structures and forms that will serve the new mission as well as the old structures served the old vision."[53] The challenge exists not only for Catholic health care, but for all religious health care. The challenge can be framed in five propositions.

1. Catholic (and other Christian health care institutions) developed in the late nineteenth and early twentieth centuries (largely) apart from government and in a low technology medical system.

2. As these institutions and the medical and policy systems evolved through the middle of this past century, religious health care grew and changed with the technology and accepted a partnership with government through programs such as Medicare and Medicaid, medical research, and medical education. Yet their advocacy assumed a position outside the policy system.

3. Today health care institutions are intimately connected with government through funding and regulation, but religious organizations must discover how to be free enough from the pressures of this intimacy and from their embeddedness in high-technology medicine to challenge both government and medicine.

4. Catholic health care is not and cannot be a separate enclave. Catholic institutions, in order to serve all people, especially the poor, must cooperate with a wide variety of religious and non-religious groups and institutions that share common goals and principles, but which do not share some important principles.

Catholic and other hospitals merge or form tight alliances, but Catholic restrictions on abortion and contraception ensure tensions within these agreements.

5. One important resource in Catholic ecclesiology is the *embrace of tension*. Catholic theology and ecclesiology are committed to the "both/and" rather than the "either/or."[54]

These propositions can be made more specific. The institutional base of religious health care is undergoing rapid change. One source of this change is the revolution in the health care markets that usually travels under the name of "managed care." Largely market-driven, contemporary changes have produced unprecedented (for recent history) pressure on the financial bottom line of health care institutions. This pressure produces closure of hospitals, emphasis on outpatient care and remote clinics (instead of in-hospital care), mergers and consolidations of hospitals, horizontal and vertical integration of hospitals with other forms of health care providers, and the movement of for-profit hospital chains into the traditional sphere of not-for-profit institutions.

The challenge to Catholic institutions is twofold. First, can they survive in this highly competitive environment? Catholic hospitals close, merge, and integrate, but it is not clear that these steps contribute to their long-run viability. Second, can Catholic hospitals maintain commitment to community service and care for the poor given the financial pressures that market forces exert? From one point of view, Catholic institutional flexibility furnishes adaptive resources not available to other religious providers. On the other hand, it is not clear that Catholic institutions are well designed for a market-oriented environment.[55]

These same pressures face Protestant and other religious hospitals and health care institutions. Does the relative isolation of Protestant hospitals from each other and the less institutional focus of Protestant ecclesiology make these institutions more vulnerable to challenges from government or the market or other providers, or does this independence facilitate creative experiments? Will Catholic hierarchical ecclesiology create inflexibilities at just the moment when maximum flexibility is demanded, or will its history of institutional creativity be the soil for new growth? If the sacramental/incarnational face of Catholicism facilitates institutional development, then the Church should encourage experimentation. But the need of a hierarchical church for unity, authority, and consistent representation of church teachings constrains against experimentation.

The tensions of a "both/and" ecclesiology could be creative or stulti-
fying.

Internal changes also pose important challenges. The religious orders of women that founded and still sponsor most Catholic hospitals
and nursing homes declined numerically during the last three decades.
Membership is smaller and the average age of members very high.
With this decline comes (potentially) significant loss of institutional
flexibility to meet new health care challenges. It is not clear where
the energies will flow. Will the remaining members of religious orders
attempt to maintain old institutional forms, or will they rediscover
vitality in inventing new forms of health care delivery? What other
institutional structures are available to take their place?

Evidence here is skimpy. Some orders have sold hospitals, using
the proceeds to fund endowments for community-based health care.
Bishops now play a greater role in health care in their dioceses. Some
lay movements and religious orders have devoted energy to "health
and spiritual wholeness" centers, prayer and healing movements, and
women's health concerns. There is historical precedent for non-
hospital based Catholic health care institutions.[56] The decline of religious orders challenges the traditional hierarchy (bishops and parishes) and lay movements to invent new forms of health care delivery for those marginalized in the new health care marketplace. Some
observers are very pessimistic about the ability of lay persons to assume leadership and maintain Catholic identity in institutions once
dominated by religious orders and clerics.[57] Yet that survival would be
one of the strongest justifications for religious institutions to maintain a highly visible, public role in any future health care system. Such
institutions can be visible witnesses, "exemplary practices," of a
health care not subservient to technological imperialism and bureaucratic, profit-oriented health care organizations.

The Catholic Health Association, as the most significant umbrella
organization for Catholic health care ministry and reflection, has
recognized the tests just described. It remains optimistic that the
challenges will be met. During the past few years, it has reorganized
itself, developed a new mission statement, initiated a "new covenant"
process to adapt Catholic health care to the managed care environment, and devoted increased attention to the canonical and other dimensions of "sponsorship," including attention to means of imbuing
lay leadership with the charisms of the religious orders that founded
the institutions. These issues are fraught with conflict and possibility.
Collaboration between Catholic health care institutions and Catholic
Charities organizations, once rare, has become commonplace. Similarly, different religious orders, which once jealously guarded their
boundaries, now cooperate in a variety of health care delivery ven-

tures.[58] Whether this response will be adequate, of course, is yet to be seen. But these institutional strengths do give Catholic health care facilities an adaptive edge over Protestant and other not-for-profits.

One clear danger in Catholic institutional ecclesiology is that commitment to the financial health of mainstream health care institutions will blunt the edge of social criticism and policy advocacy. This dulling did affect NCCB and CHA reform proposals of the late 1980s and early 1990s. The greatest general health care policy challenge of the next decade is to find ways to provide health care to the millions who now lack access and to specific marginal groups (for example, drug addicts, persons with AIDS, immigrants), while controlling costs in government programs. It is difficult for a religious spirit of protest against inadequate government programs to coexist with preserving the health of church institutions dependent upon the good will of government.[59] It seems possible that a church that has lived for decades with the tension between advocacy and service could be well positioned to meet this challenge. It will have to call upon its sacramental ecclesiology to fashion institutions that reestablish human connections in the midst of large institutions.

Religious groups play a significant role in a wide variety of policy arenas. How these groups address themselves to government and the kinds of policy positions they take are strongly influenced by their traditions of church organization. Institutions do matter,[60] not only government institutions, but also private institutions. The role that the Roman Catholic Church plays in health care policy owes much to its peculiar institutional structure, its "church polity." The test for political theorists who "take ecclesiology seriously" in the health care arena is to find middle principles or exemplary practices that link theological concepts, such as sacrament and incarnation, with the daily life and spirituality of the poor and sick and with the institutional and policy dilemmas of those who minister to them in health care institutions. New partnerships in health care (and other policy arenas) between government and religious institutions demand a new theory of institutions and a new political ecclesiology. The Catholic tradition demonstrates distinctive resources for institutional creativity facing the demands of modern health care.

Notes

1. This chapter began as a paper delivered at the 1996 annual meeting of the American Political Science Association, San Francisco. It was then revised for the 1998 annual meeting of the American Political Science Association, Boston. Its ideas were also presented to the Erasmus Institute Fellows Seminar in Fall 1998.

Thanks to APSA panelists and my Institute colleagues for important suggestions. Thanks to the Erasmus Institute at the University of Notre Dame for the Research Fellowship during 1998-1999 that allowed completion of this project.

2. On "social theology," see James L. Guth, et al., *The Bully Pulpit: The Politics of Protestant Clergy* (Lawrence: University Press of Kansas, 1997). For the importance of social theology and denominational influences within a particular policy arena, see Robin Hoover, *Social Theology and Religiously Affiliated Nonprofits in Migration Policy*. (Ph.D. Dissertation. Department of Political Science. Lubbock: Texas Tech University, 1998).

3. "Denomination" and "church," terms particular to the Christian tradition, are used here since attention focuses on that tradition. Jewish and other non-Christian religious traditions have analogous institutional forms, expectations, and identity issues.

4. For example, Robert Booth Fowler, Allen D. Hertzke, and Laura R. Olson, *Religion and Politics in America: Faith, Culture, and Strategic Choices*, 2d ed. (Boulder, Colo.: Westview Press, 1999); Kenneth D. Wald, *Religion and Politics in the United States*, 3d ed. (Washington, D.C.: CQ Press, 1997); Clyde Wilcox, *Onward Christian Soldiers? The Religious Right in American Politics* (Boulder, Colo.: Westview Press, 1996).

5. Allen D. Hertzke, *Representing God in Washington: The Role of Religious Lobbies in the American Polity* (Knoxville: University of Tennessee Press, 1988); Matthew C. Moen, *The Christian Right and Congress* (Huntsville: University of Alabama Press, 1989); Daniel J. B. Hofrenning, *In Washington but Not of It: The Prophetic Politics of Religious Lobbyists* (Philadelphia: Temple University Press, 1995).

6. Hofrenning, *In Washington*, 163-67.

7. For an account of different theological traditions and medicine, see Martin E. Marty and Kenneth L. Vaux, eds. *Health/Medicine and the Faith Traditions: An Inquiry into Religion and Medicine* (Philadelphia: Fortress Press, 1982), and Ronald L. Numbers and Darrel W. Amundsen, eds. *Caring and Curing: Health and Medicine in the Western Religious Traditions* (New York: Macmillan, 1986). A "tradition" might be thought of as ecclesiology "on the ground." On tradition, see especially Marty and Vaux, *Health/Medicine*, chapter 1.

8. J. Bryan Hehir, "Policy Arguments in a Public Church: Catholic Social Ethics and Bioethics," *Journal of Medicine and Philosophy*, 17 (1992), 347-64.

9. Christopher J. Kauffman, Ministry and Meaning: A Religious History of Catholic Health Care in the United States (New York: Crossroad, 1995); Mary J. Oates, The Catholic Philanthropic Tradition in America (Bloomington: Indiana University Press, 1995). True, one can read such themes as a kind of "subtext" in both works. But neither makes church organization an explicit theme. Thomas Jeavons ("Identifying Characteristics of 'Religious' Organizations: An Exploratory Proposal," [PONPO Working Paper No. 197. Program on Non-Profit Organizations, Yale University, 1993], 2) does ask the key question of how "being religious" makes a difference for how an organization exists and functions in the world, but his paper presents only a (useful) consideration of the meaning of "being religious." He does not get to the question of what difference it makes.

10. For example, it is evident in Oates (*The Catholic Philanthropic Tradition*) that various kinds of Catholic philanthropies have very different histories, a point that she does not draw out. Parochial schools, hospitals, colleges and universities, and charities for the poor (asylums, almshouses, orphanages, homes for young girls, etc.) did not link to the same parts of the Catholic Church. The differences were partly a function of which of these philanthropies received government assistance, but also a function of whether their origins were in parishes or dioceses, how religious or-

ders were part of their life, whether ethnic societies were committed to them, and other issues of church life.

11. Of course, there is no way to describe all of these concepts or their connections here. (See Clarke E. Cochran, "Sacrament and Solidarity: Catholic Social Thought and Healthcare Policy Reform," *Journal of Church and State*, 41 (Summer 1999): 475-98; and Clarke E. Cochran, "Institutional Identity; Sacramental Potential: Catholic Healthcare at Century's End," *Christian Bioethics*, 5, no. 1 (1999): 26-43.) Theological sources include: Francis Schüssler Fiorenza, "Church, Social Mission of," in *The New Dictionary of Catholic Social Thought*, ed. Judith A. Dwyer, (Collegeville, Minn.: Liturgical Press, 1994); E. Schillebeeckx, O.P., *Christ the Sacrament of the Encounter with God* (New York: Sheed & Ward, 1963); and John D. Zizioulas, *Being as Communion: Studies in Personhood and the Church* (Crestwood, N.Y.: St. Vladimir's Seminary Press, 1985).

12. Richard P. McBrien, *Catholicism*, New Edition (San Francisco: Harper-Collins, 1994), 1196.

13. Kauffman, *Ministry and Meaning*, 12-14.

14. Kauffman, Ministry and Meaning, 309.

15. Of course, not *only* Catholics stress the sacramental character of God's relations with humanity. See, for example, the Episcopal theologian, Robert Farrar Capon, *Health, Money, and Love: . . . And Why We Don't Enjoy Them* (Grand Rapids, Mich.: Wm. B. Eerdmans, 1990); *The Mystery of Christ: . . . And Why We Don't Get It* (Grand Rapids, Mich.: Wm. B. Eerdmans, 1993).

16. Bryan J. Hehir, "Identity and Institutions," *Health Progress*, 75 (November-December, 1995), 17-23.

17. Thanks to Wally Mead for this formulation. See, for example, H. Richard Niebuhr's classic *The Kingdom of God in America* (New York: Harper Torchbooks, 1959), where "institutionalize" is a pejorative term.

18. McBrien, *Catholicism*, 593.

19. A Catholic best-seller in the years after the Council summarized five "models" of the church (institution, mystical communion, sacrament, herald, and servant). Avery Dulles, S. J., *Models of the Church* (Garden City, N.Y.: Image Books, 1978).

20. The most convenient collection of Vatican II documents is Austin Flannery, O.P., general ed. *Vatican Council II: The Conciliar and Post-Conciliar Documents* (Northport, N.Y.: Costello Publishing Company, 1975). The text's summary follows McBrien *Catholicism*, 666-86, and *Catechism of the Catholic Church* (Washington, D.C.: United States Catholic Conference, 1994).

21. Timothy A. Byrnes, Catholic Bishops in American Politics (Princeton, N.J.: Princeton University Press, 1991); Brian J. Benestad, The Pursuit of a Just Social Order: Policy Statements of the U.S. Catholic Bishops, 1966-1980 (Washington, D.C.: Ethics and Public Policy Center, 1982); Michael Warner, Changing Witness: Catholic Bishops and Public Policy, 1917-1994 (Washington, D.C.: Ethics and Public Policy Center, 1995).

22. Oddly enough, as important as religious orders have been in the life of the church, they are often neglected in discussions of ecclesiology. McBrien, for example, devotes only about five scattered pages to religious orders in his 200 plus page discussion of "The Church" (McBrien, *Catholicism*, 620-21, 623-25, 638, and 681-82).

23. The data on hospitals and other institutions below are drawn from "Facts about the Catholic Health Association of the United States" (www.chausa.org/ABOUTCHA/CHAFACTS.ASP; accessed June 2, 1998); communications from Benjamin Aune, President and CEO of Interhealth, a now-dissolved advocacy, research, and educational alliance that joined with the former American Protestant Hospital Association in 1993; and *The Statistical Abstract of the United States, 1997*

(Washington, D.C.: Government Printing Office, 1997), Tables 185, 201, 203; and *Modern Healthcare* (May 25, 1998), 35-46.

24. The "Profile of Catholic Healthcare 1995" (St. Louis: Catholic Health Association, 1995) provided thumbnail sketches of thirty-nine such ministries that had been nominated for the CHA Achievement Citation Award.

25. For CHA's history, see Kauffman, *Ministry and Meaning*, chapters 8, 10-12.

26. Protestants have a more difficult time organizationally. In 1993, the former American Protestant Hospital Association merged with Interhealth, another body representing Protestant providers. In early 1998, that organization split into Interhealth and a new American Protestant Health Alliance (APHA). See *Modern Healthcare* (December 8, 1997), 4.

27. Kauffman, Ministry and Meaning, 63.

28. Kauffman, *Ministry and Meaning*, 34ff.

29. Kauffman, Ministry and Meaning, chapter 8; Oates, Catholic Philanthropic Tradition, chapter 4.

30. Oates, *Catholic Philanthropic Tradition*, xi, 38, and chapter 1.

31. Oates, Catholic Philanthropic Tradition, 39ff.

32. Oates, Catholic Philanthropic Tradition, 21.

33. Oates, Catholic Philanthropic Tradition, 71.

34. Oates, Catholic Philanthropic Tradition, passim; Kauffman, Ministry and Meaning, chapter 4.

35. Kathleen D. McCarthy, "Religion, Philanthropy, and Political Culture," (Working Paper No. 11. National Commission on Civic Renewal, n.d.).

36. Marvin R. O'Connell, "The Roman Catholic Tradition since 1545," in *Caring and Curing: Health and Medicine in the Western Religious Traditions*, ed. Ronald L. Numbers and Darrel W. Amundsen (New York: Macmillan, 1986), 115.

37. Kauffman, Ministry and Meaning, 49.

38. O'Connell, "The Roman Catholic Tradition," 136.

39. Niebuhr, The Kingdom of God in America, 28.

40. Gary Gunderson, Deeply Woven Roots: Improving the Quality of Life in Your Community (Minneapolis: Augsburg Fortress, 1997).

41. Hessel Bouma III, et al., *Christian Faith, Health, and Medical Practice*. (Grand Rapids, Mich.: Wm. B. Eerdmans, 1989).

42. Alastair V. Campbell, Health as Liberation: Medicine, Theology, and the Quest for Justice (Cleveland, Ohio: Pilgrim Press, 1995).

43. Numbers and Amundsen, *Caring and Curing*, 311, 339, 345, 502-3. And it may be worth mentioning that a recent, comprehensive survey of (largely) Protestant social theology in twentieth-century America has no index entries for ecclesiology, sacrament, institution, or church (Gary Dorrien, *Soul in Society: The Making and Renewal of Social Christianity* (Minneapolis: Fortress Press, 1995).

44. Ronald L. Numbers and David R. Larson, "The Adventist Tradition," in Numbers and Amundsen, *Caring and Curing*, 447-67.

45. Though small by absolute standards, the Adventist Health System of 32 hospitals, 155 home health agencies, and 27 nursing homes is large compared to its membership. For these data, see *Modern Healthcare* (October 5, 1998), 118.

46. Clarke E. Cochran, "The Common Good and Healthcare Policy," *Health Progress* 80 (May-June 1999), 41-44, 47; Cochran, "Sacrament and Solidarity"; and Cochran, "Institutional Identity."

47. On Vatican II, see Kenneth L. Grasso, "Beyond Liberalism: Human Dignity, the Free Society, and the Second Vatican Council," in *Catholicism, Liberalism, and Communitarianism*, ed. Kenneth L. Grasso, et al., (Lanham, Md.: Rowman & Littlefield, 1995), 49; on the 1971 Synod, see McBrien, *Catholicism*, 711-12; John Paul II, *The Gospel of Life* (Boston: St. Paul Books, 1995), §68-74.

48. Benestad, *Just Social Order.*

49. For example, CHA claims that its work helped to produce important modifications in the 1996 Kassebaum/Kennedy health insurance reform legislation and in the Medicaid provisions of the 1996 welfare reform legislation and the Medicare and Medicaid provisions of the 1997 Balanced Budget agreement. (See *CHA Washington Update*, August 9, 1996, and July 18, July 25, and August 1, 1997).

50. National Conference of Catholic Bishops, "Resolution on Health Care Reform," *Origins* (July 1, 1993), 97, 99-102.

51. Catholic Health Association, *Setting Relationships Right: A Proposal for Systematic Healthcare Reform* (St. Louis: Catholic Health Association, 1993). The proposal also relied far too strongly on "expert" bureaucratic determinations of risk and need and contained built-in mechanisms to "overfund" health care, given the grave consequences of "underfunding" (28-31). Both of these features reflect the church's institutional location.

52. Fine discussions of these dilemmas, from very different perspectives, are: Richard McCormick, S.J., "The Catholic Hospital Today: Mission Impossible?" *Origins* (March 16, 1995), 648-53; Richard McCormick, S.J., "The End of Catholic Hospitals?" *America* (July 4, 1998): 5-12; and Kathleen M. Boozang, "Deciding the Fate of Religious Hospitals in the Emerging Health Care Market," *Houston Law Review* 31 (1995), 1429-1516. CHA and Catholic institutions generally are aware of these issues. Indeed, this topic is much on the minds of these institutions. See for example, National Coalition on Catholic Health Care Ministry, *Catholic Health Ministry in Transition: A Handbook for Responsible Leadership* (Silver Spring, Md.: National Coalition on Catholic Health Care Ministry, 1995). The issue of Catholic "identity" is almost an obsession within CHA, and they have done creative thinking about it. But this only serves to illustrate the primary point that their location within the system produces severe tensions. See also Cochran, "Institutional Identity."

53. Quoted in Strong Partners: Realigning Religious Health Assets for Community Health (Atlanta: The Carter Center, 1998), 17.

54. McBrien, *Catholicism,* 16.

55. Catholic mergers and affiliations often seem to promise strong market positions and increased ability to cut costs while providing quality care. For examples, see *Modern Healthcare* (July 28, 1997), 20-21. On the other hand, the hierarchical institutional structure of the Catholic Church can also make mergers difficult. See, for example, the Vatican's 1997 rejection of a proposed New Jersey alliance of a Catholic hospital with a secular, non-profit hospital: Bruce Japsen, "Vatican Taking Closer Look," *Modern Healthcare* (July 7, 1997), 14.

56. Kauffman, *Ministry and Meaning,* 11-26, 82-95.

57. McCormick, "End?"

58. See, for example Kevin J. Sexton, "The Ministry Change Imperative," *Health Progress* 77 (March-April, 1996), 18-22; also the reports on the 1996 CHA Annual Assembly published in *Catholic Health World*, June 15, 1996; accounts of collaboration in *Catholic Health World*, November 15, 1996; and discussions of sponsorship issues in *Catholic Health World*, March 15, 1997, and in *Health Progress* 79 (March-April, 1998): 54-55, 60.

59. The failure of Catholic institutions, both in health care and other areas of ministry, to respond to the plight of African Americans after the Civil War points to the depth of this challenge. Fearful of upsetting important ethnic interests, fearful of their place in the structures of society, Catholics did not attend to the needs of this group (Kauffman, *Ministry and Meaning,* 94; Oates, *Catholic Philanthropic Tradition*), passim.

60. Sven Steinmo, and Jon Watts, "It's the Institutions, Stupid! Why Comprehensive National Health Insurance Always Fails in America," *Journal of Health Policy, Politics, and Law* 20 (Summer, 1995): 329-72.

Chapter 8

The State of the States: A Perspective on Federalism and Biblically Just Social Policy

Stacey Hunter Hecht

Introduction

By 1996 nearly everyone, regardless of political ideology, agreed that welfare as we knew it was in need of reform. Even those who protested in the strongest ways against the kinds of reforms enacted in the summer of 1996 admitted that the system had failed. In an article explaining his resignation from the Department of Health and Human Services due to the president's endorsement of the Personal Responsibility and Work Opportunity Reconciliation Act of 1996, (PRWORA)[1] former Assistant Secretary for Planning and Evaluation Peter Edelman, wrote, "I HATE welfare. To be more precise, I hate the welfare system we had until last August, when Bill Clinton signed a historic bill ending 'welfare as we know it.' It was a system that contributed to chronic dependency among large numbers of people who would be the first to say they would rather have a job than collect a welfare check every month—and its benefits were never enough to lift people out of poverty."[2] Consensus for change, however, rarely reflects genuine consensus about the results of the changes, and despite nearly universal acknowledgment of a problem, the "solution" proffered in the summer of 1996 fell short of nearly everyone's vision of good, realistic reform.

Nonetheless, welfare has been reformed. In response to public cynicism with "big government," and frustration with "bureaucracy," the Personal Responsibility and Work Opportunity Reconciliation Act is, among other things, a real example of making "devolution"—the returning of both programmatic and fiscal responsibility to the states—the law of the land. In a transfer of power unprecedented since the New Deal, the legal entitlement relationship between individuals and the federal government was dismantled and in its place stands a block grant program where states can redefine welfare as they see fit. Advocates of devolution trumpet reform as finally allowing the states an opportunity to design programs that fit their needs, independent of undue bureaucratic constraints.[3] Without having to meet the volume of regulations imposed by a federated system of welfare administration, states can presumably act as "policy laboratories," experimenting with different policy programs to see which ones work best. In addition, states might be better able to meet the needs of their particular constituencies, or to implement policy programs more efficiently than the federal government. Finally, the competition between the states might spark growth in the economy and/or increases in governmental and private sector efficiency as states compete to attract residents—corporate or individual—much as private sector firms compete for business. Opponents of devolution fear a return to the particularistic and prejudicial treatment of the poor and disadvantaged that characterized states welfare efforts both before and after the development of the federal entitlement program.[4]

But despite the recent attention to devolution, most Americans, and certainly most Christian Americans, seem less interested in this structural reality of American politics than they are with the general nature of public policy programs, or the amount of money that government spends on such programs. Michael Kinsley aptly expressed most Americans' perspective on the effect of federalism on public policy;

> The great questions of government are what functions it should perform and how it should perform them. Should we or should we not supply health insurance to those who can't afford it? Should we or should we not require welfare mothers to work? What *level* of government should perform these functions is an inherently less interesting, and important, question.[5]

Read one way, Kinsley's remarks, and the general lack of interest in the federal nature of policy programs—and welfare policy in particular—suggest a hopeful sign for those interested in questions of justice and the work of the government. Perhaps the method of administration of a particular policy program *is* inherently less important than the normative issues surrounding the program. But to pose the question as an "either/or" proposition—that is, that either the structure of government that determines policy or the normative choices involved in policy decisions is more important—belies the interconnectedness of structures and policymaking in the United States.

The structural dimension of policy provision has a profound capacity to affect the justness of policy programs. Must welfare policy be the same in all fifty states for it to be just? Does the potential for competition between the states bode well or ill for welfare policy? Will a diversity of approaches to welfare policy lead to more biblically just policy? All of these questions speak to the impact that the structure of federalism has on the development of just welfare policy. In order to begin to address these questions, this chapter asks the broader question, "(how) can a federal system of government administer biblically just social welfare policy?"[6]

The Context of the Problem

While block grant administration of a national welfare program is an untested proposition in the age of the welfare state, the fifty states have played a considerable role in the development of national welfare policy through this century. Though much of the history of welfare in the twentieth-century United States is a story of national level control of welfare, even when the national government was most in control, state experience has guided the setting of national policy. Indeed, the origins of the federal Aid to Families with Dependent Children (AFDC) program can be found in state mother's or widow's pension programs that spread quickly through the states in the early part of the twentieth century. Between 1911 and 1919, thirty-nine states implemented cash assistance programs for widowed mothers with dependent children in an effort to replace so-called "indoor" relief programs that dominated anti-poverty efforts in the nineteenth century.[7] By 1935, the year that the Social Security Act which created the Aid to Dependent Children (ADC) program was passed, all but two states (Ga. and S.C.) had mother's pensions, and the widespread diffusion and approval of programs to benefit mothers with young children at the state level played a role in the fairly uncontroversial acceptance of the ADC program. This general consensus in favor of welfare programs directed at mother or widows evaporated through time and by the 1950s the demographic composition of the ADC caseload had shifted from being composed nearly exclusively of so-called "worthy, white, widows," to being substantially more racially, ethnically, and demographically diverse. Because of increasing state reluctance to fund programs for populations that were either new to the state, or new to the state's welfare rolls, state welfare policies began to discriminate among public welfare recipients and to include measures intended to deter application for benefits.

In time, government at the federal level responded to the state level changes in the ADC/AFDC[8] program, and increasingly welfare policies were looked at through the lenses of the civil rights movement. Beginning with the first set of major amendments to the Social Security Act in 1962, states could experiment with their AFDC programs only in more modest ways. In order to implement changes, states were required to request that the federal government waive their compliance with certain provisions of the Social Security Act. State departments of human services, or the equivalent state agency, were given the opportunity, under section 1115 of the Social Security Act, to apply for waivers to the requirements of section 402 of the Social Security Act. These provisions dealt primarily with eligibility criteria and with the means through which recipients were paid. Beyond this, waiver programs were to have a mechanism for "rigorous evaluation" and be cost neutral to the federal government.

Although the section 1115 waivers would appear at first glance to entail only minimal tinkering with a state's AFDC program, the language of the section proved to be strangely prescient with regard to the direction that waivers would take in the future. Under section 1115, the secretary of the Department of Health and Human Services[9] could have granted a waiver for, "any experimental, pilot or demonstration project which, in the judgment of the secretary, is likely to assist in promoting the objectives . . . of the programs, including reduction of dependency, improvement of living conditions or increase of the incomes of individuals who are receiving public assistance." Some waiver programs, especially programs in the early years of section 1115, were fairly narrow in scope, mainly allowing for administrative changes at the state level such as automated re-eligibility notification, and computerization of certain state bureaucratic agency functions. But later state waiver programs also included highly visible and controversial state programs including early "workfare" projects, "two-tiered" benefit provision, and "learnfare."

The section 1115 waiver program was largely supplanted by the Temporary Assistance to Needy Families (TANF) portion of the Personal Responsibility and Work Opportunities Reconciliation Act of 1996. TANF, as discussed earlier, dismantled the AFDC program and transformed the national level welfare into a block grant program where states submit whole plans for their welfare programs to the federal government, thereby removing the necessity of applying for waivers to any federal stipulations.[10] Nonetheless, many commentators have argued that the waiver programs are both the precursors of and models for not only the present legislation, but also an earlier major federal welfare initiative, the Family Support Act of 1988.[11] Clearly state experimentation with welfare policy not only had an effect on the programs of the respective states, but it also profoundly affected the direction of national welfare policy. Thus despite the recent attention given to devolution, state welfare policy has long structured our efforts to provide relief to needy populations in the United States. In light of this reality, the recent turn to a block grant arrangement bespeaks the need to reexamine the extent to which a federalized welfare program can meet a standard of biblical justice, and if so, what structural constraints might be necessary.[12]

Biblical/Theological Principles

Above all other principles that must be discussed in order to examine the federalized welfare policy of the United States is the principle of justice. While the Bible is abundantly clear regarding the particular obligations of Christians toward the poor, the question of whether the state should be involved in the provision of welfare is an issue over which there has been a great deal of controversy, even within Christian communities.[13] This chapter appeals more broadly to a standard of public justice where the state, indeed, has a particular role to play and can act as an agent for justice. Dutch theologian and statesman Abraham Kuyper argues, in a speech concerning the role of "state aid" in addressing the problem of poverty, "God the Lord unmistakenly instituted the basic rule for the duty of government. Government exists to administer his justice on earth, and to uphold that justice."[14] This administration of justice, Kuyper suggests, entails arbitration between the various spheres of society when they come into conflict, or, in the parlance of pluralism, the maintenance of a "level playing field" among the various sectors of society.[15] Kuyper's commentary nicely crystallizes the reality that the state may have a role to play in providing for the needy in its larger role of administering God's justice on earth, and Kuyper's approach begins to speak to the requirements of biblically just public policy.

If we take the principal duty of the state to be the administration and upholding of justice, the question of what principles this entails for the making of just public policy, and specifically welfare policy, must be raised. Cochran, in a discussion of health care policy, suggests two important dimensions of public policy that are equally important in a discussion of welfare. First, just policy must ensure "equal membership of all citizens."[16] In the area of welfare policy this certainly means, as will be discussed below, that welfare programs must be governed by political bodies that are democratically organized, and which allow for involvement by the people who are affected by the results of welfare policy. The interests of one citizen, or group of citizens, must not be heard more loudly than another individual or group as policy decisions are made. Further, "equal membership of all citizens" when applied to welfare policy clearly bespeaks the need to ensure that no citizens are blocked from participation in the polity due to economic disenfranchisement. Second, Cochran suggests, government has the obligation in the provision of just policy to protect the common good. Just behavior by government entails careful attention to the management and distribution of public resources. Again, such a standard has particular implications for just welfare policy as welfare often entails redistribution of resources from some parts of society to others. In making these redistributive decisions, government takes on a no less than sacred obligation to ensure that resources are devoted to programs that contribute to the "equal membership of all citizens."

Within the foundational issue of the state's role in administering justice is the structural issue of whether one form of governmental administration is more likely to promote or enhance the cause of justice. Although the Bible does not speak to issues of federalism directly, the Old Testament is instructive with regard to the significance of the method of administration of government.[17,18] The account of Israel's transition from a nation ruled by decentralized judges to a nation ruled by a monarch centered in Jerusalem is the organizing theme of 1 and 2 Samuel, and this account can serve, at the very least, to speak to the threats and challenges posed by decentralized and centralized political rule. Although the most significant feature of this biblical narrative lies in what it reveals about the rebellious nature of the nation of Israel as it rejects God's sovereignty, this text merits some attention as it provides some limited description of the results of two forms of political rule.

In Genesis, Moses expresses his inability to adjudicate all of the cases brought before him, so he is instructed in Deuteronomy 16:18–20 as to the method through which he is to ensure just rule, and the gravity of maintaining a just political order:

> You shall appoint judges and officers throughout your tribes, in all your towns that the LORD your God is giving you, and they shall render just decisions for the people. You must not distort justice; you must not show partiality; you must not accept bribes, for a bribe blinds the eyes of the wise and subverts the cause of those who are in the right. Justice, and only jus-

tice, you shall pursue, so that you may live and occupy the
land that the LORD your God is giving you. (NRSV)

Political rule of the nation of Israel was to take place through a decentralized collection of the leaders of various tribes and their offi-
cers. In order to administer justice over a scattered people the Lord in
essence instructs Moses to federalize governmental power—that is, to
grant adjudicative power at both the tribal and municipal level. By the
time of Samuel, however, scripture reveals that the people doubted
the adequacy of these judges to govern them and demanded a king—a
centralized monarchy in Jerusalem—similar to the monarchies that
ruled surrounding nations (1 Samuel 4–5).

It is important to note that the political transition from a relatively decentralized form of government to a relatively centralized
one occurs within a social, political, and theological culture that was
and is unique to the biblical nation of Israel. Birch highlights for example, the "social and military pressures" that the nation of Israel
faced from neighboring nations—particularly the Philistines—during
this period.[19] But, reading the institution of a monarchy as purely an
act of "political or military expediency" is to misread the main thrust
of the text.[20] The institution of the monarchy, and the mirroring of
surrounding culture that it represented, led to a turning away from the
sufficiency of God's rule and the relatively egalitarian and contextually specific political rule that characterized the pre-monarchic era.
This narrative of transition is most powerful in its expression of the
risks of earthly political rule in general as such earthly rule invites the
potential for abuse, and for confusion over where sovereignty should
rightly reside—on earth or in heaven.

In this Old Testament narrative of transition from decentralized
to centralized political rule, no clear preference for centralized or decentralized administration of government is evident—despite the
warning that in seeking an earthly king the nation of Israel was in
fact rejecting the Lord (1 Samuel 7–8). Rather, the narrative speaks
to the fundamental sufficiency of God's rule of the nation of Israel,
both under the judges and under the kings. Hannah's prayer near the
beginning of the book of Samuel expresses this truth most clearly,
amid the struggles and confusion regarding the political rule of Israel.
This prayer is one of praise for the birth of Samuel, and it extols the
might and power of God. The prayer concludes, "The LORD will judge
the ends of the earth, he will give strength to his king, and exalt the
power of his anointed."[21] Above all methods of administering government, the Lord will serve as adjudicator and will empower those
whom he appoints to rule.

Still, this story makes clear that the troubles encountered by contrasting methods of governmental administration are different. The
threats posed by a certain type of centralized political rule are perhaps most evident. While Samuel's warning in 1 Samuel 8:10–18
speaks to the particular excesses of monarchic rule, it is nonetheless
clear that a centralized political power will necessitate the marshaling
of significant resources under the control of the king. Sons and daughters are to be called into service, and material resources were to be
taken for the king's use. Further, Samuel reports, complaints about
the excesses of this kind of rule will go unanswered by the Lord himself, as political sovereignty has been granted to an earthly king. In
what seems a strange response after these warnings, the Lord grants
Israel's request. Birch writes, "Kingship may be a sinful request by the
people, but if there is to be a king, then it will be God's king."[22] God's
king is given to the people, but this king is none the less, "borne of
their (the peoples') sin" and the prophecy granted to Samuel comes
true in its entirety. In short, the end of theocratic rule wreaks significant social and economic change on the people, and it alters the nature of their relationship with God.

The problems of decentralized rule by the judges are evident as
well. The final chapters of Judges tell of the moral decline of Israel,
and though the violation of the covenant with the Lord is the most
significant part of the story, the problem of coordination in a decentralized polity is clear as well. In Judges 17, and again in Judges 21 we
are told, "In those days there was no king in Israel; all the people did
what was right in their own eyes" (Judges 17: 6, 21:25). Consistent
interpretation of the law was lacking, and caused, at least in part, the
political instability in the nation of Israel that the people of Israel
perceived as contributing to their vulnerability to external foes and
thus to the need to establish a monarchy. While it bears repeating
that the principal importance of this narrative lies in the understanding that Israel's woes are the result of her having forsaken the
Lord, it seems that the lack of consistency, and the challenges of
"localism" borne of fractured political rule, bear some responsibility
as well.

These warnings concerning the resource-hungry, unjust efficiency
of centralized political rule and the problematic consistency and potential chaos of decentralized rule lead us to a broader consideration
of biblical and theological guidance in the just administration of government. As a theocracy, the nation of Israel cannot stand as a model
for either governmental resource usage or consistent political rule in
a modern, pluralistic, democratic state. We are left, then, with the
question of how these issues affect the development of just public
policy in a contemporary context. Given biblical exhortations first,

that the government is established to administer justice, and second, about the kinds of problems that flow from differing types of administration, what theological principles might provide assistance in deciding what level of government should administer a particular type of policy?

Subsidiarity is a theological concept from Roman Catholic social thought that merits particularly close attention in a discussion of federal governmental systems, and their potential for just public policy. In *Quadragesimo Anno* Pope Pius XI writes that, "it is an injustice and at the same time a grave evil and disturbance of right order to assign to a greater and higher association what lesser and subordinate organizations can do."[23] In this schema, the state is granted a particular position: "The supreme authority of the State ought, therefore, to let subordinate groups handle matters of lesser importance, which would otherwise dissipate its efforts greatly."[24] Subsidiarity seemingly has a fairly simple analog in the design of federalized governmental systems—national governments should not do those things that subnational governments can do. Three components of subsidiarity warrant closer examination when employing this concept to shed light on the appropriate role of states in a federal system in social policy provision. The first dimension is the effect that observance of subsidiarity as a norm may have on policy outcomes. The second is the role assigned to government, or, in the parlance of the encyclical, the state. Finally the question of whether, and to what extent, subsidiary arrangements make sense in the context of federalism in the United States will be examined.

Subsidiarity raises a particularly important and often neglected dimension of just policymaking—the autonomy and importance of the individual in policy decision making. This democratic impulse is expressed nicely by Greeley, who writes that subsidiarity is "a bias in favor of the maximization of participation in decision making in every sector of society."[25] Thus when applied to welfare policy, Greeley argues, "you eliminate poverty by giving the poor maximum power in making the decisions that will affect them."[26] This perspective on subsidiarity recognizes greater potential for direct democracy in situations where smaller institutions are involved. Certainly there are limits on the extent to which decision making can be delegated, as Greeley writes, "Obviously, under normal circumstances, workers in the shipping rooms cannot contribute much to the design of a new computer chip."[27] Greeley suggests that deciding what decisions should be delegated to a lower level of institution is an empirical—or perhaps prudential—question, rather than a theoretical one, with the unique nature of each decision determining the level at which decision making is to occur. Subsidiarity raises the question of whether leaving the responsibility for welfare to the states rather than to the federal government results in greater potential for democratic participation in policy decision making, and ultimately, as suggested above, a more just welfare policy.

Among the criticisms that have been leveled against subsidiarity is the problem that just as subsidiarity ensures the autonomy of the individual, it threatens the autonomy of the subsidiary institutions of society by carving out a privileged position for the state vis-à-vis these institutions in society.[28] Skillen and McCarthy make this argument, writing that subsidiarity fails because the very nature of the subunit is determined by the larger political whole of which it is a part. This poses a particular threat to institutions like the church that must therefore assume a position subordinate to the state, regardless of the institution's fitness to meet particular societal needs. Skillen and McCarthy argue that, as an institution, the state's role is the provision of justice, while other associations are better suited to meeting particular social needs that have little to do with the maintenance of a just societal order. Subsidiarity presumes that responsibilities accrue to institutions subsidiary to the state only as the state rejects them. This creates a situation, the authors argue, that acknowledges autonomy of individuals while subverting autonomy of institutions.[29] Thus, on the question of whether the states in the United States are structurally positioned to be able to administer just welfare policy, one might well examine the place provided for institutions other than the government to serve the function of administering welfare programs. In other words, do the states differ from the national government in the room that they allow for the operation of the other institutions of society in the provision of the public good?

Despite the power of this critique concerning the politicizing effect of subsidiarity on the subsidiary institutions, it fails to acknowledge fully a differentiated position for smaller units of government within the whole of the "state." Skillen and McCarthy write: "Cities and counties are lesser governmental administrative bodies which possess some autonomy (relative independence) within a single political whole."[30] This understanding may understate the potential for virtually wholly autonomous policymaking by the states, a situation that has resulted under the TANF program where fifty unique welfare plans have been developed. The ambiguity surrounding the "relative independence" of states and other "subsidiary" governmental institutions (and whether they should indeed be depicted as "subsidiary") stems in part from the ambiguous nature of the analogy between subsidiarity and contemporary federalist governmental arrangements.

Subsidiarity is mentioned most frequently in contemporary political discourse as a way of describing the arrangements among member states in the European Union. Bermann provides a useful distinction between jurisdictional and procedural subsidiarity. Jurisdictional subsidiarity is, "a principle describing the allocation of substantive authority between the Community and the member states." This type of subsidiarity has to do with the assigning of responsibilities within certain territorial borders for different governmental entities. In contrast, procedural subsidiarity asks the superior institutions in a subsidiary relationship "to engage in a particular inquiry before concluding that action at the Community rather than member State level is warranted."[31] Skillen and McCarthy would presumably argue that the Catholic Church's teaching on subsidiarity inverts procedural subsidiarity, with the state assuming complete responsibility for action save when a compelling case can be made that another institution should play this role.[32] Rejecting this part of the Catholic Church's formulary, however, neglects the jurisdictional aspect of subsidiarity as it applies to cities or states. Perhaps, just as some institutions of society are better suited to certain tasks than the government, certain levels of the government are better suited to certain substantive areas of policy concern than others.

It is surely the case that jurisdictional subsidiarity is a more apt depiction of federalist arrangements in the United States than is procedural subsidiarity. Bermann writes that, "The U.S. system offers few political or legal guarantees that the federal government will act only when persuaded that the states cannot or will not do so on their own."[33] This is equally apparent in the executive and legislative branches of government. In Congress, the operating principle is that, due to its membership composition, it will not be completely inattentive to the interests of the states in maintaining a certain degree of regulatory autonomy, yet "claiming" of credit by members of Congress still occurs largely for national level projects. No systematic evaluations of the states' capacity for addressing certain types of problems—their "procedural" capacity—occur before the Congress acts to make national policy in response to them.[34] In the executive branch, each agency is under orders to minimize the so-called regulatory burden on the states. President Bush espoused jurisdictional subsidiarity more explicitly than others in the executive branch, in executive order 12,612, drawing a distinction between national problems and those that were shared by the states.[35]

Bermann suggests that a number of fundamental values underlie subsidiary governmental arrangements, including self-determination and accountability, political liberty, flexibility, preservation of identities, diversity, and respect for internal division of component states.[36] If subsidiarity characterizes United States federalism, it reflects the value of flexibility more than any other single value. This flexibility, Bermann writes, "permits a community to reflect more closely the unique combination of circumstances—physical, economic, social, moral and cultural. . . . It may also enable the community to respond appropriately to the changes of circumstances that occur within it from time to time."[37] Historically, as noted earlier, welfare policy has entailed a certain assumption of state responsibility, and therefore varying degrees of state flexibility. AFDC policy may well have embodied subsidiary arrangements that reflect the importance of flexibility as a political value of American federalism. AFDC was set up as a matching grant program, which entailed certain obligations by the states, although the states still set benefit levels. Beyond this, as noted earlier, the states were given a certain amount of flexibility with regard to experimental projects and programs that could be conducted under section 1115 of the Social Security Act.[38] Welfare policy under the PRWORA goes a step further toward state flexibility, giving states nearly total programmatic freedom in setting up welfare programs that will be funded through a block grant by the federal government.

These issues surrounding subsidiarity provide a useful launching pad for an exploration of the adequacy of federal arrangements for administering just welfare policy. By carefully looking for the extent to which both individual and institutional autonomy are preserved, and by examining the extent to which the states are uniquely suited to the project of welfare reform, the most salient aspects of subsidiarity can be brought to bear upon the question of the effect of federalism on welfare reform. The real value of a full consideration of subsidiarity lies in its power to remind us of the divisions in political and administrative authority that shape the arrangements a society makes for administering social policy.

This brief discussion of the biblical and theological principles most important to a consideration of welfare policy in a federal system suggests three broad set of concerns that will be addressed in the final section of this chapter. First, we should be cognizant of the particular problems inherent in different kinds of governments, most notably problems with efficiency in centralized government and trouble with consistency in decentralized arrangements. Second, we should be concerned about the extent to which policymaking processes incorporate space for individual participation, and a fully differentiated role for subsidiary institutions. Finally, we must investigate whether the states are uniquely suited to certain policy tasks or, alternatively, whether certain tasks must always be accomplished by the national government. In order to assess the capacity of the federal system for making just welfare policy, these standards will be applied to the section 1115 waiver program and the TANF.

Competing Approaches to the Question of the States' Role in Welfare Policy

Three competing approaches to answering the question of whether the states can justly administer welfare policy can be identified. The first approach suggests, as discussed earlier, that this question is, for the most part, not the question to ask. The more pressing question, and therefore the more interesting one, concerns the details of the policy programs themselves—who is included, what requirements the programs will have for participation, what needs standards will be, how and whether supportive services will be provided. Devolution for many seems to be a rather unimportant issue, despite greater faith in the lower levels of government.[39] Christian commentators have often taken this approach, emphasizing justice to individuals and to "mediating structures" without a full acknowledgment of the role that the particular policy arrangements may play in meeting these goals.[40] However, leaving aside the role of federalism—both historically and currently—in an assessment of welfare policy misses an important part of the puzzle.

A second approach assumes that the states are inherently more likely to do damage to indigent populations due to structural realities of American federalism and the disincentives it creates for making just social policy.[41] These arguments can take an historical or economic form. The most straightforward historical version of the argument suggests that given a legacy of discriminatory behavior, the states cannot be trusted, and that to "rollback" welfare responsibilities to the states would be to, in effect, turn back the civil rights clock as well. The more complex and compelling argument in defense of this perspective is articulated by Paul Peterson.[42] Peterson builds a typology of public policy, based upon the policy's likely impact on the subnational governmental unit. The subnational governmental unit has a strong disincentive to create what Peterson terms redistributive policy—that is, policy that redistributes income from one group to another. This type of policy, in contrast to distributive or regulatory policy, makes a governmental entity less attractive to would-be "investors," who will be taxed to provide the funds that will be redistributed, but who will not receive any particular benefits from this type of policy. Spending money for social policy programs, according to this argument, does not make the state any more attrac-

tive to business interests who might locate in the city (or state), and
cities (or states) must attract businesses in order to remain economically viable.

Building on this understanding, Peterson and Rom extend the argument to an examination of welfare policy in a federal system in
their oft-cited book, *Welfare Magnets*. Reacting to anecdotal evidence
that states with relatively more generous welfare policy might "attract" residents of nearby states with lower benefit levels, Peterson
and Rom build a case for a national benefits standard. Using aggregate
level data on state poverty rates and the combined dollar amount of
food stamps plus AFDC benefit levels, these authors demonstrate that
states with high AFDC benefit levels experienced large increases in
their poverty rates that could not be explained through rising unem-
ployment or declining wages. From this result, the authors argue that
at least part of the increase in poverty rates for these states must be
due to the in-migration of indigent populations who were seeking
higher AFDC benefits. The practical result of their findings is, therefore, that a federal system which allows states to offer different welfare benefit levels will cause a general overall depression in benefit
levels as states seek to avoid becoming welfare magnets.[43] This approach to the question of the proper role for the states in welfare
policy would hold that, at the very least, a national minimum standard must be established for benefit levels; otherwise, the states will
compete in a "race to the bottom" to avoid having to shoulder the
burden of increasing welfare rolls.

This evidence at the aggregate level has been disputed with individual level data by Hanson and Hartmann who argue that individual
residential choices among indigent populations fail to sustain the
macro level argument. Using individual level data these authors examined the rate of interstate migration for poor women of child-
bearing age and found little migration at all. In short, these authors
allege it may not be that states were amending benefit levels in response to increases in indigent populations so much as they did so in
the face of the perception that they were "welfare magnets."[44]

The welfare magnets argument and this critique, however, ignore
the programmatic dimension of welfare policy—that is, might low
income people move to participate in a program that was considered
more likely to lead to work, more generous with regard to supportive
services, etc.? The evidence from Hanson and Hartmann concerning
the interstate migration rates of the poor would cast doubt on this
proposition, although their evidence does not allow for a complete
rejection of it. What is clear, given the Hanson and Hartmann critique and the lack of consideration of programmatic factors, is that a
wholesale rejection of a federalized welfare system on the basis of the

welfare magnets contention is not warranted. Rather, what this discussion suggests is that a cautious eye must be cast toward the structural (dis)incentives that the federal system creates for state level welfare policymaking.

A final, general approach to the question of the states' role in welfare policy suggests that there are distinct policy advantages to having fifty states attempting to address the problem in different ways. There are essentially three variants of this argument. The first approach is the so-called laboratories of democracy version of the states' role in the policy process. Justice Brandeis, in a dissenting opinion in *New State Ice Co. of Oklahoma City v. Liebman* (1932), wrote that it is one of the "happy accidents of the federal system that a single courageous state may, if its citizens choose, serve as a laboratory." Because individual states can try different policy alternatives with less risk and perhaps less effort than the nation as a whole, their policy experiments can provide comparative data concerning the likely success or failure of policy programs. With the national government presumably acting as "lab manager," the states can experiment with a variety of policy alternatives and the national government will coordinate and gather the results of the experiments. Presumably this information can then be used by other states and the national government to devise solutions to similar policy problems.

Whether this phenomenon actually occurs is the subject of scant scholarly attention. There is some evidence to support the claim that states learn from one another in a more direct fashion, adopting policy programs that fit similar needs. The speed of the spread of innovations, and the conditions necessary for the spread of innovation across the states have been thoroughly investigated, but the question of the federal government's role in the testing of policy programs is rather ambiguous.[45] While some scholars have posited a "vertical" diffusion phenomenon where policies spread from the states to the federal government, others have suggested that the vertical relationship has an impact only in those instances where particular inducements are put on the development of policy.[46] Anecdotal evidence suggests that the likelihood of the federal government serving as a clearinghouse of information on state welfare policy programs is slim. Interviews with Department of Health and Human Services officials indicate that neither the necessary resources nor incentives exist at the federal level to create such an arrangement.

Another argument for a variety of state programs is that it allows for diverse responses to diverse situations. Since states have radically different populations, sources of employment, cultures, and politics, this approach suggests that they should be given sufficient latitude to meet their various needs. This argument is used to defend devolution that leads to state approaches to policy problems that are more tai-lor-made than the programs designed at the federal level and imple-mented at the state level. While on its face this argument has par-ticular merit in the design of social policy, in contrast to regulatory policy in which states seem to enact remarkably similar policy, the question remains whether the states differ significantly enough to warrant broad latitude in policy design.

Clearly none of these three approaches provides much help in the search for an answer to the question of whether the states can ad-minister welfare policy in a biblically just fashion. Obviously the first approach falls short in that the method of administration does mat-ter, as part one of this chapter argues. The second line of argu-ment—that states will necessarily fall short in the development and administration of welfare reforms—is a line of argument that has been subject, as noted above, to a considerable amount of criticism in the scholarly literature. Finally, the argument that an approach to welfare reform that embodies diversity is the proper approach be-cause diversity in welfare policy is necessarily a worthy goal is not self-evident.

As suggested earlier, the suitability of particular levels of govern-ment to particular tasks is perhaps largely an empirical question. What this review of existing approaches to the role of the states in welfare reform seems to demonstrate most clearly is that in this field of study, ideology has often determined the way in which the search for evidence has been framed. None of the existing approaches allows for a distinctively Christian response to the devolution of welfare policymaking responsibility. An examination of previous state ef-forts and the likely direction of current proposals, in light of the standards established in the third part of this chapter may provide ad-ditional insight into the fitness of the states for welfare policy devel-opment and administration.

Public Policy Proposal

Developing a policy proposal for an appropriate role for the states in welfare policy requires an appraisal of current and past efforts by the states to enact their own welfare programs under the federal umbrella. This section applies the standards developed in the third part of this chapter to early appraisals of the TANF program, and state experi-ence with section 1115 waivers.[47] How do state welfare programs measure up against the standards of efficiency, coordination, and jus-tice to individuals and mediating structures? Do the states themselves warrant treatment as differentiated political structures? Answers to these questions give some guidance on the states' appropriate role in welfare policy development and administration.

Efficiency

The first standard against which federalized welfare policy might be judged is that of efficiency—that is, does nationalizing a program lead to greater inefficiencies than might be expected if the programs were left to the localities? There are essentially two ways to test this proposition. First, will the states use fewer resources in administering welfare programs than the federal government does? Second, will the national government save resources by further decentralizing? Examination of the cost estimates for the TANF program is necessary in order to answer these questions.

As a general proposition, it does not appear that devolution serves to conserve resources. Even under the most general terms, the likelihood that devolution can save money is small. Donahue reports that because of the fact that much of the perceived inefficiency in public spending is due to middle-class entitlements and debt service, the transfer of responsibilities to the states will have minimal impact. Were the states to assume all federal government responsibilities apart from check writing and defense responsibilities, and were the states to perform all of these duties at a 10 percent reduction in cost, Donahue reports that the total cost of government in the United States would fall by less than 0.5 percent.[48]

Whether delegating specific increased programmatic welfare responsibilities to the states will prove more efficient is more difficult to estimate. Nearly all sources, including the Clinton administration and the American Public Welfare Association, estimate that over the first six years of operation of TANF the national government will save about $55 billion over spending levels for AFDC in 1995. These savings, however, will come almost entirely from trimming the numbers of those eligible for the program: what economies may be had will not result from devolution. Furthermore, whereas AFDC was an entitlement program that, at least in theory, had a funding structure that would expand or contract with the number of individuals who were eligible for the entitlement, TANF is a fixed, block grant program that awards monies to states based upon a set formula.[49] From the perspective of cost efficiency, devolution of responsibility by itself will not yield any particular benefits that could not have been achieved without devolution of programmatic responsibility.

Coordination

Under TANF, states are required to submit a complete plan for certification to the Department of Health and Human Services in order to receive their block grant funding. A Department of Health and Human Services memo to various state welfare officials contains answers to questions from the states about the coordination of TANF. This memo makes the problem of coordinating so many state plans clear.[50] The first question in this memo asks what "completeness" means in the context of TANF plans, how long certification will take, when monies from the federal government will be received, when requirements will go into effect, and what the nature of the "comment period" for state plans should be. These questions, put most succinctly, are coordination issues—that is, what are the standards of this plan, and how will they be enforced? The response to this question is telling, as it gives only the broadest contours of what states should do, but ends with the caveat, "The determination that a plan is complete must be made on a case-by-case basis." Coordination of state efforts, which would be, by any standard, a difficult task given the ambiguity in statutory language and the enormity of the task, is clearly not being fully accomplished as state plans are judged only from case to case.

But coordination problems have historically plagued welfare programs in this federal system. Section 1115 waiver programs were similarly under- or uncoordinated efforts, with continuous internal discrepancies erupting as to the program goals, and as to appropriate state efforts in light of those goals. Internal Department of Health Education and Welfare (HEW) discussion of the waiver program in the early 1970s comments upon the lack of clear programmatic goals, which was causing "serious misinterpretation" and "abuse" of the waiver program, thereby allowing states to redefine their section 1115 waivers from a limited, experimental type program to essentially perpetual waiver programs where the "experimentation" continued indeterminately.[51]

Despite this confusion and apparent lack of coordination, no efforts were made to standardize what the priorities of the waiver programs were until the late 1970s when the Department of Health and Human Services began posting the agency's substantive priorities for section 1115 waivers in the federal register. These postings between 1978 and 1984 note the priority areas for state experimentation, and most postings included the caveat that, "unsolicited proposals of other topics will be considered only if judged to be of greater potential value" than the priorities identified by the federal government.[52] While these postings would appear to serve the goal of greater coordination, in each of these years the states were permitted to engage in many waiver demonstration projects in areas that were not listed as federal priorities.

Through the late 1980s and early 1990s, the states enacted a variety of reforms, but no attempts were made to coordinate state efforts again until 1995 when the Clinton administration created a process that shortened the period of time for review of state waiver applications. This process isolated five strategies for reform programs that would be given particular priority.[53] Increasingly, before the 1995 Federal Register notice, waiver programs had become a means for the states to engage in reforms that did not necessarily meet the spirit or the letter of federal law, and the lack of coordination prompted a thorough revamping of the waiver process, including a thirty-day turn-around on waiver reviews. The incidence of state applications for waivers rose sharply from 1992 to 1996, and while the national government finally responded with some formal means of coordination, the lack of coordination that caused the "silent revolution" in welfare reform had already occurred.

This consideration reveals that no clear preference for the states can be defended on the basis of their inherently greater efficiency, nor can federal government administration be preferred for its potential for the generation of more consistent policy. While central administration does seem to lead to certain inefficiencies, state administration is not necessarily a cure. Similarly, while decentralization causes coordination difficulties, even when the central government does make efforts to coordinate state policy programs, the states do not always respond in the expected fashion. This reality raises the question of whether state level administration should be preferred for its greater capacity for administering policy programs that do greater justice to individuals and other societal institutions.

Justice to Individuals

In section three of this chapter, the concept of subsidiarity was raised as one possible standard against which the decision to further decentralize welfare policy might be judged. While subsidiarity falls short in its treatment of societal institutions other than states, it nonetheless highlights an important dimension of public policymaking in a democratic polity—a maximizing of individual participation in policymaking by those affected by the policy. In theory, as decisions are left to the subsidiary institutions—provided the institutions are democratically organized—in society, it becomes more possible and plausible that individuals will be able to act to shape the policies that affect them. Whether this is likely is the question to be addressed in this section.

On first glance, it seems rather evident that state administration of welfare policy does little more to advance democratic participation in the policy process than does policymaking at the national level. Section 1115 waiver applications were sent from state departments of human services, and TANF proposals are developed in a similar fashion. Although state efforts to move welfare recipients from welfare to work have often involved programs which engage the individual in direct ways in an employment search, it is by no means clear that moving policymaking responsibility to the state level will necessarily result in more democratic decision making, or in greater inclusion of those who will be affected by public policy in the decision making process.

This said, however, the sheer numbers of different kinds of projects conducted by the states, particularly under the section 1115 waiver program, led to a few programs that did increase the participation of individuals in implementing solutions to the policy problem. While perhaps not as impressive an achievement as actually including those affected by a policy in the design of a program that will affect them, granting increased flexibility in the implementation of policy programs allows for more sensitivity to individual idiosyncrasies, and perhaps for a better likelihood of successful policy intervention.

Notable among these programs was an effort in the late 1980s by five states that engaged in a self employment section 1115 waiver project. While lack of full coordination of these efforts makes it difficult to assess the success of these programs, the inclusion of a potential for more active recipient involvement in decision making was inherent in the program's design. In these demonstration projects, the states developed a program for self-employment for certain AFDC recipients, thereby rather intimately involving the individuals who would be affected by a policy program in the implementation, if not the design, of the program itself.

Still, this particular program is more the exception than the rule and current stipulations for TANF are not uniformly centered on individual involvement even in the implementation process. In order to meet the federal government's criteria for "work activities" under TANF, states will only be allowed to include 20 percent of their caseloads in vocational training or secondary educational programs for teen parents. And, despite language in the statute that suggests that states *can* develop personal responsibility plans for recipients, the states are only required to make "an initial assessment of the recipients' skills." States are therefore under considerable constraints, and are not provided with any particular incentives to develop policy that incorporates increased space for individual action in the implementation of policy. Flexibility in and of itself may occasionally, as with the self-employment waivers, lead to policy that incorporates more space for individual involvement, but such an occurrence is by no means a foregone conclusion.

Further, the increased flexibility given the states may to some degree do more harm to individuals than may be first perceived. Though the point here may be a semantic one, it resonates throughout our policy discussions and decisions. With uncoordinated flexibility, the states can increasingly narrow and vary the ways in which the poor are defined, thereby creating a situation where increasingly punitive policy becomes nearly a foregone conclusion. Due to the existence of at least fifty different approaches to welfare policy, it will become less possible to dispute inaccurate characterizations of welfare recipients that follow from limited state experience or from unfortunate naming of programs. Without better coordination and enforcement than has been witnessed to date at the federal level, the attention of both advocates for the needy, and of the needy themselves, will increasingly be cast in many directions in an effort to stem the damage to individuals, rather than directed toward the coordinating entity in an effort to enact more just policy.

Justice to Societal Institutions

On the basis of the perception that the states are less "bureaucratic" and perhaps more likely to be subject to regional cultural affinities that would support the activities of a variety of societal institutions, some might argue that there is sufficient prima facie evidence for the states creating a more hospitable environment than the federal government for these institutions. The reality, however, is that state and local bureaucracies have witnessed growth rates four to five times the growth rates of the federal government, employing around 15 million people in contrast to the nearly 3.1 million employed by the federal government.[54]

Theda Skocpol, in a set of reflections on the revival of civic life in the United States, has suggested that the belief that voluntary associations flourish in an environment of "small" government is a nostalgic view with limited empirical support.[55] Rather, she notes, the "era of association" from the 1820s to the 1840s was an era that saw not only the rise of voluntary associations, but also the rise of political structures and political activity—a growth in political parties and a continuing spread of adult male suffrage. Skocpol examines a variety of other periods in our history, concluding that there is no inverse relationship between the growth of voluntary associations and the development of political structures. Thus, the positing of an easy relationship between state level government—presuming that government at the state level means "less government"—and more just treatment of nongovernmental societal institutions is perhaps too facile a connection to make. Rather, of much greater importance is the nature of each government's perception of its responsibilities and the extent to which the processes established by the government will make room for the operation of these other institutions.

The question of whether state level administration of welfare programs will provide a more hospitable environment for the activities for nongovernmental societal institutions is an empirical question that is difficult to address given the limited experience that the states have in this regard. Section 1115 waiver programs were only made available for use by state departments of social services or the equivalent state level agency. The PRWORA, in contrast, contains a provision that invites the states to consider the use of charitable and faith-based institutions in their efforts to serve needy populations. This "charitable choice" provision provides a hopeful, if untested, window into a fuller flourishing of nongovernmental institutions' activities in addressing needy populations.[56]

In an interesting recent development, the lines between "private" and "public" institutions have begun to be drawn in an effort made by Texas to use private sector firms in the administration of its welfare program. Under the Texas plan, private businesses rather than states employees would interview applicants and make eligibility determinations for the approximately $8 billion that the state distributes. In a broader sense, this plan was seen primarily as a threat to the nation's 200,000 public employees who administer welfare programs, but one of the concerns that bears upon the discussion at hand is the worry that states would create incentives for private entities to contain costs—by subtly denying benefits or discouraging applications. The Texas proposal, and a compromise measure offered by HHS, were rejected by the Clinton administration in a gesture that begins to draw the line as to what this particular administration will allow by way of "privatization." While seemingly ready to allow the states to experiment with a variety of other reform proposals, the administration through this decision has, in a practical sense, constrained the authority to privatize their welfare programs granted them in the PRWORA.[57] While this case deals with a for-profit, "private" entity, it nonetheless may speak to the caution surrounding efforts to involve nongovernmental players.

Are the States Differentiated Political Structures?

Finally, the questions as to whether the states themselves should be conceived of as differentiated political institutions and whether they are uniquely suited to the making of welfare policy deserve attention. Certain commentators have argued that among the more ingenious features of the founders' design for government is that we have been provided with a "spare" in the event that one level does not respond to the political process in appropriate ways.[58] But do the states necessarily show a particular proclivity for the making of social policy, and welfare policy in particular?

Evidence discussed earlier suggests that the states may have disincentives for the creation of social policy that will be perceived as overly generous because of the inevitable "competition" that ensues between the states. Beyond this, however, the political structures in the states may also contribute to a context in which the influence of particular interests is more intense than it might be at the federal level. Indeed, there is some evidence to suggest that the states may be more susceptible to the will of organized interests than the federal government. While the nationalization of interest groups is a well-documented phenomenon, and while old tales of "business capture" of state legislatures are no longer entirely true, some evidence exists that the states may demonstrate meso-corporatist arrangements where certain "peak" institutions may exert control over the political structures in the states.[59]

Further, the history of state experimentation with welfare policy through the section 1115 demonstration projects suggests that state efforts at reform are largely of the "try anything" variety. Rather than systematically learning from one another or from guidelines established by the federal government, states seem to respond to particular political pressures in order to create policy that suits their electorates, independent of the evidence of a particular policy program's success or failure. Research on state policy innovation has consistently shown that nearly regardless of policy type, both necessity as the "mother of invention" and the presence of slack resources affect the course of public policy in the states.[60]

Thus, while the states add another layer of political institutions to the development of welfare policy in a federal system—with state legislatures and executive branch agencies exercising a fair measure of control—their activities seem rather more oriented toward expediting the political process than toward developing any particular policy expertise. In short, it seems that although the welfare policy efforts by the states may show certain idiosyncratic features that might appear to be an attempt to meet a particular set of concerns in a state, the resultant policy itself may be more likely to be a gesture to give the "squeaky wheel" grease, rather than an attempt to address the root of the problem. States rarely seem to be more hospitable environments for the making of welfare policy than the federal government, and they may be a good deal less so.

Conclusion

This chapter presents initial evidence to demonstrate the extent to which reforming the nation's welfare system depends upon careful consideration of the role of the states in the development and administration of welfare policy. While the argument that the states provide us with a "spare" government to turn to for hopeful signs of efficiency and creativity in an era of federal gridlock and waste holds a certain appeal, this portrayal is not necessarily accurate, nor should it, on its face, constitute the foundation for a Christian perspective on the issue of devolution and welfare reform. Consideration of the extent to which the federal system fosters policy that does justice to individuals and the institutions of society, and of whether the states should have separate standing as differentiated political structures, reveals a far more complex picture.

Rather than providing an invective for or against state administration and development of welfare policy, my argument shows that the policy context posed by each of the states warrants attention. There is no "silver theological bullet" that allows for a quick and sure assessment of the necessity of a highly centralized or highly decentralized system of welfare policy administration for the making of biblically just welfare policy. However, given the track record of inefficiency, poor coordination, and policies which seem to fall short of a standard of justice to both individuals and groups, the history of federalized welfare policy in this country is not one about which much satisfaction can be expressed. What is necessary above all is attentiveness to the particular policies enacted by the states under TANF as they develop through the coming years' and careful analysis of the results of those reforms.

An encouraging sign regarding this first step in full assessment of the impact of devolution on welfare reform is the fact that a good deal of centralized data collection and coordination among organizations collecting data has already begun. Christian analysts and other welfare watch groups are carefully cataloging the implementation of TANF and its various provisions through the states, and their efforts at better and more thorough data collection will enable better and more thorough appraisals by Christians concerned about just welfare policy.[61] From this evidence we can begin to develop careful, prudential, empirically grounded conclusions about the extent to which centralized control is needed in order for welfare reform to meet the requirements of biblical justice.

Appendix A

A Brief Glossary of Selected Welfare-Related Terms

ADC   Aid to Dependent Children. This was the name given to the original federal government cash assistance program under the Social Security Act of 1935, which provided income to children and mothers who did not have the support of a male income earner.

AFDC Aid to Families with Dependent Children. This program supplanted the original ADC program in 1950 as Congress amended the Social Security Act to include so-called caretaker grants to mothers of dependent children.

Block Grant   A block grant is a transfer of money from the federal government to the states that allows the states a great deal of discretion in determining how the money will be spent. Under a block grant the states are given a set of basic guidelines from Congress as to how monies may be used.

Entitlement   A legal relationship between individuals and government under which individuals are legally entitled to certain benefits from government should they meet eligibility criteria.

Learnfare   Learnfare programs were intended to provide incentives for AFDC families to ensure that school-aged children were attending school regularly. These programs either provided cash awards to families whose children met attendance standards or imposed sanctions on families whose children did not.

PRWORA   Personal Responsibility and Work Opportunity Reconciliation Act. This law, signed in 1996, creates the TANF program, which is described below. Other significant changes were made to other dimensions of public welfare, including child care, child support enforcement, benefits for legal immigrants, the Food Stamp Program, and SSI for children.

TANF Temporary Assistance to Needy Families. This program is the centerpiece of PRWORA and eliminates AFDC, JOBS, and Emergency Assistance (EA) and replaces them with a block grant to the states. States will be required to demonstrate that certain percentages of their recipient populations are participating in work activities according to a schedule stipulated by the legislation. Further, cash assistance under TANF is of a time-limited nature. The amount of a state's block grant is computed by adding its previous expenditures in AFDC, EA, and JOBS.

Two-Tiered Benefit   These kinds of programs provided different cash benefit levels to welfare recipients who were residents of a state prior to applying for welfare benefits than to those who moved to a state immediately prior to applying for benefits. The intent of this program was to reduce the "welfare magnet" effect where indigent populations would move to a state with higher benefit levels for the purposes of increasing their income.

Section 1115 Waivers The 1962 amendments to the Social Security Act allowed states to request that the federal government exempt them from compliance with certain requirements of the AFDC program. State departments of human services, or the equivalent state agency, could apply for waivers to the provisions of the program that dealt with eligibility criteria and with the means through which recipients were paid. Beyond this, waiver programs were to have a mechanism for "rigorous evaluation" and be cost neutral to the federal government.

Workfare   In the most general sense workfare programs require welfare recipients to work in order to receive a cash benefit. These programs go beyond the requirements of the Job Opportunities and Basic Skills program, which required work readiness and education activities for AFDC recipients, to require that welfare recipients accept employment rather than just engage in preparation for future employment.

Notes

This chapter was originally developed as a Crossroads Doctoral Scholar monograph. The author gratefully acknowledges the careful reading and thoughtful comments of

Clarke Cochran and Darren Walhof, and helpful and interesting discussions with Keith Pavlischek, Stanley Carlson-Thies, the 1996 class of Crossroads Doctoral Scholars, and Crossroads Conference attendees. I also wish to thank the staff and leadership of Evangelicals for Social Action, and the Pew Charitable Trusts for their facilitation of the Crossroads Program. Scripture quotations contained herein are from the New Revised Standard Version Bible, copyright, 1989, by the Division of Christian Education of the National Council of the Churches of Christ in the U.S.A. Used by permission. All rights reserved.

1. See Appendix A for a glossary of technical, legal, and statutory terms relating to welfare policy.

2. Peter Edelman, "The Worst Thing Bill Clinton Has Done," *The Atlantic Monthly* 279, no. 3 (March 1997): 43–58. Edelman resigned with two other high profile HHS officials—Mary Jo Bane, Assistant Secretary for Children and Families, and Wendell Primus, Deputy Assistant Secretary for Human Services Policy. Primus defends his resignation noting, "The bill could have been significantly better. We should have provided the funding that was necessary to move recipients to work rather than merely mandating that they do so. The political system, however, that wanted to balance the budget was convinced that social policy was not working. From a Christian perspective, we are called to have compassion for all of our neighbors." James Skillen, "Not All Welfare Needs To Be Reformed: An Interview with Wendell Primus," *Public Justice Report* 20, no. 2 (March–April 1997): 4. A similar statement by Primus appears in *Discernment* 4, no. 3 (Fall, 1996). For Bane's explanation of the reasons for her resignation see "Stand By for Casualties" *New York Times*, November 10, 1996, E13.

3. Public support for devolution is both widespread and strong. A 1995 Washington Post/Kaiser Foundation/Harvard University poll found that 61 percent of respondents agreed that their state governments could be trusted to "do a better job running things" than the federal government, compared to 21 percent who thought the federal government would do a better job. All subgroups of this sample, except black and Jewish voters, agreed that the states were more trustworthy. John D. Donahue, "The Disunited States," *The Atlantic Monthly* 279, no. 5 (May 1997): 19–22.

4. Prior to significant amendment of the Aid to Families with Dependent Children provisions of the Social Security Act in 1962 and 1967, respectively, states routinely instituted punitive measures to reduce the number of welfare recipients and deter applicants. Residency requirements intended to prevent migration from southern states to northern states, and so-called suitable home provisions, which included "man in the house" rules in which the presence of any man regardless of his economic condition or relationship to the family in the home rendered it "unsuitable" ostensibly because financial need could not exist, were instituted as the demographic nature of the AFDC program changed from a program composed primarily of white widows to one with greater racial diversity.

5. Michael Kinsley, *Time,* January 16, 1995, 78.

6. The justice of particular substantive types of welfare reform programs is not the subject of this chapter, and although the substance of various programs necessarily impacts the degree to which welfare policy is judged to be just, this chapter's purpose is to address the narrower question of the effect of the structure of federalism on the justice of welfare reform(s). Various Christian scholars and activists have considered the justness of a variety of welfare reforms and have considered the particular need for welfare programs in a just polity. This literature is too voluminous for a full review or discussion in here. For an excellent introduction to a variety of Christian approaches to this subject see *Welfare in America: Christian Perspectives on a*

Policy in Crisis, ed. Stanley Carlson-Thies and James Skillen (Grand Rapids, Mich.: Wm. B. Eerdmans, 1996).

7. For a more complete depiction of the substance of mother's/widow's pensions, and their position in the evolution of social welfare programs, see William I. Trattner, *From Poor Law to Welfare State: A History of Social Welfare in America* (New York: Macmillan, 1989), especially chapter 10. For an account of the mechanism behind the rapid diffusion of mother's pensions through the states, see Theda Skocpol, Christopher Howard, Susan Goodrich Lehmann and Marjorie Abend-Wein, "Women's Associations and the Enactment of Mother's Pensions in the United States," *American Political Science Review* 87, no. 3 (1993): 686–701.

8. The name of the program shifted from the Aid to Dependent Children program to the Aid to Families with Dependent Children program in 1950. The AFDC program was the cash portion of the federal welfare program. This program was developed to provide income to children and their guardians in the event that the principal wage earner was unemployed, dead, incapacitated, or not present. Under AFDC a legal entitlement relationship was made between the recipient and the federal government. If a person met the eligibility requirements for AFDC—essentially income limits set by the states—that person was entitled to receive a cash benefit. Under the TANF (Temporary Assistance to Needy Families) program, no legal entitlement relationship exits. Rather, the states, within federal guidelines, set the terms under which persons may receive any cash assistance. No person is automatically entitled to a benefit merely by meeting certain eligibility requirements.

9. Initially, this section of the Social Security Act applied to the Department of Health, Education and Welfare, the precursor to the Department of Health and Human Services.

10. For a more complete discussion of the options available to the states with section 1115 waivers in operation at the time of the enactment of the new law see Mark Greenberg and Steve Savner, *Waivers and the New Welfare Law: Initial Approaches in State Plans Center for Law and Social Policy* (Occasional Paper Center for Law and Social Policy, 1996).

11. The fact that policies spread from one state to another, and that their spread can affect federal policymaking has been well established by many scholars. In fact, Hanson and Heaney argue that a "silent Revolution" in welfare policy occurred through the waivers granted during the Bush administration and Clinton's first team (Russell L. Hanson and Michael T. Heaney, "The Silent Revolution in Welfare: AFDC Waivers during the Bush and Clinton Administrations." Unpublished paper presented at the 1997 meeting of the Midwest Political Science Association, Chicago, Ill.).

12. Focusing on the section 1115 waiver programs and the TANF program provides a means for assessing the effect on the federal system on welfare policies, as both of these programs entailed some action on the part of the states, as well as nominal approval by the national government. State general assistance programs, the part of welfare controlled exclusively by the states, are too idiosyncratic to warrant drawing any broader conclusions. As of the summer of 1996, 42 states had a general assistance program, but only 33 of these programs were in operation throughout the state. Nine states have abolished their general assistance programs entirely, among them the state of Michigan. Of the 42 states with general assistance programs only 12 states provide assistance to all financially needy persons who do not receive some federal aid. For a more thorough description of state general assistance programs, see Cori E. Uccello, Heather R. McCallum, and L. Jerome Gallagher, *State General Assistance Programs 1996,* Urban Institute, no. 6719, (1996). The scope of state effort for general assistance programs in contrast to their efforts under AFDC and TANF is also rather small, with spending on general assistance programs in

1992 amounting to only 4 percent of state and local spending on programs for low-income persons. (Mark Rom, "Health and Welfare in the American States," in *Politics in the American States: A Comparative Analysis*, ed. Virginia Gray and Herbert Jacob [Washington, DC: Congressional Quarterly Press, 1996], 401–5).

13. A full consideration of the various meanings of justice and the requirements of justice with respect to the poor in the Bible is beyond the scope of this chapter. Some commentators have argued that justice or righteousness takes on a specialized meaning relating to giving alms or charity. Regardless of whether this is the principal aim of just behavior, it is nonetheless clear that there is room for a meaning of justice beyond the judicial connotation that is prevalent in the Old Testament. The exhortations of Isaiah 1:17 to "Seek justice, encourage the oppressed," is clearly in keeping with the New Testament sense of justice that embodies a kind of compassionate consideration, as exemplified through the life of Christ. Even at the moment of his crucifixion, when one of the criminals to be crucified remarks that his punishment is just as he is receiving the punishment due him, Christ tells him, "today you will be with me in paradise" (Luke 24:4).

14. Abraham Kuyper, *The Problem of Poverty*, ed. James Skillen (Grand Rapids, Mich.: Baker Book House, 1991), 71.

15. For a fuller articulation of sphere sovereignty, and an application of this argument to various public policy issues, see James W. Skillen, *Recharging the American Experiment: Principled Pluralism for Genuine Civic Community* (Grand Rapids, Mich.: Baker Books, 1994).

16. Clarke E. Cochran, "Balancing Care and Cure: The Place of Health Care Reform in the Welfare Reform Debate," in Carlson-Thies and Skillen, *Welfare in America*, 519.

17. As this issue is a seemingly undertilled field, I have deliberately devoted more attention to the development of these ideas in this chapter than I have to other issues that have been well covered by other commentators. Bauckham (1989) suggests that the Old Testament speaks to questions of "the ordering of Israel's political life, the formulation of policies, the responsibilities of rulers as well as subjects, and so on" (p. 3). Thus, despite obvious difficulties due to dispensational differences, the theocratic rule of the Old Testament, and the like, I turn first to the Old Testament for guidance on issues on political structure. Richard Bauckham draws a careful and useful distinction between use of the Old Testament as a set of *instructions* in contrast to use of the Old Testament as an *instructive* tool for the modern exegete, advocating the latter perspective, which will be employed here. (Richard Bauckham, *The Bible in Politics: How to Read the Bible Politically* [Louisville, Ky.: Westminster/John Knox Press, 1989]).

18. For reasons of space, I do not justify the potential for the "redemption" of political structures, although the following account is informed by the understanding that the existence of political structures themselves does not preclude the development of a just political order—that is, that political structures are not "post-fall" phenomena that are by definition unjust. For a more complete and persuasive articulation of this perspective see Richard Mouw, *Politics and the Biblical Drama* (Grand Rapids, Mich.: Baker House Books, 1983).

19. Bruce Birch, *Let Justice Roll Down: The Old Testament, Ethics, and Christian Life* (Louisville, Ky.: Westminster/John Knox Press, 1991), 198.

20. Birch, *Let Justice Roll Down*, 207.

21. (1 Samuel 2:10 NRSV)

22. Birch, *Let Justice Roll Down*, 208.

23. Pope Pius XI, *Quadragesimo Anno* (New York: Benzinger Brothers, 1943), §79.

24. *Quadragesimo Anno*, §80.

25. Andrew Greeley, *America* (11/9/85) 153(13): 292. It should be noted that *Quadragesimo Anno* was written in response to the totalitarian states in Europe at this time, and therefore the stress on the power of the individual vis-à-vis the state should be to some extent understood contextually.

26. Greeley, *America*, 293.

27. Greeley, *America*, 293.

28. These "subsidiary institutions" have been called "mediating structures," a termed coined by Peter Berger and John Neuhaus in their classic, *To Empower People: The Role of Mediating Structures in Public Policy* (Washington, D.C.: American Enterprise Institute, 1977). Their terminology again tends to reify the preeminence of the state, as other institutions in society serve the role of mediating between the public and the state. To argue that these institutions must mediate is again to put the state in a position of greater importance than the other institutions that share no special designation save "mediation."

29. James W. Skillen and Rockne M. McCarthy, "Subsidiarity, Natural Law and the Common Good," in *Political Order and the Plural Structure of Society* (Atlanta, Ga.: Scholar's Press, 1991).

30. Skillen and McCarthy, "Subsidiarity," 385.

31. George A. Bermann, "Taking Subsidiarity Seriously: Federalism in the European Community and the United States," *Columbia Law Review* 94, no. 2 (March, 1994): 331–456 (336).

32. These authors would presumably advocate a universal kind of procedural subsidiarity where all institutions—not just the state—would engage in an inquiry as to their warrant to act.

33. Bermann, "Taking Subsidiarity Seriously," 403.

34. Bermann, "Taking Subsidiarity Seriously," 408.

35. Bermann, "Taking Subsidiarity Seriously," 407.

36. Bermann, "Taking Subsidiarity Seriously," 340–42.

37. Bermann, "Taking Subsidiarity Seriously," 341.

38. AFDC policy has been described as embodying a kind of putative partial preemption given the requirements that the states needed to adhere to in order to receive federal monies. This discussion leaves aside a consideration of the preemption more technically understood. Preemption occurs when within a particular category of governmental activity the national government assumes the complete sole right to make policy, thus the state's ability to make policy in that area is "preempted." Preemption explicitly entails the national government's right to act first rather than to ask for a warrant to act in the first place.

39. See footnote two.

40. In part this may be due to the fact that the questions concerning justice to individuals and institutions as broad questions are considered to be somewhat prior to the more empirical question as to how the unique structural features of a government affect the potential for meeting such a standard of justice. As an example of the omission of this dimension of the welfare policy problem, the quite comprehensive and thoughtful volume, *Welfare in America: Christian Perspectives on a Policy in Crisis*, ed. Stanley W. Carlson-Thies and James W. Skillen, does not discuss the structural effect that federalism has on welfare policy, save to discuss "the state" and its problems generally (see selections by Stackhouse, Mott, Monsma, and Carlson-Thies) or to look to particular local level programs as exemplars for potential national policy (see Sider and Rolland). While these dimensions of the welfare problem are vital to the framing of a Christian response to contemporary policy debates, to ignore the more specific political context in the United States, and the extent to which it shapes the policy agenda, is to present a politically naïve picture of the potential for reform.

41. The following discussion is borne of the literature on state public policy innovation and diffusion. For the classic discussion of this phenomenon see Jack Walker, "The Diffusion of Innovations among the American States," *American Political Science Review* 63(1969), 880–99, and Virginia Gray "Innovation in the States: A Diffusion Study," *American Political Science Review* 67 (1973): 1174–1193. For a full review of this literature see Frances Stokes Berry and William Berry, "Innovation and Diffusion Models in Policy Research," in *Theories of the Policy Process*, ed. Paul Sabatier (Westview Press, forthcoming).

42. Paul E. Peterson, *City Limits* (Chicago: University of Chicago Press, 1981).

43. As a case study these authors examine the state of Wisconsin, long known as a state in the forefront of reform efforts. As a state with higher benefit levels than its neighbor, Illinois, Wisconsin has argued that it is a magnet for AFDC recipients who live on the edges of the Chicago metropolitan area.

44. Russell Hanson and John T. Hartmann, "Do Welfare Magnets Really Attract?" (Institute for Research on Poverty Discussion Paper #1028–94, University of Wisconsin at Madison, 1994).

45. See Berry and Berry, forthcoming, for a full discussion of this literature.

46. For a discussion of vertical diffusion see Keith Boeckelman, "The Influence of States on Federal Policy Adoptions," *Policy Studies Journal* 20 (September 1992): 365–75. For a discussion of the effect of federal inducements or constraints on state level policymaking see Susan Welch and Kay Thompson, "The Impact of Federal Incentives on State Policy Innovation," *American Journal of Political Science* 24 (November, 1980): 715–29.

47. The TANF program is still in its infancy, and data concerning the effects of its implementation is at the time of this writing only beginning to become available.

48. Donahue, "Disunited States," 20.

49. Federal grants to the states will be computed based upon the amount that the states received from the national government under AFDC according to one of three rules. States will receive the greater amount of: the average of their 1992, 1993 and 1994 AFDC awards, their 1994 award plus 85 percent of the emergency assistance grant for 1995, or 4/3 of the amount of their award for the first three-quarters of 1995 plus the amount of their Job Opportunities and Basic Skills (JOBS) program grant for 1995.

50. Letter from Olivia A. Golden, Acting Assistant Secretary for Children and Families to Martha S. Nachman, Commissioner, Alabama State Department of Human Resources, October 9,1996.

51. Department of Health, Education and Welfare memo, dated 1971.

52. *Federal Register*, vol. 43, p. 17061.

53. *Federal Register*, vol. 60, p. 42754.

54. B. Guy Peters, *American Public Policy: Promise and Performance* (Chatham, N.J.: Chatham House, 1993), 32.

55. Theda Skocpol, "What Tocqueville Missed: Government Made All That 'Volunteerism' Possible" *Hey Wait a Minute Slate* <http://www.slate.com/ HeyWait/96-11-14/HeyWait.asp>, November 14, 1996 (Accessed 11/15/96).

56. For a full description and cogent explanation of the charitable choice provisions of PRWORA, see, *A Guide to Charitable Choice: The Rules of Section 104 of the 1996 Federal Welfare Law Governing State Cooperation with Faith-based Social-Service Providers.* (Published Jointly by the Center for Public Justice, Washington, D.C. and The Center for Law and Religious Freedom, Annandale, Va., 1997). The Center for Public Justice is currently engaging in a national study of the implementation of the Charitable Choice provisions of the PRWORA.

57. Sam Howe Verhovek, "Clinton Reining in Role for Business in Welfare Effort," *New York Times*, May 11, 1997, A1, 14.

58. Donahue, "Disunited States," 20.

59. For a full articulation of this perspective see Virginia Gray and David Lowery, "The Corporatist Foundations of State Industrial Policy," *Social Science Quarterly* 71 (1990): 3–24.

60. Virginia Gray, "Innovation in the States: A Diffusion Study," *American Political Science Review* 67 (1973): 1174–1193.

61. The Welfare Information Network, working with the Center on Law and Social Policy has developed a website to facilitate the exchange of information tracking the implementation of welfare reform. Such groups as the American Public Welfare Association, Congressional Research Service, United States General Accounting Office, National Conference of State Legislatures, National Governor's Association, National Research Forum on Children, Families and the New Federalism, Rockefeller Institute, and the Urban Institute are all tracked on this site. The URL of this website is www.welfareinfo.org.

Chapter 9

The Christian Case for Humanitarian Intervention[1]

Daniel Philpott

Introduction

In sixteenth- and seventeenth-century Europe, the medieval unity by which all Christians lived in a common *respublica*, bound by natural law, yielded to independent sovereign states. With the inception of modern international relations Christian philosophers faced novel political questions, most important, the limits to be placed on sovereign states. Were their rulers still publicly obligated by the common natural law, or were they, as Jean Bodin and contemporary publicists thought, unchallengeable in their divinely sanctioned authority, supreme among humans, limited only by whatever scruples natural law might arouse in their consciences? Was sovereignty absolute? Were any of the ruler's actions subject to check?

The question was most salient, the Christian conscience most disturbed, when a monarch was extraordinarily cruel to his subjects or impotent to prevent lawlessness or inordinate suffering. In such cases, was it permissible for outsiders to undertake what modern international lawyers call humanitarian intervention? Could other sovereign nation-states interfere in another state's territory, by means of armed force if necessary, to prevent suffering or execute justice within another state?

Until recently, the question of humanitarian intervention has virtually hibernated. Its recession from discourse can be traced to the 1648 Peace of Westphalia, whose modern prescriptions of state sovereignty and nonintervention persisted right up through the United Nations Charter, the document that ensconced them in post-World War II international legitimacy. But once again, humanitarian intervention is a crucial issue, arising as the United Nations, other international organizations like NATO, and their proxy armies respond to starvation, anarchy, and the denial of human rights and democracy. In Iraqi Kurdistan, Somalia, Bosnia, Rwanda, Haiti, the U.N. has authorized armed combat against internal injustice; in Kosovo, NATO has done the same. They have done so—and this is the crucial novel characteristic—without seeking the consent of the local parties.

Whether humanitarian intervention will become widely endorsed, regularly practiced, and universally accepted as the new orthodoxy is uncertain. The new interventions have enjoyed mixed success, and progress in international relations is manifestly reversible. But these post-Cold War aberrations together represent a historic trend, evoking the memory of early modern Europe, when state sovereignty was spreading yet intervention was still practiced and theorized. Of course, international relations are now moving in the opposite direction, away from sovereignty. But if we are again facing the dilemma of humanitarian intervention, then we ought again to ask how Christians should respond.

But what exactly *is* the dilemma of humanitarian intervention? That the capable and fortunate ought to assist the needy and afflicted, that there is a duty to relieve suffering, is hardly troubling. The rub lies in the means. Humanitarian intervention is usually a form of war, or at least heavy-handed police action, and thus invokes coercion's attendant moral problems. Is enforcing justice in other lands interfering in "their affairs"? Are armies and navies of strong nations morally or practically suited to end starvation, civil war, and genocide among weaker nations? Can we depend on strong nations, given that their usual foreign predilections are for territory, wealth, and might, not justice?

Most intervention, indeed, is not humanitarian. In early modern Europe, monarchs typically intervened not to alleviate suffering, but to proselytize and to pursue more ordinary forms of power, eliciting bloodshed on a scale easily rivaling that of twentieth-century world wars. Against this precedent, Westphalian nonintervention appears not as an amoral barrier to accountability, but as a sane modus vivendi, a truce upholding at least a modicum of reciprocal moderation. Our perplexing quandary, then, is to find, if possible, principles that justify and properly delimit the armed delivery of respite without also plucking away standards of nonintervention that support whatever precarious restraint exists.

But if this is our dilemma, what makes it a particularly Christian question? The dilemma, in fact, is not only one for Christians. The institutions behind intervention and the moral flaws limiting it are fully accessible to, and fully demanding upon, all reasoning humans, unaided by special revelation. General accessibility, though, does not obviate the need for specifically Christian reflection, and I want to argue that a particular Christian case for humanitarian intervention complements the more widely accessible one. Why Christians need both types of reflection, and how the two can be linked, depends upon a certain view of the relationship between the scriptural Gospel and natural law.

I will briefly highlight the tenets of this view. Natural law is that part of God's moral law that is apparent to all humans by virtue of their rational capacity. Though natural law is discernible without knowledge of the Gospel, Christians should not view it as contradictory to the Gospel, but as complimentary. Scripture itself suggests in several places that God's moral law is accessible to reason. In his letter to the Romans, St. Paul tells us that "when the Gentiles, who do not have the law, by nature do things in the law, these, although not having the law, are a law unto themselves, [w]ho show the work of the law written in their hearts."[2] Reason, or reflection upon this law, can also aid Christians in interpreting the moral precepts revealed to us in scripture—for instance, natural law philosophers help us understand some of the ambiguities in Romans 13 toward political institutions. A full understanding of natural law requires awareness of its divine source; a sufficient understanding of its content and its obligatory force, however, is available without such as awareness. The case for humanitarian intervention developed in this chapter is rooted in both the Gospel and in the natural law, yet allows that a sufficient argument is available through natural law alone.[3]

The first part of the chapter constructs this moral foundation, borrowing heavily from the early modern Christian natural law philosophers who faced the question in a quite similar, but not identical, form.[4] The second part seeks to show that trends in international law are establishing the U. N. as a proper legal authority to authorize humanitarian intervention. Finally, the third section considers some problems in implementing intervention that may detract from its generally just character. The justice of humanitarian intervention must, in the end, be qualified.

The Moral Case for Humanitarian Intervention

The sixteenth-century Huguenot Hubert Languet argued in his *Vindiciae Contra Tyrannos* that a prince is obligated to defend the subjects of a neighboring prince who is tyrannical. He who "fails to stand up against injuries, if he can, is as much at fault as if he deserted his parents, or his friends, or his country."[5] What is the basis of such an obligation? Behind the parable of the Good Samaritan (Luke 10:30-37), Languet argues, is the precept of benevolence, analogous to Christ's command to love one's neighbors, to promote their welfare and alleviate their suffering regardless of their culture or community. Languet relies on this precept in making his argument for aid across borders.

Christ says that a Jew is not only the neighbor of a Jew, but also of a Samaritan and of any other man; and that we should love a neighbor as ourselves. And so a Jew is bound, if he wants to fulfill (*sic*) his office, to rescue from a robber not only another Jew, but also a foreigner and stranger, if he can do so. Nor will anyone who judges it just to protect himself dispute whether it is lawful to defend another: for it is clearly much more just to defend another than oneself, since what pure charity does is considered more just than what anger, revenge, or any other disturbance of the mind does; and since no one observes moderation in avenging his own injuries, whereas with regard to the injuries of others, although much more serious, the most immoderate are able to observe moderation.[6]

Benevolence is both Christ's command and a precept of practical reason, one which Thomas Aquinas and Immanuel Kant defend systematically. David Singer, a proponent of global distributive justice, elucidates this precept vividly through the example of an able-bodied person walking past a lake where a child is drowning: Is one not obligated to save the child?[7] Benevolence, though, is a principle of the most general sort. It says nothing about who among us should attend to which sorts of injuries, and nothing about the role of institutions. In contrast, a doctrine of humanitarian intervention must be quite specific about who may intervene, about the conditions requiring intervention, and about how intervention may be conducted—matters of political authority, requiring a theory of political authority.

The most direct biblical teaching on the state, important in the political thought of Aquinas, Luther, and Calvin, among others, is Romans 13. In verse one, Paul writes, "[E]veryone must submit himself to the governing authorities, for there is no authority except that which God has established. The authorities that exist have been established by God." In verse four, Paul tells us God's purpose in instituting authority: "For he is God's servant to you for good. But if you do wrong, be afraid; for he does not bear the sword for nothing. He is God's servant, an agent of wrath to bring punishment on the wrongdoer."[8]

Here, we are commanded to "submit to" government and told the purpose of our obedience: the authorities are divinely ordained to promote our good. The Christian natural law tradition grounds the nature of this good philosophically as the common good, or the set of social conditions that promote the virtuous life of the individual.[9] The value of political authority is thus instrumental. The precise content of the good life is, of course, a complicated matter—and it has been diversely formulated, even within the natural law tradition: for Aquinas, the good life culminates in the "beatific vision," or knowledge of God; for latter-day natural law theorist John Finnis, it consists additionally of seven "basic goods," including friendship, married life, and involvement in a religious community.[10]

While I will not specify exactly what the good life entails or how it is to be promoted politically, several ideas that run throughout the tradition are relevant to humanitarian intervention. First, at the very least, government must safeguard what Augustine called the *tranquillitas ordinis*, or public peace. Without this, life itself, and still more the virtuous life, is precarious. Second, there are certain things that government ought never to do, that are always incompatible with promoting the good life for individuals. These include killing, torture, inflicting bodily harm, and starvation. The modern natural law tradition also includes respecting other aspects of human dignity, including the pursuit of truth according to one's conscience.[11] The common good, then, includes both peace and justice.[12]

To the degree that a government violates these precepts, it fails in its ordained duty to promote the common good. It is no longer just. The questions of what actions ought to be taken to enforce justice upon these governments, and who may take them, however, are not answered merely by the nature and purpose of government's authority; they require additional argument. Since humanitarian intervention is almost always a form of war, and inevitably challenges the authority of the target state's government, it forces us to confront another of Paul's admonitions in Romans 13: "[C]onsequently, he who rebels against the authority is rebelling against what God has instituted, and those who do so will bring judgment on themselves. For rulers hold no terror for those who do right, but for those who do wrong."[13] The history of Christian political philosophy, especially as it has focused on questions of rebellion, obedience, and authority, is in no small part a debate on this verse of Romans 13. Are there any conditions in which one may justly oppose government?[14]

Certainly most interpreters of Romans 13 make a distinction between "submission" to the authorities, or the abjuration of active resistance to which the scripture clearly calls us, and "obedience," the following of the commands of authorities, which Christians clearly cannot do when government asks them to do wrong. Since submission means forswearing rebellion, permissible disobedience can only mean civil disobedience, the kind in which the objector is willing to accept punishment. What Christian philosophers have disagreed upon, however, are the conditions in which the command of submission applies, which in turn depend on how one interprets "authority." If authority means *all* existing governments, then resistance to any government is always forbidden. If, though, authority embodies a notion of legitimacy—making "authority" equivalent to "legitimate power"—then it is only forbidden to resist legitimate governments, that is, those that in fact promote the good (which we may think of as the common good). Illegitimate governments, in this interpretation, either are not among those authorities that God has ordained, or fail to rule according to their ordained purpose. My own view is that authority indeed embodies a notion of legitimacy; only this interpretation can make sense out of Paul's description of authority as "God's servant to you for good." Since there clearly exist tyrannical governments that do very little to serve, and much to undermine, "our good," Paul's teaching can only be valid if authority means legitimate authority.[15]

Intervention is not the same thing as rebellion from within, but since it also challenges the authority of a state's government, it must be shown to be compatible with submission to authority. Both of the above interpretations of Romans 13 can allow humanitarian intervention, although not for identical reasons or under identical circumstances. If it is forbidden to resist all existing "governing authorities"—the first interpretation—then only an international body that itself possesses the authority to use force against states may intervene. It is a product of our modern Westphalian system that we assume governing authorities to be sovereign states, but they need not be. The United Nations and the European Union, for instance, hold certain prerogatives over their member states, and they are every bit as much governing authorities, even though their authority is restricted to certain areas of policy. If a body such as the United Nations has the authority to intervene under some circumstances, then states do not have the authority to resist this intervention of another governing authority.

If, though, we accept the second interpretation of Romans 13, namely, that illegitimate governments are not included among the authorities that God ordains for our good, then we do not need a higher international authority to justify intervention against these governments, for they have already forfeited their prerogatives. We are also open to considering a more broadly claimed right to intervention. Such an approach has a historic pedigree. Its Golden Age was the sixteenth century; its proponents were Calvinists, Catholics, and Anabaptists, who often invoked violence against tyranny, and who almost always claimed faithfulness to Romans 13.[16] This tradition justifies the vigilante, the lone enforcer of justice, and such a figure indeed captures some portion of our moral imagination. When princes or dictators starve or kill or ethnically cleanse their people, and when no international law or authority's feeble condemnations reveal its impotence, then those who take the law into their own hands tug on our sympathy.

But the vigilante also gives us pause and stretches our sense of justice. Illegitimate governments may, as the second interpretation suggests, lose their immunity from intervention by their very illegitimacy, yet the authority of those who would intervene may still require a separate justification. Intervention, after all, is the enforcement of justice, and by any interpretation of Romans 13, justice should be the work of "governing authorities," ones who are established lawfully, not impulsive volunteers. Moral prudence also questions the vigilante. Vigilantes frighten us. We nervously suspect their lack of impartiality, of judiciousness, and of a pure motive of justice uncorrupted by an *animus dominandi* toward land, wealth, and power. And history grounds our suspicion. Even those interventions that have overthrown tyrants or ended massacres have typically remunerated the intervening states with an even greater measure of worldly treasures.

But what if no effective authority exists to intervene against illegitimate governments? Or what if international law even forbids intervention? Here we are faced with a dilemma, and it is exactly the dilemma that Christian ethics poses to the state in the Westphalian system: the state has a moral duty to assist those in need, illegitimate governments have no immunity from the intervention, and yet international law does not grant states that authority to intervene. The choice is between culpable passivity and unlawful action. Can intervention without international legal sanction be justified?

The best solution, I believe, derives from the distinction between submission and obedience. The authority of the tyrannical or impotent state is illegitimate, and does not require submission. States, however, ought to submit to the authority of international law, which is presumably generally just. But they should not necessarily obey. That is, a state that has the opportunity and capability of intervening to quell colossal suffering ought to do so, even if the law forbids it. But out of respect for the law, it should be willing to accept the judgment of an international legal body upon its action. This judgment may not amount to much of a punishment—states do not go to prison—and given current international equivalent of civil disobedience, the state that carries it out is the equivalent of a conscientious objector rather than a vigilante.

These conclusions, it is important to emphasize, do not necessarily translate into an imperative for international law to allow intervention. Not all morality should be legislated, and the historically typical aims of intervening states constitute a good reason not to institutionalize intervention in law (as will be argued below). But if the question of intervention is put to the moral philosopher rather than the lawmaker, if it is asked by the conscientious state contemplating intervention rather than the state looking for a rationale, then we can allow that under some circumstances, even unlawful intervention is morally justified.

So far, I have argued that humanitarian intervention is an expression of the duty of benevolence that ought to be the work of a legally authorized international governing body. At least under one interpretation of Romans 13, however, states may morally intervene when such a body does not exist or fails to act. And yet, even if this establishes the authority to intervene, it does little to justify intervention as a particular means of promoting justice. Intervention usually (but not always) involves combat, and in Christian political thought, combat has always required special justification. The just war tradition, the richest Christian tradition of thought on the morality of combat, provides such a justification. Rooted in (but not exclusively reliant upon) natural law thinking, the just war tradition begins with a presumption against war, then proposes an account of *jus ad bellum*, that is, the reasons for which war may be fought.[17] The central just cause, especially in the modern tradition, is defense of the political community against an attack from the outside. Such attacks are unjust because, as natural law theory claims, the political community is the upholder of the common good, the necessary social condition for the good life. This is the core of the arguments of current authors like Paul Ramsey, James Turner Johnson, and the United States Catholic bishops.[18]

Christian thought, however, has not always restricted just cause to self-defense. During the Middle Ages, war was also justified as a police action within Christendom, and as a means of protecting Christians abroad or even of converting Muslims. Medieval police action, however, was fitted for a unified political realm, and became obsolete in the

Westphalian world of sovereign states and nonintervention. When early modern Europe was sundered by religious conflict, some English Puritans, Catholics, and others espoused the holy war, which called for armed punishment of heretics. Holy war also became obsolete, both for pragmatic reasons—the Thirty Years' War led Christians to see the futility of conversion through arms—and for more principled reasons, as the notion that political authorities cannot coerce the conscience became more widespread.[19] Among the just causes of war, only self-defense survived into the modern tradition.[20]

During early modern Europe, several Christian philosophers espoused a different reason for going to war, one quite like humanitarian intervention. It was not exactly a police action, for similar to the doctrine of self-defense, it presumed that the state's normal, regular, and just function is to promote the common good within its own realm. But when egregious injustice prevailed within a state, either through the ruler's commission or omission, then Christian love and the universal mutual duties of the natural law required neighboring rulers to intervene through arms. Arguing some version of this case were Spanish Dominican Franciscus de Victoria and Spanish Jesuit Francisco Suarez, and Protestants Alberico Gentili, Hubert Languet, and Hugo Grotius. Each of these philosophers rejected war to convert foreigners or enforce the practice of religion. They held rather that politics and war are to be governed by moral precepts written on the hearts of all humans, accessible to all reasoning beings:[21] the natural law. They believed in Christian truth, but argued, with some variation among them, that a certain portion of it, the natural law, was to be the basis of relations between people of different creeds (the *jus inter genes*).

According to these philosophers, sovereignty is the presumed entitlement of all political authorities, but is restricted in some areas, in some situations. At the very least, natural law implied something like "the common rights of mankind."[22] The moral status of any political authority rested upon the fulfillment of its purpose to protect these common rights, and princes might justly intervene upon other princes who fail to uphold them. As the common rights of mankind are few and essential, including the right to life, freedom from bodily harm, and basic public order, instances of just intervention are rare. The natural law theorists envisioned them as rare not only on grounds of first principle but also for fear that the right to intervene would be abused by rapacious, pretext seizing princes. Benevolent intervention was, for the natural law theorists of this time, not merely a moral duty but also a legal obligation, just as the natural law that implied the authority to enforce it. This was clearly a holdover from the medieval *Respublica Christiana*, in which nobody's authority was absolutely supreme, but in which every-body was to some degree responsible for justice within the realm.

On the exact conditions warranting intervention, the theorists differed: Victoria envisioned intervention when missionaries were harassed, Christians persecuted by unbelievers, seekers of the faith hindered from converting, or innocent lives threatened by human sacrifice or cannibalism, or when a population was incapable of self-government.[23] Suarez, more circumspect, was wary that intervention would become vain pretext, another predatory rationale. He allowed intervention only when a prince forced his subjects to practice idolatry.[24] Gentili was the strongest proponent of the "common rights of mankind," and allowed intervention to promote them; however, he provided no elaborate list of what they included, mentioning only the honor of women, and more generally the victims of "immoderate cruelty and unmerciful punishment."[25] Grotius allowed intervention "on account of injuries which do not directly affect [kings or their subjects] but excessively violate the law of nature or of nations in regard to any persons whatsoever."[26]

All of the important assumptions that led these early modern philosophers to endorse humanitarian intervention persist in modern natural law thinking.[27] The precept of Christian benevolence is alive and well. The ideas that government's purpose and duty is to promote the common good, that governments are limited by this same purpose and duty, and that all citizens have rights, now thought of as human rights, that give them corresponding claims against government are enthusiastically argued in papal encyclicals (most prominently by Pope John XIII in *Pacem in Terris*), and endorsed in the thought of natural law philosophers like Jacques Maritain and John Finnis.[28] Since the Second World War, the just war tradition has also been received, mostly but not exclusively, within the Catholic natural law tradition. Little is heard, though, of the concern for humanitarian intervention voiced by Grotius, Gentili, Languet, Victoria, and Suarez.

The modern sleep of humanitarian intervention probably has much to do with the victory of the doctrine of state sovereignty at the 1648 Peace of Westphalia. In international relations, sovereignty meant that the state held the highest authority; no outside institution or individual could make claims upon it, at any time, for any reason. First ensconced in the Peace of Westphalia, accepted into international law in the subsequent century and a half, and lasting right up to the present day, state sovereignty became the overwhelmingly dominant principle in international relations. Escorting it into dominance was an accompanying shift in the philosophy of international law during the seventeenth and eighteenth centuries: the replacement of natural law with positivism, the doctrine that states are only obligated by the law to which they agree. Although they may still be obligated morally by natural law (over this, philosophers disagreed), they could only enforce upon one another law that was codified. And that law, with only a few exceptions, has allowed sovereign states almost complete liberty in their affairs.

If we are to be true to our Christian tradition, rooted in scripture and developed through natural law thinking, we must acknowledge and attempt to remedy the troubling dissonance between the Westphalian norm and the duty of humanitarian intervention. Just war theory is rooted in the imperative to promote justice, and if we are to keep it true to this mission, we should reformulate it in accordance with the insights of the early moderns, recognize that sovereignty is conditional upon justice, and set forth carefully the nature of the authority who would intervene and the conditions under which force might justly be used against unjust states. The next section turns to the nature of the intervening authority.

The Legal Case for Humanitarian Intervention

A key assumption of the early modern theorists, even the later ones like Grotius, was that there still existed a common legal community within Christendom. Even if political authority was fragmented among sovereigns, legal and moral obligations still bound Europe together. These obligations were not originally codified (the work of Grotius, and perhaps Gentili, might be seen as the first attempt to codify them), but existed by dint of the common assent of Christians. It was on these consensual norms that the justification for humanitarian intervention rested. Today, no such implicit consensus exists. Rather, as positivism holds, states regard themselves as legally obligated only by those laws to which they explicitly agree, or, in the case of customary law, habitually acknowledge in practice.[29] These laws, until recently, have not acknowledged the legitimacy of humanitarian intervention.

As I have argued above, legal authority is an essential element of just intervention; according to one's interpretation of Romans 13, it is either required or highly desirable. The just war tradition has generally echoed this view by posting "right authority" as a *jus ad bellum* criterion.[30] Positive law has not always been the basis of legitimate authority—in other ages, natural law, tradition, or the divine right of kings have served as foundations—and scripture says little about how we are to know exactly which authorities are to count as ordained by God. We are left with the general consensus of our age about legitimate authority, which amounts to a positive doctrine of law. This does not mean that powers that exist by positive law are always legitimate; they could be deeply inimical to the common good. The common good alone, however, says little about exactly which authorities ought to hold power. Positive law, as long as it is generally compatible with the justice as defined by the common good, is one of several ways of determining who holds authority.

What, then, does international law say about humanitarian intervention? An answer must surely begin with the United Nations Charter, international law's foundational document (1945). In several places, the charter points to a principle of nonintervention. Article 2(4) prohibits unilateral intervention in the form of "the threat or use of force against the territorial integrity or political independence of any state, or in any other manner inconsistent with the Purposes of the United Nations." Article 2(7) is specifically directed against the intervention of the United Nations:

> [N]othing contained in the present Charter shall authorize the United Nations to intervene in matters which are essentially within the domestic jurisdiction of any state or shall require the Members to submit such matters to settlement under the present Charter; but this principle shall not prejudice the application of enforcement measures under Chapter VII.

Subsequent U.N. documents even more directly condemn intervention, especially unilateral intervention. General Assembly Resolution 2131, passed in 1965, for instance, reads:

> No State has the right to intervene, directly or indirectly, for any reason whatever, in the internal or external affairs of any other State. Consequently, armed intervention and all forms of interference or attempted threats against the personality of the State or against its political, economic, or cultural elements are condemned.
> No State may use or encourage the use of economic, political or any other type of measure to coerce another state in order to obtain from it the subordination of the exercise of its sovereign rights, or to secure from it advantages of any kind. Also no state shall organize, assist, foment, finance, invite or tolerate subversive terrorist or armed activities directed toward the violent overthrow of the regime (government) of another state or interfere in civil strife in another state.[31]

The same clause appears in the 1970 U.N. "Declaration on Principles of International Law concerning Friendly Relations and Cooperation among States."[32] In addition, in 1981, the General Assembly passed a "Declaration on the Inadmissibility of Intervention and Interference in the Internal Affairs of States," in which it proclaimed the "duty of a State to refrain from the exploitation and distortion of human rights issues as a means of interference in the internal affairs of states."

Scholars generally share the interpretation that the charter rules out unilateral military intervention.[33] The charter's provisions on force and intervention, however, are not without ambiguities, and one might interpret them as allowing some room for intervention. Charter 2(4)'s prohibition of the use of force by states closes with the words, "in any manner inconsistent with the purposes of the United Nations." Does this mean that states can take it upon themselves to defend the U.N.'s purposes? What might these purposes be? The charter's preamble states that "We the Peoples of the United Nations are determined . . . to reaffirm faith in fundamental human rights, in the dignity and worth of the human person, in the equal rights of men and women," while Article 1(3) defines one of the U.N.'s purposes as "promoting and encouraging respect for human rights and for fundamental freedoms for all without distinction as to race, sex, language, or religion." Articles 55 and 56 go even further, calling on members to take "joint and separate action in cooperation with the Organization" to further "equal rights and self-determination of peoples," and "universal respect for, and observance of, human rights." In subsequent decades, the U.N. further strengthened its commitment to human rights, in the 1948 Universal Declaration on Human Rights, which was a declaration of principles, and in its 1996 "Covenant on Political and Civil Rights" and "Covenant on Economic and Social Rights," which created monitoring mechanisms.[34] If furthering human rights is a purpose of the U.N. charter, should states be allowed to intervene on behalf of human rights?

Commitments to human rights, even legally binding ones that go beyond declarations of principle, do not alone imply any particular method of monitoring or enforcement. Such mechanisms must be further spelled out, and presently no mechanism allows states to enforce human rights unilaterally through arms. The statements against intervention in the above General Assembly declarations make it even clearer that no unilateral right to intervene exists in international law. During the Cold War, this interpretation was also generally upheld by U.N. member states in every situation in which it was put to the test. In the three most prominent instances of intervention against human rights violators—cases in which the suffering was in fact colossal, and in which the interventions succeeded in ending the suffering—the intervening powers did not even claim to be protecting human rights, but pleaded the more traditional U.N. principle of self-defense, and they received little support from other states or from the U.N. India's invasion of Pakistan in 1971, Tanzania's invasion of Uganda in 1978, and Vietnam's invasion of Cambodia in 1978 could have quite plausibly qualified as humanitarian intervention had such a doctrine been in favor. Instead, India just barely avoided a U.N. Security Council demand for its withdrawal before it defeated Pakistan's armies, and was actually condemned by the General Assembly; Tanzania was widely criticized; and Vietnam was condemned for its invasion and punished with sanctions (although this was partly due to the fact that it remained in Cambodia long after it defeated Pol Pot's Khmer Rouge, the perpetrator of the genocide).[35] Other Cold War interventions against lesser evils—the United States' 1983 invasion of Grenada, for instance—have likewise received little support within the U.N.

What about multilateral intervention that is endorsed by the U.N.? For this, there seems to be more provision within the charter. Like article 2(4), article 2(7)—the one forbidding U.N. intervention in affairs "within the domestic jurisdiction of any state"—concludes with a permissive clause: "but this principle shall not prejudice the application of enforcement measures under chapter VII." Here, we may question what is in the "domestic jurisdiction of any state" and what is provided for in chapter VII. In fact, chapter VII, the section of the chapter that provides for enforcement of U.N. law, helps answer both questions. The operative phrases occur in article 39: "The Security Council shall determine the existence of *any threat to the peace, or act of aggression* and shall make recommendations, or decide what measures shall be taken . . . *to maintain or restore international peace and security.*"[36]

Clearly, the charter is intended to address crimes between states rather than human rights violations wholly within states. Yet human rights abuses, especially the more colossal ones, often produce masses of refugees, malignant armed conflicts, ethnic strife, and environmental and health problems that do in fact spill across borders, giving weight to the argument that U.N. intervention may at times be legal.[37] During the Cold War, chapter VII was invoked only in a few cases, which are quite revealing: resolutions to impose binding economic sanctions on Rhodesia in 1966 and 1968 and an arms embargo on South Africa in 1977. The 1968 justification held that human rights violations created a threat to the peace, while the 1977 mandate cited only "the situation in South Africa." In either case it is difficult to imagine the target government's threat as being anything but domestic.[38] These incidents are few, isolated, and seemingly inconsistent with the charter, but they do suggest a weak precedent for intervention on behalf of human rights within states.

Finally, an impressively clear right of armed humanitarian intervention exists in the 1948 Genocide Convention, whose article VIII states that "Any Contracting Part may call upon the competent organs of the United Nations to take action as they consider appropriate for the prevention and suppression of acts of genocide."[39] The act requires U.N. authorization, and to my knowledge has never been invoked, but it nevertheless permits intervention. Like chapter VII, it suggests some conditions under which Westphalian state sovereignty might be abridged, but has meant very little in practice during the Cold War.

It seemed anomalous, then, when the United Nations Security Council authorized western allied troops to deliver relief to the Iraqi Kurds after the Persian Gulf War in 1991; the suffering of the Kurds was an internal affair. But then U.N. forces intervened in Somalia and then in Yugoslavia; not long after, the U.N. sanctioned intervention in Rwanda and Haiti; more recently, NATO has authorized intervention in Kosovo—all to counter starvation or human rights violations occurring largely within a single set of borders. Grounds for hesitancy exist. That the Security Council still cites a "threat to international peace and security" in each case reveals its refusal to endorse intervention openly in the affairs of a single state. But in crucial respects each intervention has also been a departure from Westphalian sovereignty: each was far more intrusive, and was directed at an injustice far more confined to a state's internal affairs, than any Cold War-era intervention.

Again, Iraq was the first target of this new sort of intervention. After allied troops forced Saddam Hussein out of Kuwait in the spring of 1991, he cruelly quelled an uprising of Kurds that the West had in fact done much to encourage. The U.N. Security Council, which had authorized the resolution to fight Hussein in Kuwait, responded on April 5, 1991, with Resolution 688, calling for Iraq to "end this repression," to "ensure that the human and political rights of all Iraqi citizens are respected," and to "allow immediate access by international humanitarian organizations to all those in need of assistance in all parts of Iraq and to make available all necessary facilities for their operation."[40]

Resolution 688 admittedly fails to prescribe humanitarian intervention paradigmatically. It ritually genuflects to "the maintenance of international peace and security," and fails to invoke chapter VII to authorize military enforcement (although the buzz-phrase "international peace and security" is taken from chapter VII). Yet innovation abounds in the resolution. The intervention called for is nonforcible, but novelly intrusive; it demands that supplies rather than attacks be delivered, yet notably fails to demand the consent of an important local ruler and combatant, namely, Saddam Hussein. The scope of demands on a domestic government and the scale of an operation within a single state were also both unprecedented.[41] "Some 13,000 U.S. troops and 10,000 soldiers from twelve other nations delivered 25 million pounds of food, water, medical supplies, clothing, and shelter to protected areas carved out of northern Iraq," motes one pair of analysts.[42] All of these efforts aimed to counter, in the resolution's words, "the repression of the Iraqi civilian population in many parts of Iraq, including most recently in Kurdish populated areas." Although the Security Council adds "the consequences of which threaten international peace and security in the region" (again ritually to acknowledge nonintervention's status), the evil is clearly domestic.[43]

Despite the absence of chapter VII enforcement provisions in Resolution 688, the actual intervention relied upon forceful measures, including allied military operations to create a security zone in Northern Iraq, threats to prevent Iraq from using its air force, and the deployment of U.N. guards to protect humanitarian relief workers.[44] Although U.S. President George Bush acted improperly by invoking Resolution 688 to use force (only the Security Council may authorize combat), the armed assistance of Britain, France, and The Netherlands, along with the Security Council's acquiescence and the General Assembly's refusal to censure formally the armed support, suggests that most other nations did not view the military component of the intervention in Iraq as a breach of legitimacy.[45] It follows, then, that the entire operation was something very similar to legitimate humanitarian intervention.

In Somalia, the U.N. operation looked even more like humanitarian intervention. Authorizing the use of force to protect the delivery of relief supplies against armed warlords, the Security Council approved Resolution 794 on December 3, 1992. Legal scholar Gregory Fox notes that the Somalia mission was remarkable in three ways: (1) it was the first time that the U.N. has ever sent a large-scale military force on a humanitarian mission without attaining the open consent of the target state's government; (2) the Security Council interpreted chapter VII innovatively, counting a humanitarian crisis as a legitimate threat; and (3) for the first time, the U.N. committed itself to rebuilding a state's government without the approval of local warring parties or influential neighboring powers.[46]

Fox notes the importance of the departure: taken together, these factors suggest the United Nations is prepared to discard both substantive and procedural barriers to intervening in a humanitarian crisis. These barriers—here, the requirement of prior consent, the exclusion of domestic crises from "threats to the peace" and the existence of a negotiated settlement—derived from a traditional concept of the states as a legal entity possessing certain immutable rights of sovereignty. The Somalia mission has evinced little regard for those traditional rights, expressing instead direct concern for the welfare of individual Somalis.[47]

That Somalia had no actual state, or at least no strong one, does not diminish the importance of the U.N. intervention. To invoke chapter VII in order to end conflict and stabilize institutions within a state's borders, without the consent of the warring parties and whatever government exists, remains a novel policy.

In response to disasters in the former Yugoslavia, Rwanda, and Haiti, U.N. resolutions also authorized the use of force. Each case had its idiosyncrasies, but all fit the pattern of innovation in intervention. In Yugoslavia, the U.N. authorized force to protect already existing peacekeeping and relief operations. In Rwanda and Haiti, powerful nations' armies, not U.N. troops, did the intervening. Haiti is also notable for the (relative) mildness of the disaster evoking intervention—not genocide, civil war, nor mass starvation, but the regime's denial of democracy and killing of its political opponents. If Haiti proves a model, the legal grounds for intervention could be considerably widened. In Kosovo, the U N. Security Council could not agree to authorize intervention due to the refusal of Russia and China. There, it was NATO that approved, and carried out, military action. Several statements and documents by the U.N. Secretary General, the Security Council, and key member states reflect the growing legitimacy of humanitarian intervention.[48]

Together these interventions and their accompanying statements suggest an emerging right authority. Right authority is lawful authority. As the use of military force to remedy injustices and suffering internal to states (which the Security Council is now willing to consider a "threat to international peace and security") gradually becomes a part of customary law, humanitarian intervention becomes a legitimate action. It is legitimate, though, only when carried out by a certain party, namely, the U.N. Security Council, whose right to authorize force is prescribed by chapter VII of the U.N. charter. Several qualifications are relevant. First, not everyone approves of the new pattern of intervention. Countries like China consistently voice dissent. China and Russia both refused to sanction intervention in Kosovo in the Security Council; China, Russia, and France have opposed U.S. intervention against Iraq to enforce restraints on nuclear weapons. Notably, though, all five permanent Security Council members have refrained from vetoing any of the other interventions mentioned above. Second, although the U.N. may make references to "international peace and security" to avoid embracing intervention too directly and heartily, each of the largely internal crises so far has to some extent actually spilled across borders, either through the spread of combat or through refugees. In a hypothetical case in which suffering was not in any conceivable way international (a possible, but rather rare scenario),[49] it is not certain that intervention would elicit support. Despite these caveats, humanitarian intervention—widely endorsed and significantly practiced—is now well within the Security Council's legitimate authority.

Developing a Just Policy of Intervention

The bombing of U.N. troops in Sarajevo and the appearance on CNN of a dead U.S. soldier being dragged through the streets of Mogadishu, Somalia, illustrate that even humanitarian intervention that is just in aim and sanctioned by a right authority is hardly immune from thorny moral problems. Recent interventions have revealed the persistent relevance of two tenets of just war theory, proportionality and discrimination (between combatants and noncombatants). Questions about the profligate use and cynical abuse of the principles also arise, and beg consideration.

However, the first, most basic, question in developing a sound policy is: To exactly what sort of evil and disasters should intervention respond? Remedying injustice, alleviating suffering, and restoring the common good have been established as intervention's just purpose, but little has been said about exactly what sort of injustices, suffering, and defects in the common good this includes. Defining a universal conception of justice or specifying exactly which human rights everyone ought to enjoy are notoriously difficult tasks, which cannot be undertaken fully here. The complexity is lessened by the fact that humanitarian intervention is aimed at suffering on the largest scale, the sort that "shocks the conscience of mankind." Upon the evil of this level of harm, almost all will agree.

Several distinct types of this calamity exist (in reality, they often sadly come together). One is mass starvation that a domestic government is either unable or unwilling to prevent (for example, Somalia). Another is genocide or systematic ethnic cleansing (Rwanda, Pol Pot's Cambodia, Bangladesh, and Bosnia). Another is mass migration or refugee crisis (Kurdistan). Finally, a man-made or natural disaster may also warrant intervention, although in these cases it is often not military force but a noncoercive relief operation that is required (for example, flooding in Bangladesh or some African famines). These sorts of cases provide a starting point: if intervention cannot be proportionate, discriminate, and so on here, then it will hardly meet these tests in cases of less colossal violations.

But what about these milder cases? If intervention can stop the killings of dissidents and the denial of democracy in Haiti, why should it be ruled out? On the basis of first principles, I do not believe that it should be ruled out; if modern Christian natural law is clear about the justice of human rights and democracy, then an intervention that promotes it might very well be just.[50] Yet the question of the justice of intervention does not simply involve the evil being targeted. Evil consequences also arise from interventions, and these become weightier when the injustice is smaller.

The moral dilemmas of their execution indeed encumber all humanitarian interventions, regardless of the injustice being addressed. One of the most frequently voiced apprehensions is about the motives of intervening states, which are more often the old desire for territory, wealth, and might than they are those of justice and succor. But what exactly the dilemma of motives amounts to is not always clear, and is posed in disparate ways. In one view, states' mixed motives, mostly having to do with power, make intervention morally dubious. There are few cases of genuine humanitarian intervention. This argument notes that the interventions of India, Vietnam, and Tanzania in the 1970s—the three most likely humanitarian cases during the Cold War—were motivated by fear at best and the desire to control neighboring states at worst.[51]

To deny that intervention is genuinely humanitarian on account of motives, though, seems mistaken, not least because mixed motives run through virtually every moral action, whether that of a state or an individual, and because motives are nearly impossible to assess. A disturbing possibility is the state that claims to intervene for humanitarian reasons, but in fact seeks to install a puppet government, occupy the target state, or extract unjust concessions. This criticism, however, does not depend on any reference to motives. An act is just or unjust according to its observable character. Without examining the consciences of Vietnam's leaders, then, one can argue that Vietnam was just in overthrowing Pol Pot, but culpable for maintaining a puppet government in Cambodia for the next decade.

A more subtle and compelling argument about motives is troubled not by the mere fact of mixed motives, but by the possibility that in a world in which states are typically spurred by power, legalized humanitarian intervention would too readily legitimate subdual and extraction. Mixed motives do not in themselves make humanitarian intervention less than humanitarian, but given that states' motives *are* mixed, a law allowing humanitarian intervention might provide a veil of legitimacy that would make it easier for states to intervene for purposes having little to do with a humanitarian one. The principle would be abused.

Underneath this criticism lies a key assumption: that states' incentives to intervene depend in part on whether principles of intervention become international law, either customary or codified. As Jarat Chopra and Thomas Weiss argue: "Codification would lead to further abuse as states could base their actions on interpretations of legal provisions, rather than mere rhetorical proclamations. As such, law would be used by the strong against the weak. It would serve power politics and no longer protect the weak against the strong." They also raise a related problem: "[T]he prohibition on the use of force and intervention under Charter Article 2(4) is fragile enough and so often breached that codification of another exception would only erode it further."[52] Customary law would probably have the same hypothesized effect.

Codification of humanitarian intervention is a distant prospect given the current thinking of the Security Council and general U.N. opinion. Whether it is codified or legitimated by customary law, though, it is not clear that it would be abused as feared. It could well be true that law has little effect on states' decisions to intervene in the first place. Even if it does, much will depend on how the law is formulated.

A central barrier to abuse would be the requirement that humanitarian intervention be authorized by the U.N. Security Council (though not necessarily carried out by the U.N. troops). This multilateral forum would not guarantee that intervention will never be for motives of power, but it could provide an effective check.[53] The western powers, Russia, and China are wary enough of each others' interventions that they would likely be cautious about endorsing interventions that directly favor the others' interests. Of course, disputed interventions could encourage mutually permissive bargaining. Some commentators have speculated that in the summer of 1994, the United States tacitly agreed with Russia to support Russian intervention in Georgia in return for support of American intervention in Haiti, but extant suspicion will likely limit the scope of such deals.[54] In general, the practice of humanitarian intervention since the end of the Cold War has been mostly consistent with humanitarian purposes. The United States and France may have derived some small extra-humanitarian benefit in Haiti and Rwanda, but it is difficult to see how interventions there, or in Somalia, Iraq, Bosnia, or Kosovo, serve these interests directly or significantly enough to justify the risks involved. The purposes of the intervening parties have, on the whole, been genuinely humanitarian. A principle permitting humanitarian intervention is not inevitably abused.

The principle's future integrity, though, will depend on how it is treated. Will the Security Council continue to authorize interventions only in genuine humanitarian crises or will it degenerate into backing the grasping forays of the most powerful states? Preventing abuse by the powerful is another reason that the more "ordinary" sort of human rights violations occur regularly all over the globe. On the egregiousness of intervention of the most troubling disasters, and on the appropriateness of intervention, most of the world is likely to agree. Interventions here are least likely to induce cynicism and most likely to strengthen the legitimacy of the norm.[55]

Moral failure, though, is still manifestly possible in individual cases of intervention even if it does not result from general law, and it has several potential sources. One is that military force does not prove appropriate for solving humanitarian problems. Some critics of humanitarian intervention argue that the violation of human rights within a state is a problem that outside states are ill-equipped to solve.[56] This dismissal seems too sweeping, for there are cases of successful intervention, but formidable obstacles to assistance doubtless exist, and they must be considered. Here, the *jus ad bellum* criterion "probability of success" is germane.

It is difficult to generalize, though, about the prospects for success. It depends on the task, which may range from the comparatively easy job of protecting the delivery of supplies from marauders, to the more daunting business of imposing a cease-fire or creating domestic institutions. The trouble is that these challenges, for example, led to the delivery of food to the starving in Somalia only to find that preventing future starvation required at the very least bringing an end to fighting between warlords, and possibly also creating a functioning government, both tasks requiring far more treasure, troops, and time than originally envisioned.[57] Similarly, protecting safe havens in Bosnia has proved to require repelling invading Serbian troops.[58] Combatting forces who would prevent relief and even changing the character of institutions is not out of the question; securing relief for the Kurds against Hussein's attacks has proven attainable, as has overthrowing the dictatorship of Raoul Cedras and installing a nascent democracy in Haiti. In Kosovo, intervention succeeded in expelling the forces of Yugoslavia, who had committed atrocities against ethnic Albanians. The long-term results of these operations are yet to be seen, but there are no a priori grounds for ruling out the success of any particular endeavor. While providing relief is doubtless easier than resolving conflict or building governments, the difficulty of any particular task depends on its magnitude and the strength of its opponents. Nor is it inevitable that one task will lead to others.

During the summer of 1994, France successfully provided medical supplies and food to refugees in Rwanda without trying to end the civil war
with its own troops or rebuild Rwandan institutions, both of which
would have been impossible, at least without a massive commitment of
resources.

Thus, probability of success is often also relative to the resources
states are willing to commit, making the question one of proportionality,
another *jus ad bellum* criterion. In order to achieve the just end of intervention, how much may states sacrifice in terms of other values? Lives
on both sides are the most obvious of these values, but there are others.[59]
Since the common good of its own realm is the first responsibility of a
state, domestic consequences for intervening states are also an important
consideration. The United States's war in Vietnam, for instance, also
deeply harmed American civic health. In general, it is extremely difficult
to calculate with any precision what is proportionate and acceptable.
Certainly the greater the humanitarian disaster, the higher the acceptable
cost, and the less harm likely to result from the intervention, the more
acceptable it is; but quantifying benefits and costs, justice and harm, is a
most difficult task. Beyond calling for realism about what can be accomplished with a given number of forces, we can make few systematic
statements; the ethics of this question is baffling and situational.

Success depends not only on the nature and costs of the task but on
the capability of the intervening forces to bring it about. This suggests
another problem that has arisen in post-Cold War U.N. operations: the
lack of a unified command structure. Operations in both Somalia and
Yugoslavia suffered from conflicts of authority within multinational
coalitions, both between commanders of different national forces and
between national commanders and U.N. commanders. Yet, international
coalitions remain normatively attractive. Just as the Security Council's
multilateral nature is a moral check on the just aims of operations, so
there is moral appeal when forces of diverse religions, regions, and standards of living intervene in Somalia or Yugoslavia.

Is there a way to lessen this tradeoff between success and impartiality? Reformers have proposed to place multinational forces under a single command, an intuitively reasonable proposal, but one that great
powers are reluctant to adopt both because they fear losing sovereignty
and because they perceive a lack of accountability in such proposals.
The same holds for the proposal of Secretary-General Boutros Boutros-
Ghali, U.N. scholar Brian Urquhart, and others to create a standing U.N.
volunteer rapid deployment force.[60] The problems of sovereignty and
accountability are both conceptual ones, related to the way that political
leaders and the public think about authority, and opinion about such

matters changes only in the long term. It is a goal, though, for which activists, scholars, and far-sighted public figures may labor.

In the shorter term, reliance upon regional organizations like NATO may be another way to mitigate the command structure problem while maintaining a multilateral character. Here too, however, coordination problems persist, in this case between the U.N. Secretary-General and regional organizations' commanders. In the international operation in the former Yugoslavia, crossed signals between the U.N. and NATO commands frequently hampered day-to-day battle operations. Improving command and coordination here, though, is not a gargantuan political or conceptual matter, mainly requiring more effective and efficient military routines.

The most easily commanded interventions, of course, are unilateral. As I have argued, they are also the most morally suspicious. Yet they may be morally, though not legally, justified when the suffering is colossal, intervention feasible, and the Security Council unresponsive. If such intervention is to be undertaken, certain criteria can help to ensure their moral character. David Scheffer offers the following seven guidelines:

> The Security Council is deadlocked indefinitely on the issue and has not explicitly prohibited intervention to meet the humanitarian crisis. . . .
>
> Alternative peaceful remedies, including economic sanctions, have been exhausted within the period of time during which humanitarian need had not reached crisis dimensions.
>
> The severity of the human rights violations is apparent.
>
> The effort is made to diversify the intervening forces among many nations. A unilateral intervention can only be justified if efforts to create a multinational force have failed.
>
> The humanitarian purpose and objective of the intervention is paramount.
>
> The intervention will have a convincingly positive effect on human rights in the target country. In other words, more good than harm will come of the intervention.
>
> The long-term political independence and territorial integrity of the target state will not be imperiled by the intervention.[61]

Most of the criteria have the character of the "last resort" measures, although some also deal with the implementation of intervention. Although I regard these criteria as moral ones, Scheffer actually proposes them as law. To his first criterion concerning Security Council deadlock, Scheffer adds:

> In the law of self-defense, there is the right of immediate unilateral or collective action until the Security Council activates the collective security system (until the Persian Gulf War, a rare event indeed). But with respect to humanitarian intervention, an inverted procedure might be more appropriate: first, await action, if any, by the Security Council, and when no such action occurs, a right to intervene for humanitarian purposes without Council approval might arise, depending upon the circumstances.[62]

Would such legal reform be wise? Legalizing what is moral may indeed further justice, although warrant for caution exists. Scheffer's criteria could be complex in their application, and might be subject to the abuse to which unilaterally applied mechanisms are prone. Supposedly any unilaterally intervening state should open its actions to the legal scrutiny of a body such as the International Court of Justice, but it is not clear that states would permit such judgment, or that being judged would affect their actual calculations to intervene. The brightest prospects for a set of laws permitting unilateral intervention lie in the gradual development of customary law. Over time, through a series of cases of interventions that meet Scheffer's criteria and elicit the endorsement of key great powers, a preponderance of the General Assembly, and the International Court of Justice, legitimacy in the eyes of most states and the meaningful censure of powerful states upon intervening states that do not comply.[63] Were this to occur, individual states might be effective enforcers of justice in the affairs of other states.

Motives, probability of success, proportionality, adept command, effectiveness—each of these issues affects the justice of any particular intervention and the wisdom of institutionalizing intervention in law. Several more general issues relating to the use of force on behalf of justice remain to be considered. One is the question of last resort, another old *jus ad bellum* standard. Humanitarian intervention has been defined in this chapter as military intervention, and this is consistent with the way in which the term is usually used. But intervention—interference in the internal affairs of other states—does not always have to be military, and it is imperative that Christians advocate every plausibly effective nonviolent means of ending suffering before they urge force. Scheffer points out that the International Committee of the Red Cross (I.C.R.C.) and Medicins sans Frontières have operated inside states without government consent. Consent may be impossible to obtain because a government does not exist, or because permission to deliver aid is required from rebel forces in control of certain areas within a country. In Resolution 688, the Security Council itself called for non-forcible intervention, establishing "an unprecedented set of rights and obligations for aid agencies and the host government," although these proved to require (unauthorized) military force to back them up. The case of Iraq revealed what often proves true for nonforcible interference—that armed support turns out to be necessary after all. But the imperative of nonviolence persists nevertheless.[64]

Consistency is another issue around which discussions of intervention center. It is closely related to the issue of motives, for motives other than the moral motive lead states to favor one case over another on grounds other than justice. That the U.N. seeks to end ethnic conflict in Bosnia but not the Sudan, that the United States intervenes in Haiti but not Myanmar, raises issue of partiality and possibly ethnocentrism. Impartiality is indeed of fundamental importance—it is part of what defines common morality—and yet is often a more complex matter than "if here, then why not there?" criticisms imply.

Measuring consistency involves assessing a prospective intervention thoroughly and considering carefully proportionality, probability of success, and so on, in addition to the nature of the evil involved. It is only if, all things truly being equal (which they rarely are), intervening parties favor one case over another that the criticism of impartiality applies. This will mean, for instance, that given similar evils, interventions in which the military task is easier may also be more just; overthrowing a dictator in Haiti would likely involve much less loss of life than deposing one in Myanmar, and is thus a more just endeavor, despite the fact that Haiti is also more strategically important to the United States.

An especially difficult problem arises, however, when prospective interventions are morally unequal not by virtue of "the facts as they stand," but of the decision of someone in the intervening country to make them unequal. For instance, the media might publicize the suffering in one locale while ignoring a similar, separate, tragedy evoking domestic support for intervention in one place but not the other, thus making unequal the domestic costs of intervening. The dilemma is that the moral facts of the two cases are different, but the disparity is parasitic upon unjustly biased attention. How policymakers treat the situation depends on exactly whose obligations they have in mind. For the authorities considering the intervention, the uneven media exposure and resulting skewed domestic support are not facts that they have created, but are part of the given set of consequential considerations which they must take into account. They are justified, then, in favoring the more exposed suffering (again, all else being equal). The media, however, and to a lesser extent the public as a whole, are obligated to cover suffering wherever it occurs, to the degree it can. To the extent that exposure affects the moral calculus of intervention, they are responsible.

The problems of consistency, along with potential for abuse, proportionality, last resort, and so on, are most troubling when combat is contemplated, for combat is one of the most troubling actions faced by Christians. Then again, the disasters that humanitarian intervention aims to relieve are among the most troubling evils faced by Christians. For the Christian, Christ's love expressed as benevolence and the conditional sovereignty of the state together suggest the justice of humanitarian intervention. But we must remember the hazards and proceed with circumspection. The kingdom of heaven will not be humanly consummated before Christ's intervention (humanitarian?), and we should not try to usher it in through plan or reform. In early modern Europe, Christian advocacy of humanitarian intervention was muffled by religious wars, interventions that were for particular causes, laced heavily with territorial and economic ambition, and brought massive bloodshed. True humanitarian intervention is still rare, but is becoming more common. That it might effectively end suffering in a few of the world's disasters is as much as we can hope for.

Notes

1. For their helpful comments, I would like to thank the members of my monograph committee: Luis Lugo, David Lumsdaine, Larry Adams, and Glen Stassen.

2. Romans 2:14-15. All scriptural citations are quoted from the New International Version Bible.

3. The *locus classicus* for Christian natural law is the writings of Thomas Aquinas. See Paul Sigmund, trans. and ed., *St. Thomas Aquinas on Politics and Ethics* (New York: W.W. Norton & Company, 1988). I also rely heavily upon the modern natural thought on morality and politics of John Finnis, especially his *Natural Law and Natural Rights* (Oxford: Clarendon Press, 1980). On politics, see particularly, 134-371.

4. That is, they faced a world that is morally and institutionally similar to our own. It was a world where sovereign states were increasingly the de facto form of authority, yet where some echo of the consensus on previous moral and legal unity existed. Today, sovereign states are still the de facto form of authority, while the role of global legal norms and shared moral consensus is significant, if still precarious.

5. Hubert Languet, *Vindiciae Contra Tyrannos*, ed. and trans. George Garnett (Cambridge, England: Cambridge University Press, 1994), 181.

6. Languet, *Vindiciae Contra Tyrannos*, 181.

7. That benevolence is a principle of "common morality," sharing Thomistic, Kantian, and Judeo-Christian bases, is the argument of Alan Donagan, *The Theory of Morality* (Chicago: University of Chicago Press, 1977). Singer's argument is in his "Famine, Affluence, and Morality," in *International Ethics*, ed. Charles R. Beitz, Marshall Cohen, Thomas Scanlon, and A. John Simmons (Princeton, N. J.: Princeton University Press, 1985), 247-61.

8. Romans 13:1, 4.

9. See *St. Thomas Aquinas on Politics and Ethics*; also see Finnis, *Natural Law and Natural Rights*, particularly, 134-371.

10. See *St. Thomas Aquinas on Politics and Ethics*; in Finnis's *Natural Law and Natural Rights*, see chapters III and IV on the basic goods, and chapter VI on the common good. Another modern theorist of the common good is the French Catholic natural law philosopher Jacques Maritain. See his *Man and the State* (Chicago: University of Chicago Press, 1950).

11. In modern natural law tradition, basic goods underlie "natural rights" to certain forms of treatment which individuals may claim against governments. See Finnis, *Natural Law and Natural Rights*, chapter VIII, as well as the Papel encyclical, *Dignitas Humanae*, in *The Documents of Vatican II*, ed. Walter M. Abbot, S. J. and Joseph Gallagher (New York: America, 1966).

12. The dual importance of peace and justice is stressed throughout the natural law tradition. Most recently, the United States Catholic Bishops articulated the concept of "shalom" as including both peace and justice. See The United States Catholic Bishops, *The Challenge of Peace: God's Promise and Our Response*, reprinted in *Catholic Social Thought: The Documentary Heritage*, ed. David J. O'Brien and Thomas A. Shannon (Maryknoll, N.Y.: Orbis Books, 1992). Also helpful on the relationship between peace, justice, and law within the Christian tradition is Paul Ramsey, *The Just War* (New York: Scribner's, 1968).

13. Romans 13:2.

14. John Calvin, *Commentaries on the Epistle to the Romans*, ed. and trans. John King (Grand Rapids, Mich.: Zondervan, 1954); Reinhold Niebuhr, *The Nature and Destiny of Man*, vol. 2 (New York: Scribner's, 1964), John Howard Yoder, *The Politics of Jesus* (Grand Rapids, Mich.: Eerdmans, 1994). On Calvin's and Luther's views of authority, see Quentin Skinner, *The Foundations of Modern Political Thought* (Cambridge, England: Cambridge University Press, 1978), especially chapters 1 and 7.

15. Notice that Paul writes that authority *is*, not *ought to be*, "God's servant to you for good."

16. See Skinner, *The Foundations of Modern Political Thought*, chapters 7-9.

17. Not all Christians thought on war falls in the just war tradition. Major alternatives are pacifism and the holy war tradition. Although I briefly mention the holy war tradition, I do not have room here for a defense of the just war tradition against its competitors. However, the natural law basis for humanitarian intervention can serve as a foundation for a just war approach. On competing traditions in Christian thought on war, see James Turner Johnson, *Ideology, Reason, and the Limitation on War* (Princeton, N. J.: Princeton University Press, 1975) and Roland Bainton, *Christian Attitudes toward War and Peace* (New York: Abingdon Press, 1960).

Likewise, the Christian natural law tradition is not the only source of thought for the just war tradition. One of the most systematic studies to date is the work of Michael Walzer, rooted in a communitarian approach. See Michael Walzer, *Just and Unjust Wars: A Moral Argument with Historical Illustrations* (New York: Basic Books, 1977).

18. Augustine, *The City of God*, ed. Marcus Dods, introduction by Thomas Merton (New York: Modern Library Edition, 1993); Aquinas, *St. Thomas Aquinas on Politics and Ethics*; Paul Ramsey, *The Just War*, James Turner Johnson, *Just War Tradition and the Restraint of War* (Princeton, N.J: Princeton University Press, 1981); the United States Catholic Bishops, *The Challenge of Peace*. Michael Walzer also places self-defense of the community at the center of his argument, although his defense of the value of community falls outside the Christian natural law approach. See *Just and Unjust Wars*, 53-55.

19. The claim that conscience cannot be coerced is made strongest in the encyclical *Dignitas Humanae*.

20. Humanitarian intervention differs from medieval police action in that it is normally carried out by a body that must authorize intervention in particular instances, rather than simply enforce the law at its will, and which enforces only selected violations of the law, rather than regularly enforcing all violations of the law that occur.

21. The phrase is from Romans 2:14-15.

22. For a helpful account of limitations on sovereignty and the common rights of mankind, see Theodor Meron, "Common Rights of Mankind in Gentili, Grotius, and Suarez," *American Journal of International Law*, 85, no. 1 (January 1991):, 110-16.

23. See Francisco de Victoria, *Political Writings*, ed. Anthony Pagden and Jeremy Lawrence (Cambridge, England: Cambridge University Press, 1991). Victoria's concern for Christians being persecuted and seekers of the faith being hindered from converting may sound at first like precepts that could only grow out of specific revelation, but in fact he saw them as generally accessible issues of the conscience.

24. Suarez, in the same spirit as Victoria, thought this right to be defensible according to natural reason. See Francisco Suarez, *Selections from Three Works of Francisco Suarez*, S.J. (New York: Oceana, 1964).

25. Meron, "Common Rights of Mankind," 115. Quoted from Albreico Gentili, *De jure belli libri tres*, trans. J. C. Rolfe (Oxford: Clarendon Press, 1993), 74.

26. Meron, "Common Rights of Mankind," 112. Quoted from Hugo Grotius, *De jure belli ac pacis libri tres* (London: Clarendon Press, 1925), bk. II, chap. XXV, pt VIII(4).

27. These natural law thinkers may not have been the only school of thinking to relate the above propositions about the basis of authority, the nature of justice, and the justice of intervention in the way just described. Seventeenth-century Puritans such as Richard Overton, for instance, were early proponents of human rights and conditionally just government. For an account of their thought, see Glen Stassen, *Just Peacemaking: Transforming Initiatives for Justice and Peace* (Louisville, Ky: Westminster/John Knox Press, 1992.)

28. Pope John XXIII, *Pacem in Terris*, in *Catholic Social Thought*, ed. David J. O'Brien and Thomas A. Shannon (Maryknoll, NY: Orbis Books, 1992), 129-62; Finnis, *Natural Law and Natural Rights*; Maritain, *Man and the State*.

29. For a good account of traditions within international law, see Walter Schiffer, *The Legal Community of Mankind* (New York: Columbia University Press, 1954).

30. The United States Catholic Bishops endorse "competent authority" in *The Challenge of Peace*, 512.

31. G.A. Res. 2131, U.N. GAOR, 20th sess., at 11, U.N. Doc. S/6014 (1965).

32. G.A. Res. 2625, U.N. GAOR, 25th sess., at 121, U.N. Doc. A/8082 (1970).

33. International legal scholar Lori Fisler Damrosch, "Commentary on Collective Military Intervention to Enforce Human Rights," in *Law and Force in the New*

International Order, ed. Lori Fisler Damrosch and David Scheffer, (Boulder, Colo.: Westview Press, 1991), 215-23; and human rights scholars Kelly Kate Pease and David Forsythe, "Human Rights, Humanitarian Intervention, and World Politics," *Human Rights Quarterly* 15 (1993), 290-314.

34. 993 United Nations Treaty Series, 3 December 1966. The strongest human rights monitoring mechanisms are regional. Western Europe, the Western Hemisphere, and Africa all have regional human rights treaties. The treaties in Western Europe and the Western Hemisphere create monitoring agencies, and the Council of Europe and the Organization of American States have set up human rights courts. See Pease and Forsythe, "Human Rights," 295-96. On the internationalization of human rights, see also Jack Donnelly, *Universal Human Rights in Theory and Practice* (Ithaca, N.Y.: Cornell University Press, 1989), and David P. Forsythe, *The Internationalization of Human Rights* (Lexington, Mass.: Lexington Books, 1991).

35. On these cases, see Tom J. Farer, "An Inquiry into the Legitimacy of Humanitarian Intervention," in Damrosch and Scheffer, *Law and Force in the New International Order*, 193.

36. Italics added.

37. This is the argument of David Scheffer in "Toward a Modern Doctrine of Humanitarian Intervention," *The University of Toledo Law Review* 23 (Winter 1992): 253-94, 287.

38. Pease and Forsythe, "Human Rights," 302-3.

39. "Convention on the Prevention and Punishment of the Crime of Genocide," art. VIII, 78 United Nations Treaty Series, 9 Dec. 1948, 277.

40. U.N. Doc. S/RES/688 (1991).

41. Scheffer, "Toward a Modern Doctrine," 267.

42. Jarat Chopra and Thomas G. Weiss, "Sovereignty Is No Longer Sacrosanct: Codifying Humanitarian Intervention," *Ethics and International Affairs* 6 (1992), 95.

43. U.N. Doc. S/RES/688 (1991).

44. Scheffer, "Toward a Modern Doctrine," 268.

45. Scheffer suggests that Bush had other legal rationales open to him, even without seeking Security Council approval ("Toward a Modern Doctrine," 268).

46. This contrasts even with the U.N.'s operation in Cambodia, which was in many ways quite intrusive, involving the U.N.'s creation of state institutions and performance of domestic roles such as policing. In Cambodia, though, the consent of the local parties was obtained.

47. Gregory H. Fox, "New Approaches to International Human Rights: The Sovereign State Revisited," paper prepared for the Social Science Research Council/MacArthur Foundation Symposium in Sovereignty and Security in International Affairs, revised manuscript, September 1993.

48. Scheffer, "Toward a Modern Doctrine," 262. Former Secretary-General Javier Perez de Cuellar, both in an address at the University of Bordeaux, and in his 1991 annual report on the work of the United Nations, proposed striking a new balance between the rights of the individual and the rights of states, showing favor toward humanitarian intervention. At Bordeaux, he stated, "We are clearly witnessing what is probably an irresistible shift in public attitudes towards the belief that the defense of the oppressed in the name of morality should prevail over frontiers and legal documents." See *Secretary General's Address at University of Bordeaux*, U.N. Press Release SG/SM/4560 (1991); J. Perez de Cuellar, *Report of the Secretary-General on the Work of the Organization* (1991), 11-13. At a Security Council summit, several heads of state called for new approaches to sovereignty and intervention on behalf of human rights (Scheffer, "Toward a Modern Doctrine," 283-85). See *United*

Nations Security Council Summit Opening Addresses by Members, Federal News Service, January 31, 1992, at VP-5-1, 3-4.

49. Scheffer argues that few cases of large-scale suffering are likely to be confined to borders ("Toward a Modern Doctrine," 287).

50. There is considerable debate between Michael Walzer and his critics on the level of human rights violations required for intervention to be warranted. Walzer wants to restrict intervention to colossal humanitarian disasters, while his critics want to allow intervention against more "ordinary cruelty." See Walzer, *Just and Unjust Wars*, 101-08; see also David Luban's critiques with Walzer's response, collected in Beitz, Cohen, Scanlon, and Simmons, *International Ethics* (Luban, "Just War and Human Rights," 195-216; Walzer, "The Moral Standing of States: A Response to Four Critics," 217-37; and Luban, "The Romance of the Nation-State," 238-43.

51. See Michael Akehurst, "Humanitarian Intervention," in *Intervention in World Politics*, ed. Hedley Bull (Oxford: Clarendon Press, 1984), 95-118, 96-99.

52. Chopra and Weiss, "Codifying Humanitarian Intervention," 99-100. Chopra and Weiss raise these as examples of objections to a codification of humanitarian intervention, but also mention arguments in favor of codification, and generally support codification.

53. Lori Fisler Damrosch is more skeptical about multilateral forums serving as a check. See Damrosch, "Commentary on Collective Military Intervention," 220.

54. Another potential check is the central authorizing role of Chapter VII of the U.N. Charter and its "international peace and security" clause. Although most civil wars and humanitarian disasters have an international component and can be construed as an international threat, the clause may still help prevent Security Council powers from making strategic gains the object of their intervention.

55. This conclusion might seem to cast doubt on the wisdom of the fall 1994 U.N. authorized U.S. intervention in Haiti, where there was no humanitarian disaster on the scale of a Somalia or Rwanda. The legitimacy of this intervention, though, was enhanced by the original U.N. mandate to monitor the Haitian elections of 1990. Since the winners of this election were later overthrown in a coup, the U.N. authorized intervention can be seen as an enforcement of its previous mandate.

56. See Damrosch, "Commentary on Collective Military Intervention," 220-21.

57. On the U.N. operation in Somalia, see Jeffrey Clark, "Debacle in Somalia: Failure of the Collective Response," in *Enforcing Restraint: Collective Intervention in Internal Conflicts*, ed. Lori Fisler Damrosch, (New York: Council on Foreign Relations, 1993), 205-41.

58. On the U.N. operation in the former Yugoslavia, see James B. Steinberg, "Yugoslavia," in *Enforcing Restraint*, 27-76.

59. As in the just war tradition, non-combatant immunity can be considered a necessary standard of just intervention.

60. See Brian Urquhart, "For a U.N. Volunteer Force," *New York Review of Books* 40 (10 June 1993): 3-4, and Boutros Boutros-Ghali, "An Agenda for Peace: Preventive Diplomacy, Peacemaking and Peace-Keeping," *Report of the Secretary-General Pursuant to the Statements Adopted by the Summit Meeting of the Security Council on 31 January 1992* (New York: United Nations Publications, 1992).

61. Scheffer, "Toward a Modern Doctrine," 290-91.

62. Ibid., 291.

63. The presumption in these cases is that the Security Council has not approved of the intervention. Cases where the Security Council rejects an intervention that elicits general approval elsewhere are likely to be uncommon.

64. Scheffer, "Toward a Modern Doctrine," 266-67.

Index

About the Contributors

Paul A. Brink is a Ph.D. candidate at the University of Notre Dame. He is currently working on a dissertation examining John Rawls's doctrine of public reason as a response to the challenges of pluralism.

Clarke E. Cochran is professor of political science and adjunct professor, Department of Health Organization Management, at Texas Tech University. Professor Cochran's primary fields of teaching and research are religion and politics, political philosophy, and health care policy. He is the author of *Character, Community, and Politics* (University of Alabama Press, 1982), *Religion in Public and Private Life* (Routledge, 1990), (co-author) *American Public Policy: An Introduction* (St. Martin's Press, 6th ed., 1999), and numerous articles, including articles in the *American Political Science Review*, *Journal of Politics*, *Journal of Church and State*, *Christian Bioethics*, and *Polity*.

Thomas Heilke is associate professor of political science and director of graduate studies in the Department of Political Science at the University of Kansas. His primary fields of teaching and research are religion and politics and the history of political thought. He is the author of *Eric Voegelin: In Search of Reality*; *Nietzsche's Tragic Regime: Culture, Aesthetics, and Political Education*; and various other books and articles.

Stacey Hunter Hecht is an instructor in political science at Bethel College in St. Paul, Minnesota. She is currently completing her dissertation on welfare policy in the American states. Her work on public policy, Christianity and politics, and undergraduate teaching has been presented at several national conferences.

Michael Le Roy is associate professor of political science at Wheaton College. He has recently published *Comparative Politics: An Introduction Using MicroCase*, and articles in the *Journal of Comparative Politics*.

Daniel Philpott is assistant professor of political science at the University of California, Santa Barbara. He is the author of *Revolutions in Sovereignty*, (Princeton University Press, forthcoming) and several articles on sovereignty and self-determination in international relations.

Timothy Sherratt is professor and chair of the political studies department at Gordon College, where he teaches American politics, constitutional law, and political theory. He is the author, with Ronald P. Mahurin, of *Saints as Citizens: A Guide to Public Responsibilities for Christians* (Baker, 1995).

Ashley Woodiwiss is an associate professor of political science at Wheaton College. His research areas include contemporary political thought, political theology, and democratic theory. He is presently at work on a reader, *Political Theory after Liberalism*.